Value-Packed Booktalks

Value-Packed Booktalks

Genre Talks and More for Teen Readers

Lucy Schall

LIBRARIES UNLIMITED

AN IMPRINT OF ABC-CLIO, LLC
Santa Barbara, California • Denver, Colorado • Oxford, England

Library of Congress Cataloging-in-Publication Data

Schall, Lucy.
    Value-packed booktalks : genre talks and more for teen readers / Lucy Schall.
        p. cm.
    Summary: "In this guide, 100 recommended books and booktalks offer
the perfect way to start value discussions with teens and teen/adult
book groups"— Provided by publisher.
    Includes bibliographical references and index.
    ISBN 978-1-59884-735-2 (pbk. : acid-free paper) — ISBN 978-1-59884-736-9
(ebook) 1. Book talks—United States. 2. Teenagers—Books and reading—
United States—Bibliography. 3. Young adult literature, American—
Bibliography. 4. Values—Fiction—Bibliography. I. Title.
    Z1003.15.S33   2011
    028.1'625—dc22   2010053243

ISBN: 978-1-59884-735-2
EISBN: 978-1-59884-736-9

15   14   13   12   11   1   2   3   4   5

This book is also available on the World Wide Web as an eBook.
Visit www.abc-clio.com for details.

Libraries Unlimited
An Imprint of ABC-CLIO, LLC

ABC-CLIO, LLC
130 Cremona Drive, P.O. Box 1911
Santa Barbara, California 93116-1911

This book is printed on acid-free paper ∞

Manufactured in the United States of America

To Betsy Holloway, a good friend, who has read with me, suggested new books, and helped me clarify my thinking during long and pleasant walks.

Contents

Acknowledgments

I wish to thank Barbara Ittner, my editor, for her insight, encouragement and patience; Linda Benson, formerly of *VOYA*, for the generous sharing of her expertise; Lisa Kurdyla of *VOYA* for her continued encouragement and support; and Joice Imel of the Meadville Public Library for her suggestions about teen reading and book selection.

The staffs of the following libraries and media centers have provided me with resources and support: St. Petersburg Public Libraries in St. Petersburg, Florida; the growing teen section in the Meadville Public Library; and the Meadville Middle School and High School Media Center in Meadville, Pennsylvania.

Introduction

Value-Packed Booktalks: Genre Talks and More for Teen Readers provides high-quality books for booktalks, coordinated displays, book club programs, and lesson plans. It is organized by the values on which each genre seems to focus: Self-Respect/Issues; Balance/Contemporary; Courage/Action, Adventure, Survival; Problem Solving/Mystery, Suspense; Imagination/Fantasy, Science Fiction, Paranormal; Heritage/History; and Openness and Tolerance/Multiple Cultures.

Of course, books classified by one value certainly address other values. While preparing this book, I read *Today I Will: A Year of Quotes, Notes, and Promises to Myself* by Eileen and Jerry Spinelli. Published by Alfred A. Knopf, it targets a middle school and junior high audience but addresses the process that brings all of us, day by day, to what eventually becomes our value system. It is a book for young people, parents, and teachers to own, ponder, and share. As the authors suggest in their daily meditation format, we act on or against a value we have been given, live through the consequences, and perhaps develop a new value or a new perspective from that consequence. Throughout their book, they recommend reading books and going to the library—a smart way to extend firsthand experiences. Since different families and groups hold different values, watching the mistakes and triumphs of others is sometimes as good as learning though our own experiences. Developing values, or the *why* behind our actions, can make us more comfortable with our lives, or as a very street-smart student of mine once commented, "happy in our skins." Hopefully, the books in this volume will lead young readers to that destination.

The bibliography information for featured books, published primarily between 2006 and 2010, and "Related Works" include the author name; book title; publisher and date of publication; number of pages; price and ISBN; a bracketed fiction, nonfiction, graphic novel, or reference designation; and a reading level suggestion.

C   = children
M   = middle school
J   = junior high
S   = senior high
A   = adult
G   = girls
B   = boys
CG = cross gender

Cross gender designations may also include the phrases "with high interest for boys" or "with high interest for girls." The abbreviation "pa." indicates paperback.

Remember—since teen readers, like adults, have a broad range of purpose and preference in their reading, these reading level designations are only *suggestions*. And since everyone does not hold the same values, some of the selections and conclusions could be considered acceptable in some groups and controversial in others. The "Themes/Topics" listing and the summary give the book's basic content and ideas. Following the summary is a brief values statement that explains what values or ideals the work's content and themes address.

Following the theme/topic designation and summary, each selection includes a "Read Aloud/Reader Response" section that lists at least five specific passages for sharing aloud, reflecting for discussion or writing, or presenting dramatic readings or performances. The "Read Aloud/Reader Response" entries, according to the book's plan, include a chapter, section, division, or page designation; a beginning and ending phrase for locating the passage; and a brief comment on the content. Some passages are attention-getting statements for classroom or book display posters. Others are natural springboards for discussions or substitutions for booktalks.

Booktalks highlight good books teens might overlook in a well-developed library collection. They advertise both the book and the library. Teachers supplementing textbook information will find that booktalking makes that supplemental reading list a personalized reference document as students note their preferences during the presentation. Booktalks in this volume can be considered ready-mades or springboards for writing another booktalk according to personal style or purpose. Presenter directions for some of the booktalks are in italics. Short enough to hold a teen audience's attention, several booktalks from different genres can be included in one forty-five-minute program. Individual booktalks might introduce or conclude a class period or library program. Easily adapted for a school's morning announcements or the school newspaper, the booktalks are also appropriate for local public service announcements, newsletters, Web sites, or a multi-media kiosk in the library. Nonprofit use is permitted and encouraged.

Every booktalker has a distinct style and favorite methods. The following are some suggestions I can pass on from my own experience.

- Read every book you booktalk.
- Booktalk only the books you respect and with which you feel comfortable.
- Include books from several genres.
- Tell your audience how a book from one genre relates to a book in another.
- If you are planning a full program of booktalks, invite your audience to select the books they want to hear about from the books that you bring.
- Display the books so that the covers hold the audience's attention.
- Hand out an annotated list at the beginning of the program for the audience to refer to and visit later.
- Keep the booktalk short.
- Hold the book while you speak.
- Have extra copies so that (if you are lucky) you have a replacement for the one snatched by an eager reader.
- Involve your audience, if only with a rhetorical question, at least every five minutes.
- Keep in mind that in this age of testing and assemblies, forty-five-minute presentations may not be possible.
- Adapt as needed.
- Remember to use technology and the teen customers who use it so well to extend your booktalks.
- Train some of those teens to be booktalkers.

"Curriculum Connections" present individual and group projects based on the book and "Related Works" and will help teachers and media specialists connect books with classroom objectives. The "Curriculum Connections" include discussion topics; ideas for journals, longer papers, poems, or other creative writing; panel discussions; presentations; graphic arts projects; or cross-curriculum collaboration—visual, oral, or both. Some may provide a basis for independent studies, portfolios, or senior projects. Most will encourage conversation among generations or within teen book clubs. Works mentioned in "Curriculum Connections" are listed in "Related Works."

"Related Works" include sources for expanded learning or further reading. The listings include books as well as short stories, plays, poems, articles, and Web sites. These sections will help build book programs, units of study, and inter-genre relationships. They also will guide instructors, librarians, and parents to additional reading or information sources. The index includes authors, titles, and topics for a quick overview of a work's relationships to others mentioned in this volume.

As the quantity and quality of teen literature grows (not to mention the size of individual books), the professional recommendations from YALSA, *VOYA, Booklist, School Library Journal,* the *ALAN Review,* as well as award lists and "best" booklists become even more valuable to me. Recommendations from my reading, family, friends, and audiences are more frequent. Getting involved in and excited about teen books, they are even more aware that teen publication is a distinct publication division, rather than an add-on to the children's section or an adapted adult publication. Hopefully, this volume gives you useful tools for motivating more readers as you continue to explore recent texts and encourage customers to share their own values and the experiences that built them.

Self-Respect: Issues Books

Issues books confront topics such as identity, abuse, dependency, dysfunctional families, and disease. Each involves self-respect. With stark, controversial circumstances, authors challenge readers to value themselves: physically, emotionally, and mentally. To respect who they are, to remain physically and emotionally healthy, teens redefine friendships and question authority that protects or threatens them.

Health

⚜

Anderson, Laurie Halse. **Wintergirls.**
New York: Viking, 2009. 278p. $17.99.
ISBN 978 0 670 01110 0. [fiction] JS, G

Themes/Topics: anorexia nervosa, death, blended families, friendship, identity

Summary/Description

When Lia's best friend Cassie dies of complications from anorexia and bulimia, eighteen-year-old Lia escalates cutting and anorexia. She recalls their abusive relationship and the parental actions and peer pressure that fueled their pursuit of control. Because Lia was hospitalized, she now lives with her father, step-mother, and her eight-year-old step-sister, Emma. She manipulates the scale and her eating behavior, enjoys mothering Emma, and refuses to visit her physician mother. Haunted by messages Cassie left on the answering machine, Lia visits the motel where Cassie died and connects with Elijah, a motel employee who called her with a message from Cassie. After he tells her that the

1

message was about Lia winning their control contest, she cuts herself open. Emma finds her. The family decides to hospitalize her. She tries to run away with Elijah, but he robs her and leaves her with enough money to call for help. Alone in the motel, she enters a dream state, almost dies, and then calls for help.

Values: Lia's lack of self-worth almost kills her, but the unconditional love she receives from and has for her little sister Emma inspires her to keep living.

Read Aloud/Reader Response

1. 003.00, pages 7 to 9, beginning with the chapter and ending "into my empty veins . . ." Lia describes the precipitating event that led to her parents discovering her disease.
2. 004.00, pages 10 to 13. In this chapter, Lia recalls her break-up with Cassie and the unanswered phone calls before Cassie died.
3. 006.00, page 19, beginning "'Dead girl . . .'" and ending ". . . contagious." Lia identifies herself in relation to her peers.
4. 034.00, pages 145 to 148, beginning with the chapter and ending ". . . off my eyes . . ." Lia describes her discovery that Cassie was bulimic.
5. 062.00, pages 268 to 273, beginning "I peek inside" and ending with the chapter. Confronting Cassie's ghost, Lia decides to live.

Booktalk

Thin is in. Right? (*Show a series of pictures from teen and fashion magazines.*) Cassie and Lia have it down to a science. They can eat and purge. They can pretend to eat, and they can refuse to eat. Big sweatshirts hide the bones. Quarters in their pockets cheat the scales, and the Internet overflows with weight-loss hints and encouragement. Anorexia is their third musketeer. Then Cassie dies, alone in a motel room. Cassie's voice is on Lia's answering machine: thirty-three messages that Lia did not answer the day Cassie died. But Cassie doesn't give up. She keeps talking to Lia. The more weight Lia loses, the more she hears dead Cassie. Even a stranger's voice promises a special message from Cassie. If Lia loses enough weight, she may just quietly disappear, no punishment for her betrayal required. If she cuts herself, she can bleed to death, the ultimate weight-loss diet. Enough laxatives can do the job too. She will be clean, pure, and light—all well and perfect. Lia knows how she can do it and why she can do it, and now she is looking for when. She is one of the *Wintergirls*.

Curriculum Connections

1. (Research, biology) Learn more about the emotional roots of eating disorders and the effects the disorders have on the body. Act as a resource person for the group.
2. (Create, biology and art) Create a display illustrating the information that you learned in Curriculum Connection 1. Consider using photos, graphs, or medical illustrations.
3. (Discuss, mental health and language arts) Does *Wintergirls* have a happy ending? Be sure to support your answer with specifics from the novel.

Related Works

1. Anderson, Laurie Halse. **Speak.** New York: Farrar, Straus and Giroux, 1999. 198p. $16.00. ISBN 0 374 37152 0. [fiction] JS, G (*Booktalks and More,* 2003, pages 75 to 77.) After Melinda Sordino is raped, she withdraws until a teacher and two students draw her out by advice and example. Telling her story changes her life.
2. Hautman, Pete. **Sweetblood.** New York: Simon & Shuster Books for Young Readers, 2003. 180p. $16.95. ISBN 0 689 85048 4. [fiction] S, G (*Teen Genre Connections,* 2005, pages 6 to 8.) Sixteen-year-old Lucy almost dies by denying her diabetes and discovers that the parents and friends she resented are the people trying to help her stay alive.
3. Kalodner, Cynthia. **Too Fat or Too Thin? A Reference Guide to Eating Disorders.** Westport, CT: Greenwood Press, 2003. 228p. $51.95. ISBN 0 313 31581 7. [reference] JS, CG Kalodner defines various eating disorders and explains the medical care, health issues, education, and cultural issues surrounding them.
4. Littman, Sarah Darer. **Purge.** New York: Scholastic Press, 2009. 234p. $16.99. ISBN-13: 978 0 545 05235 1. [fiction] S, CG with high interest for girls. After an attempted suicide, sixteen-year-old Jane Ryman is committed to an eating disorder facility where she learns to face her bulimia and the life issues behind it.
5. McCormick, Patricia. **Cut.** Asheville, NC: Front Street, 2000. 168p. $16.95. ISBN 1 886910 61 8. [fiction] (*Booktalks and More,* 2003, pages 169 to 171.) Fifteen-year-old Callie cuts herself in reaction to her parents' neglect and accepts therapy after her father admits his own responsibility for problems in the household.

❦

Bray, Libba. Going Bovine.

New York: Delacorte Press, 2009. 479p. $17.99.
ISBN 978 0 385 73397 7. [fiction] S, CG with high interest for boys

Theme/Topics: mad cow disease, dwarfs, gnomes,
disabilities, automobile travel, death

Summary/Description

Sixteen-year-old Cameron expends a minimum of effort. He resents his career mother, the father he thinks is having an affair, and his popular sister. He contracts mad cow disease, is given four to five months to live, and begins a coma journey with a midget, a dwarf, and an angel who help him realize the joy in life. As he helps each of them and sees his family's love, he struggles to live but accepts that death is part of and an extension of the life flow.

Value: A cynical Cameron learns that love is the most important part of life.

Read Aloud/Reader Response

1. Chapter 10, pages 72 to 73, beginning "My mouth is . . ." and ending ". . . NOW, KIDS." Cameron sees Dr. X on "followthefeather. com."
2. Chapter 12, pages 96 to 98, beginning "Day Eleven," and ending " 'tell them!' " Cameron meets the old lady who wishes to die by the sea.
3. Chapter 19, pages 152 to 157, beginning "The bodyguard . . ." and ending "Exactly." Cameron meets Junior Webster.
4. Chapters 24 and 25, pages 199 to 225. Cameron is rescued by the *Church of Everlasting Satisfaction and Snack-'N'-Bowl*.
5. Chapter 48, pages 449 to 250, beginning "I'm a roadrunner . . ." and ending " '. . . one more time.' " Cameron dreams through the relationship between the roadrunner and the coyote.

Booktalk

His parents live for their jobs. His sister lives for the in-group, and sixteen-year-old Cameron aims his life under the radar. But, suddenly, he is on everyone's radar. He gets fired from his job for throwing food and thrown out of school for fighting. A major fit in the family kitchen takes him to the doctor's office. The word from the doctor is mad cow disease and four to six months of life as his brain turns into a sponge. Cameron will spend his last days in a hospital, or will he? He decides on a road trip instead. He takes a dwarf with him and picks up a gnome on the way. Where is he going? He doesn't know. An angel tells him to follow the signs and feathers. Why is he going? To save the world of course. Why give Cameron, "the Great Mess-Up," that job? He never does anything right. But maybe life will change while he is *Going Bovine*.

Curriculum Connections

1. (Research, biology) Using your library resources, learn more about mad cow disease. Share your findings with the group.
2. (Research, religion) Using your library resources, find the after-life concepts of as many religions as you can. Share your findings with the group.
3. (Discuss, language arts) What is the importance of Cameron's journey?

Related Works

1. Albom, Mitch. **The Five People You Meet in Heaven.** New York: Hyperion, 2003. 196p. $19.95. ISBN 0 7868 6871 6. [fiction] JS/A, CG (*Booktalks and Beyond,* 2007, pages 35 to 37.) In the after-life, eighty-three-year-old Eddie learns there are no random acts.
2. Jenkins, A. M. **Repossessed.** New York: HarperCollins/HarperTeen, 2007. 218p. $15.99. ISBN-13: 978 0 06 083568 2. [fiction] JS, CG (*Genre Talks for Teens,* 2009, pages 35 to 37.) Kiriel, a fallen angel, enters the body of teenage Shaun to experience the Seven Deadly Sins but grows to appreciate God's creation.
3. Woodson, Jacqueline. **Behind You.** New York: G. P. Putnam's Sons, 2004. 128p. $15.99. ISBN 0 399 23988 X. [fiction] JS, CG (*Booktalks and Beyond,* 2007, pages 43 to 45.) In a series of first-person essays, Jeremiah Roselind, who is mistakenly killed, and the people who love him work through losses and transitions.
4. Zevin, Gabrielle. **Elsewhere.** New York: Farrar, Straus and Giroux, 2005. 277p. $19.95. ISBN 0 374 32091 8. [fiction] MJS, G (*Booktalks and Beyond,* 2007, pages 188 to 190.) Killed in a traffic accident, Liz begins life in Elsewhere where she becomes younger each day and learns about her spirit, which will return to earth.
5. Zusak, Markus. **I Am the Messenger.** New York: Alfred A. Knopf, 2002. 357p. $20.50. ISBN 0 375 93099 X. [fiction] S, CG (*Booktalks and Beyond,* 2007, pages 143 to 146.) Average nineteen-year-old Ed becomes a hero and receives Aces that direct him to help people.

CRCD

Lawrence, Iain. The Giant-Slayer.

New York: Delacorte Press, 2009. 292p. $16.99.
ISBN 978 0 385 73376 2. [fiction] MJ, CG

Themes/Topics: 1950s, poliomyelitis, storytelling, disabilities, fathers and daughters, friendship

Summary/Description

Eleven-year-old Laurie Valentine learns that her eight-year-old friend has polio, visits the iron-lung ward against her father's wishes, and begins a story for her friend and the other two patients about a giant-slayer. They identify with characters, add to the plot, grow closer, and reveal their own troubled lives. Laurie receives the first batch of vaccine, which gives her polio. She returns to the ward as a patient where her father learns the value of her visits and storytelling. Fearing that ending the story will end her life, the group waits for her to regain consciousness. She recovers and finishes the story. One boy learns to walk again; a once hostile, now kinder, fourteen-year-old girl joins her family; and two other boys move to new hospitals. Laurie reconnects with her workaholic father who resolves to spend more time with Laurie.

Values: Laurie proves her loyalty to her friend with her stories. Her contact with patients gives her empathy and the courage to fight her own disease.

Read Aloud/Reader Response

1. Chapter 5, pages 87 to 88, beginning "At just that moment . . ." and ending with the chapter. Laurie describes Khan the hunter, and Dickie names him.
2. Chapter 7, pages 118 to 121, beginning "As though he'd been . . ." and ending with the chapter. Jimmy seeks the swamp witch, and the story becomes personal to Carolyn.
3. Chapter 9, pages 144 to 146, beginning "At last . . ." and ending "'Poor Jimmy.'" Jimmy meets the swamp witch, and the question about how much she can affect the future arises.
4. Chapter 12, pages 197 to 199, beginning "It was nine days later . . ." and ending "'. . . scared to drive it.'" James tells his story, which parallels Jimmy's.
5. Chapter 14, page 234, beginning "Dickie lay staring . . ." and ending "'. . . the giant's got her.'" The patients ponder what the giant symbolizes.

Booktalk

Ask the group to share what they know about polio. If no one in the group has information, briefly explain the virus's effects. Show a picture of an iron lung.

Because of a man named Jonas Salk, who discovered the polio vaccine, we do not fear polio, but in the 1950s, it was a real threat. Laurie Valentine is eleven years old in the 1950s. Her father works for the March of Dimes, an organization that supports polio research and helps its victims. When polio strikes Laurie's eight-year-old friend, Dickie, there isn't much she can do. He needs an iron lung to breathe, and he is getting weaker every day. Her father doesn't want her near anything or anyone who has the disease, but Dickie is her only friend, so she goes to the polio ward. Laurie can't think of anything to say at first. Two other patients are there: Carolyn, a beautiful, obnoxious fourteen-year-old; and Chip, a boy with a questionable past. Everyone in that room just concentrates on surviving, on breathing. Then Dickie begs her to do what she does best, tell a story. She begins the tale of Collosso the fearsome giant, and Jimmy, a tiny cursed boy born to fight and destroy him. An impossible task? Like recovering from polio? Maybe, but as Laurie tells the story, she and her audience seem to forget the disease. They can control the story. They add plot, characters, creatures, and ideas, and they see themselves in this plot. But someone may die in this adventure. Don't both fighters and patients sometimes die? Fiction, fact, and fear collide in the world of *The Giant-Slayer*.

Curriculum Connections

1. (Research, science) Using your library resources, learn more about polio and the March of Dimes. Share the information with the group during discussion.
2. (Discuss, language arts) What does the giant symbolize? You may want to refer to Read Aloud/Reader Response 5.
3. (Follow-Up, language arts) Choose one character. On the basis of what you know about polio, finish the character's personal story.

Related Works

1. Farmer, Nancy. **The Land of the Silver Apples.** New York: Atheneum Books for Young Readers/A Richard Jackson Book, 2007. 491p. $18.99. ISBN-13: 978 1 4169 0735 0. [fiction] MJ, CG with high interest for boys. (*Genre Talks for Teens*, 2009, pages 202 to 205.) In his journey to rescue his sister, Jack learns that both beauty and fear are in the eye of the beholder. This is the sequel to *The Sea of Trolls*.

2. Farmer, Nancy. **The Sea of Trolls.** New York: Atheneum Books for Young Readers/A Richard Jackson Book, 2004. 459p. $17.95. ISBN 0 689 86744 1. [fiction] MJ, CG with high interest for boys. (*Booktalks and Beyond,* 2007, pages 160 to 162.) Captured when Berserkers raid his Saxon village, eleven-year-old Jack learns that understanding good means acknowledging evil.

3. Giff, Patricia Reilly. **All the Way Home.** New York: Dell Yearling, 2001. 169p. $5.99pa. ISBN 0 440 41182 3. [fiction] MJ, G Eleven-year-old Muriel, a polio victim, seeks the mother she remembers from the polio hospital and discovers that her adopted mother nursed her in the hospital.

4. Hostetter, Joyce Moyer. **Blue.** Honesdale, PA: Calkins Creek Books, 2006. 193p. $16.95. ISBN-13: 978 1 59078 389 4. [fiction] MJS, G (*Genre Talks for Teens,* 2009, pages 225 to 227.) Thirteen-year-old Ann Fay Honeycutt becomes the man of the house when her father leaves for World War II. She battles polio, which paralyzes her and kills her little brother. Like *The Giant-Slayer,* this story also deals with prejudice.

5. Leavitt, Martine. **Keturah and Lord Death.** Asheville, NC: Front Street, 2006. 216p. $16.95. ISBN-13: 978 1 932425 29 1. [fiction] JS, G (*Genre Talks for Teens,* 2009, pages 178 to 180.) Sixteen-year-old Keturah Reeve slowly falls in love with Lord Death because he gives her reprieves from death so that she can help others.

Sonnenblick, Jordan. **After Ever After.**

New York: Scholastic Press, 2010. 272p. $16.99.
ISBN 978 0 439 83706 4. [fiction] MJS, CG

Themes/Topics: cancer, eighth grade, friendship, conduct of life, love, family

Summary/Description

Jeffrey Alper, from *Drums, Girls and Dangerous Pie,* is in eighth grade. Another cancer survivor, Thaddeus Ibsen, is his best friend, and Lindsey Abraham, a new girl from California, is his romantic interest. Because of heavy chemotherapy he received under treatment, Jeffrey lacks memory and may not graduate eighth grade because of a required standardized math exam. The challenge forces him to work through his feelings about family, cancer, friendships, and Steven, who is in Africa for a year. Thaddeus tutors him, and Jeffrey helps wheelchair-bound Thaddeus build the strength to walk across the graduation stage. Thaddeus and Lindsey organize a protest that eliminates the test as a graduation requirement. Thaddeus contracts a rare form of leukemia. Jeffrey raises money for him, but Thaddeus dies in treatment. Jeffrey collects both diplomas and concludes that no life should be pointless.

Values: Jeffrey learns the importance of working hard, being open, and embracing small joys.

Read Aloud/Reader Response

1. "the handsome babe magnet rides again," pages 62 to 63, beginning "'Ha-ha. I think . . .'" and ending with the chapter. Tad tells how the Lindsey/ Jeffrey relationship helps him.
2. "night of the living waterfowl," pages 86 to 88, beginning with the chapter and ending ". . . slow dance?" Jeffrey writes about the Halloween dance.
3. "challenges," pages 122 to 131. A class assignment highlights the differences between normal life and cancer challenges.
4. "on the treadmill," pages 200 to 210. Tad and Jeff sort out personal responsibility.
5. "perpetual care," page 258, beginning "I sit some more" and ending ". . . life wasn't pointless." Jeffrey reflects on the meaning of life.

Booktalk

Hold up a copy of Drums, Girls and Dangerous Pie.

Any of you who have read this book know Jeffrey Alpert and his older brother Steven. Jeffrey is the little brother with cancer. Steven is his hero—the one who understands him, takes care of him, and raises money for him. In this story, Jeffrey is a healthy teenager. Steven is in Africa finding out who he is. Jeffrey is on his own and finding out who Jeffrey really is. The school district just announced that everyone must pass a standardized test to move to high school. The chemo didn't leave Jeffrey's brain ready for that challenge, especially if he takes the test with hundreds of other kids. The sympathy train that Jeffrey rode so long has left the station. His father says try. It will make him stronger. His teachers say try. It will make him pass. His friends say try. Then he will be like everyone else. But it turns out that this year, the math monster is going to be the least of his worries. Life and death write another chapter in Jeffrey's life *After Ever After*.

Curriculum Connections

1. (Research, science) Learn more about the effects of cancer treatments on the body. Act as a resource person for the group.
2. (Discuss, language arts, life skills) Note the instances of beau geste, or "beautiful gesture," in the novel. Discuss what the gestures do for each character. Continue to research the relationship between *After Ever After* and *Cyrano de Bergerac*.
3. (React, language arts) What does this book teach us about living? Use specifics from the novel to support your opinion.

Related Works

1. Leavitt, Martine. **Keturah and Lord Death.** Asheville, NC: Front Street, 2006. 216p. $16.95. ISBN-13: 978 1 932425 29 1. [fiction] JS, G (*Genre Talks for Teens,* 2009, pages 178 to 180.) Sixteen-year-old Keturah Reeve receives reprieves from Lord Death that allow her to achieve generous tasks for others.
2. Prose, Francine. **Bullyville.** New York: HarperTeen, 2007. 260p. $16.99. ISBN-13: 975 0 06 057497 0. [fiction] MJ, CG with high interest for boys. (*Genre Talks for Teens,* 2009, pages 16 to 19.) Thirteen-year-old Bart Rangely receives a scholarship to an exclusive boys' school where he bonds with a terminally ill sister of the boy who bullies him.
3. Rostand, Edmond. Gertrude Hall (trans.). **Cyrano de Bergerac.** New York: Barnes and Noble Classics, 2004. 208p. (Barnes and Noble Classic Series) $5.95pa. ISBN-13: 978 1 59308 387 8. [classic] JS/A, CG The poor but noble Cyrano is generous with his money, life, and love.
4. Sonnenblick, Jordan. **Drums, Girls and Dangerous Pie.** New York: Scholastic Press, 2005. 288p. $16.99. ISBN 0 439 75519 0. [fiction] MJS, CG Thirteen-year-old Steven, a talented drummer, learns to handle his conflicts and emotions as he helps his family cope with his four-year-old brother's battle with leukemia.
5. Sonnenblick, Jordan. **Notes from the Midnight Driver.** New York: Scholastic Press, 2006. 272p. $16.99. ISBN 0 439 75779 7. [fiction] JS, CG with high interest for boys. (*Genre Talks for Teens,* 2009, pages 82 to 84.) Sixteen-year-old Alexander Gregory learns to live life to the fullest.

❧❧

Tharp, Tim. The Spectacular Now.

New York: Alfred A. Knopf, 2008. 294p. $16.99. ISBN 978 0 375 85179 7.
[fiction] S, CG with high interest for boys.

Themes/Topics: self-destructive behavior, dating, substance abuse, stepfamilies, Oklahoma

Summary/Description

Sutter Keely, a life-of-the-party senior, denies his destructive behavior and hides his father's desertion of the family behind a lie about his father's business success. When Sutter's girlfriend breaks up with him, he begins to date an intelligent, meek, and abused girl. As their relationship develops and their behavior deteriorates, his friends encourage him to end it. The girl pushes him to move away, live with her after graduation, and reunite with his father. Sutter agrees to the reunion and finds a thoughtless, self-destructive drunk. On their way home, the girlfriend is hurt in an accident. Sutter understands how he harms her and briefly commits to sobriety, but when he breaks off their relationship, he starts drinking. Controversial language and situations require a mature audience.

Values: Sutter never achieves self-respect. His caring and responsibility extend to ending the relationship with his girlfriend. His lack of values should promote discussion about the need for them.

Read Aloud/Reader Response

1. Chapter 4, pages 18 to 22. In this chapter, Sutter rationalizes his drinking.
2. Chapter 9, pages 40 to 45. This chapter introduces Bob, a stable influence in his life.
3. Chapter 23, pages 98 to 103, beginning "When I get my pitcher . . ." and ending with the chapter. Ricky commits to building his life with elements that last.
4. Chapter 34, pages 145 to 147. Sutter and Ricky discuss relationships.
5. Chapter 66, pages 291 to 294. In this last chapter, Sutter returns to drinking alone.

Booktalk

Sutter is a senior and the life of the party as long as his glass is full. Sutter tells the best jokes and controls the room. But lately, he isn't controlling his life. His gorgeous girlfriend cuts him loose. The new one isn't half as pretty or with it, but she'll drink. His best friend has a new girlfriend too and a new life that includes sobriety. That cuts drastically into Sutter's social life. Sutter's mother is into her new husband's money and the social ladder. She may put Sutter out to the curb just like she did Sutter's father, the workaholic executive who creates big deals at the top of the Chase building. Even Sutter's older sister, with her designer clothes, house, and husband doesn't have time for Sutter. So how is Sutter going to keep that party, and the buzz, alive? He has vision. It's a privileged understanding of the world and all the fun that is in it. It's all about *The Spectacular Now*.

Curriculum Connections

1. (Research, mental health) Using your library resources, learn more about teen drinking. Act as a resource person during the group discussion.
2. (React, language arts) Will Sutter become his father? Be sure to use specifics from the book to support your answer.
3. (Research, language arts) Find the definition of "unreliable narrator." Rate Sutter's reliability. Use one as the lowest and ten as the highest.

Related Works

1. Alexie, Sherman (text), and Ellen Forney (illus.). **The Absolutely True Diary of a Part-Time Indian.** New York: Little, Brown & Co., 2007. 228p. $16.99. ISBN-13: 978 0 316 01368 0. [fiction] JS, CG with high appeal for boys. (*Genre Talks for Teens*, 2009, pages 269 to 272.) Intellectually gifted, but physically challenged Arnold Spirit (a.k.a. Junior) decides to leave the life of poverty and alcoholism on his reservation.
2. Covey, Sean. **The 6 Most Important Decisions You'll Ever Make: A Guide for Teens.** New York: Simon & Shuster/Fireside Books, 2006. 319p. $15.95. ISBN-13: 978 0 7432 6504 1. [nonfiction] JS, CG Using the seven habits, Covey addresses the issues of school, friends, parents, dating and sex, addictions, and self-worth.
3. Davis, Deborah. **Not Like You.** New York: Clarion Books, 2007. 268p. $16.00. ISBN-13: 978 0 618 72093 4. [fiction] JS, G (*Genre Talks for Teens*, 2009, pages 9 to 11.) Fifteen-year-old Kayla moves frequently because her mother drinks, loses jobs, and builds debt. Kayla struggles to be different but discovers that she may be like her mother.

4. Friend, Natasha. **Lush.** New York: Scholastic Press, 2006. 178p.
    $16.99. ISBN 0 439 85346 X. [fiction] MJ, G (*Genre Talks for Teens,*
    2009, pages 14 to 16.) Eighth-grader Samantha Gwynn lives with
    her mother, four-year-old brother, and father, a successful architect,
    who is an abusive alcoholic.
5. Rapp, Adam. **Under the Wolf, Under the Dog.** Cambridge, MA:
    Candlewick Press, 2004. 310p. $16.99. ISBN 0 7636 1818 7. [fiction]
    S/A, CG Seventeen-year-old Steve Nugent, writing a journal in a
    rehab facility for drug users and possible suicides, recalls his mother's
    death from cancer, his brother's drug-induced suicide, and his own
    personal physical and emotional deterioration. The situations, lan-
    guage, and graphic sexual descriptions require a mature audience.

Friendship

ෆ෩

Dessen, Sarah. **Lock and Key.**

New York: Viking, 2008. 422p. $18.99. ISBN-13: 978 0 670 01088 2. [fiction] JS, G

Themes/Topics: family, friendship, abuse, conduct of life

Summary/Description

When her mother deserts her, seventeen-year-old Ruby lives with
the sister she has not heard from in ten years. Used to a life of
poverty, lies, drinking, and drugs, Ruby attempts to run away from her
sister's affluent life but in her flight encounters the affable next-door-
neighbor who becomes her friend, confident, and boyfriend. She rejects
her old lifestyle, makes unlikely friends at her new private school and
part-time job, discovers how her mother lied to keep her daughters
apart, and learns that any life must include love, openness, and giving
to achieve happiness.

Values: As Ruby lives with her high-achieving sister and gets to know
her seemingly worry-free but coping-with-life's-problems neighbor, she
learns to respect herself and take responsibility for her own happiness.

Read Aloud/Reader Response

1. Chapter 2, pages 34 and 35, beginning "By the end . . ." and
    ending ". . . even began." Ruby contemplates the joy of finding
    something valuable that has been lost.

2. Chapter 5, pages 129 to 130, beginning "I'd never been much . . ." and ending ". . . like you were slumming." Ruby makes her first trip to buy clothes.

3. Chapter 8, pages 216 to 223, beginning "The first thing I saw . . ." and ending ". . . hardest of all." Nate rescues Ruby after her drug-and-alcohol reunion with her old friends, and she re-thinks friendship.

4. Chapter 10, pages 258 to 259, beginning "In the end . . ." and ending "'. . . want to be.'" Ruby challenges Nate's positive attitude.

5. Chapter 16, page 387, beginning "Later, up in my room . . ." and ending ". . . there at all." Ruby ponders "distance and accomplishment."

Booktalk

Seventeen-year-old Ruby is a loner. Some would say a loser. She lives with her mom. Dad left. Then Ruby's older sister Cora left. So Ruby and Mom drift from one dead-end job and one low rent to another. Then Mom leaves. Ruby can make it. She talks to the workmen or landlords who come to the door, anyway. She took her mom to work, stayed, and did most of the work. But Ruby's nosey landlords discover her secret. Social Services find Cora, her long-lost sister. They are going to live together after ten years apart. Cora is a married, rich lawyer. Ruby has a new, private school—all rich kids. Nobody or nothing in Cora's plans leaves Ruby too many choices. Then she meets Nate, the "everything-is-great-with-the-world" next-door-neighbor. How can Miss Problem ever relate to Mr. Problem-Free? Ruby plans to live just as she always has. Real feelings and future plans are better just kept under *Lock and Key*.

Curriculum Connections

1. (Research, Create, and Discuss, language arts) When Ruby draws the word *family* to define, Olivia draws the word *money*. Follow the same assignment structure and define the word *wealth*. Be sure to consider the rich and poor people in the story. Compare your definition with that of others in the group.

2. (React, language arts) Why are the pictures of Jamie's family and Ruby's eighteenth birthday important?

3. (Discuss, language arts) List the different jobs in the story. Consider why Dessen chooses each one for each particular character.

Related Works

1. Anderson, Laurie Halse. **Prom.** New York: Viking Press, 2005. 215p. $16.99. ISBN 0 670 05974 9. [fiction] JS, G (*Booktalks and Beyond,* 2007, pages 56 to 58.) Eighteen-year-old Ashley Hannigan plans the school prom and discovers her leadership and planning abilities.
2. Davis, Deborah. **Not Like You.** New York: Clarion Books, 2007. 268p. $16.00. ISBN-13: 978 0 618 72093 4. [fiction] JS, G (*Genre Talks for Teens,* 2009, pages 9 to 11.) Fifteen-year-old Kayla rejects her alcoholic mother's behavior but under the influence of an older man steals and runs away.
3. Dessen, Sarah. **Just Listen.** New York: Penguin Group/Speak, 2006. 371p. $8.99pa. ISBN-13: 978 0 14 241097 4. [fiction] JS, G (*Genre Talks for Teens,* 2009, pages 24 to 27.) Thrown out of the in-group because of a vicious rumor, Annabel Green develops an unlikely friendship with the "Angriest Boy in School" who helps her express her feelings.
4. Hyde, Catherine Ryan. **Becoming Chloe.** New York: Alfred A. Knopf, 2006. 215p. $17.99. ISBN 0 375 93258 5. [fiction] S, CG with high interest for girls. (*Genre Talks for Teens,* 2009, pages 32 to 34.) Seventeen-year-old gay Jordon and a fragile, possibly suicidal street girl team up to find the beauty in the world.
5. Woodson, Jacqueline. **Miracle's Boys.** New York: G. P. Putnam's Sons, 2000. 131p. $15.99. ISBN 0 399 23113 7. [fiction] MJS, CG with high interest for boys. (*Teen Genre Connections,* 2005, pages 28 to 30.) Three orphaned brothers work through the grief of losing their parents. The oldest brother takes on the burden of being the family guardian.

ℭℑℭ

Koja, Kathe. Headlong.

New York: Farrar, Straus and Giroux/Frances Foster Books, 2008. 195p. $16.95. ISBN-13: 978 0 374 32912 9. [fiction] JS, G

Themes/Topics: friendship, boarding schools, social class, family life, orphans, coming of age

Summary/Description

Lily Noble, a lifer and legacy at the Vaughn School, befriends Hazel Tobias, a new scholarship student. Lily's teachers and parents disapprove as Lily moves away from her friends and family to spend more time with Hazel's family comprised of her gay brother and his partner.

Gradually, Lily rebels against her mother's expectations and questions whether she belongs at Vaughn. Hazel receives a summer internship from her former school to mentor bright students. By the end of the internship, she has positive recognition as well as new, positive friends and returns to her "ghetto" high school. Lily stays at Vaughn after all but, like Hazel, builds new friendships.

Values: Both girls gain self-respect and clear identities by opening themselves to new experiences in spite of outside expectations.

Read Aloud/Reader Response

1. Chapter 1, pages 3 to 4, beginning with the chapter and ending ". . . vestal's right eye." Lily is finishing her end-of-the-year vestal project.
2. Chapter 4, pages 53 to 58, beginning "Duncan Tobias" and ending ". . . I wouldn't smile." Hazel talks about her family, and she and Lily bond.
3. Chapter 6, pages 97 to 100, beginning "The club was called . . ." and ending ". . . started laughing again." Hazel takes Lily to a party where she is snubbed by the "in" group of Hazel's social set.
4. Chapter 10, pages 136 to 139, beginning with the chapter and ending with "It's cold." Lily's roommate drops out, and Lily realizes her part in the girl's leaving.
5. Chapter 13, pages 194 to 195, beginning "The art room . . ." and ending with the chapter. Lily finds her place at Vaughn.

Booktalk

Two sophomore girls: Lily has a perfect life—the right family, great grades, and status friends—just like her mother. Hazel has a good but not-so-perfect life: scholarship, orphan, mediocre grades, and lots of attitude. Both attend Vaughn, a school that searches the world for students who fit the institution and each other perfectly. Lily was born into the in-group. She knows all the rules. Hazel doesn't care if she fits. Her older brother wants her to be at Vaughn. With Lily known as a Vaughn Virgin and Hazel considered a ghetto girl, these social paths shouldn't cross. But the girls not only get along, they also create their own social circle. Are they strong enough to control the problems that their commitment brings when they ignore the unspoken rules and get to know each other, heart to heart, and *Headlong*?

Curriculum Connections

1. (Research, counseling) Using library resources, research the entrance requirements for private schools in your area. Share the information with the group.
2. (Research, social studies) Choose a corporate, media, or political group. Using library resources, research the schools that some of the members attended. Share your information with the group.
3. (Discuss, counseling) If you had been Lily or Hazel, what do you think you would have learned about yourself during your sophomore year?

Related Works

1. Green, John. **Looking for Alaska.** New York: Dutton Books, 2005. 224p. $15.99. ISBN 0 525 47506 0. [fiction] S, CG (*Booktalks and Beyond,* 2007, pages 37 to 40.) Sixteen-year-old Miles Halter attends his father's alma mater, Culver Creek, and bonds with three students who help him explore the meaning of life and death.
2. Koja, Kathe. **Buddha Boy.** New York: Farrar, Straus and Giroux/ Frances Foster Books, 2003. 117p. $16.00. ISBN 0 374 30998 1. [fiction] MJS, CG (*Booktalks and Beyond,* 2007, pages 40 to 43.) Jinsen, an obvious misfit, attends affluent Edward Rucher High School where he deals with bullies by relying on his Buddhist beliefs.
3. Marchetta, Melina. **Saving Francesca.** New York: Alfred A. Knopf, 2004. 243p. $17.99. ISBN 0 375 92982 7. [fiction] JS, G (*Booktalks and Beyond,* 2007, pages 52 to 54.) Sixteen-year-old Francesca, a student at a traditionally all-boys school for one semester, bonds with other female students, who were in the out-group at her former school.
4. Oates, Joyce Carol. **Black Girl, White Girl.** New York: Harper Collins, 2006. 272p. $25.95. ISBN-13: 978 0 06 112564 5. [fiction] S/A, CG with high interest for girls. A financially privileged 34-year-old woman recalls her friendship with her underprivileged black college roommate that led to the white girl's coming of age.
5. Zevin, Gabrielle. **Memoirs of a Teenage Amnesiac.** New York: Farrar, Straus and Giroux, 2007. 271p. $17.00. ISBN-13: 978 0 374 34946 2. [fiction] JS, G (*Genre Talks for Teens,* 2009, pages 61 to 64.) High school junior Naomi Paige Porter hits her head and forgets her life from puberty on. She discovers and reevaluates her choices.

 GG

Naylor, Phyllis Reynolds. Cricket Man.

New York: Atheneum Books for Young Readers/Ginee Seo Books, 2008. 196p. $16.99.
ISBN 978 1 4169 4981 7. [fiction] JS, CG

Themes/Topics: heroes, neighbors, family life,
skateboarding, pregnancy, schools

Summary/Description

Kenny Sykes moves into a new neighborhood in the summer before eighth grade, saves crickets from dying in the family pool, reinvents himself as a superhero called Cricket Man, and discovers his power to help his friends, family, and eventually the depressed high school junior neighbor girl. Kenny, as Cricket Man, defends his friend from bullies, saves a boy from drowning, helps his little brother adjust to second grade, and rescues his sister's wedding. He befriends the beautiful, sad girl across the street and discovers that she has been hiding a pregnancy. By the end of the novel, Kenny knows that people do not fit neat classifications, and that a true hero reaches out to help everyone.

Value: Through fantasy and accident, Kenny realizes that heroism requires empathy.

Read Aloud/Reader Response

1. Chapter 2, pages 13 and 14, beginning "Anyway, in this . . ." and ending with the chapter. Kenny reflects on his summer.
2. Chapter 6, pages 38 to 44. In this chapter, Kenny describes the first day of school.
3. Chapter 12, page 91, beginning "The locker room . . ." and ending "Life's amazing." Kenny reflects on the possibly unloved at the public pool.
4. Chapter 13, page 101, beginning "*Some* times . . ." and ending ". . . would I tell *you*?" Jodie brings up the topic of erasing unpleasant memories.
5. Chapter 23, pages 188 to 196. In this final chapter, Jodi explains her decision to have the baby and give it away. Kenny starts to realize his true power.

Booktalk

Kenny Sykes wants a little summer excitement while waiting for eighth grade to start. This will be a new school. His only friends so far are his skateboard buddies and, *well*, the crickets. Every morning Kenny saves them before they swirl to a certain death in the Sykes's family pool. Kenny is the god of their world, a superhero. Then he notices another place to channel those superpowers. The gorgeous girl across the street is on her roof, in her underwear. He watches her. She surprises him and waves good-bye. Interesting. He thinks that he will watch her again, but he doesn't like what he sees. She looks sad. The boyfriends stop coming. She doesn't go out with girlfriends. Shouldn't a superhero do something about that? Before he crafts a plan, she says "Hi," invites him over, and talks to him. Why would a gorgeous high school junior want to talk to him? And when she does talk to him, she laughs, and sometimes she cries, too. Kenny isn't sure what or when he should do something. Maybe this is a job for someone with greater powers than Kenny Sykes. Maybe this is a job for *Cricket Man*.

Curriculum Connections

1. (Research, mental health) Using library resources, learn more about depression and how someone might help a depressed person. Act as a resource person for the group.
2. (Discuss, language arts) Is Kenny a superhero? Support your answer with specifics from the novel.
3. (Create, language arts, art) Explain or draw the superhero you are or would like to be.

Related Works

1. Dr. Seuss. **Horton Hears a Who!** New York: Random House Books for Young Readers, 1954. 72p. $11.96. ISBN-13: 978 0 39480 078 3. [fiction] C, CG The lovable and huge Horton protects the tiniest of creatures and is referred to in *Cricket Man*.
2. Hornby, Nick. **Slam.** New York: G. P. Putnam's Sons, 2007. 309p. $19.99. ISBN-13: 978 0 399 25048 4. [fiction] JS, CG (*Genre Talks for Teens*, 2009, pages 69 to 71.) Sixteen-year-old Sam, a top skateboarder, plans to break the family's bad decisions record by going to college but discovers that his former girlfriend is pregnant with his baby.
3. Leavitt, Martine. **Heck Superhero.** Asheville, NC: Front Street, 2004. 144p. $16.95. ISBN 1 886910 94 4. [fiction] MJ, CG with high interest for boys. (*Booktalks and Beyond*, 2007, pages 28 to 30.) Thirteen-year-old Heck, abandoned by his depression-prone mother, copes by moving back and forth between real and hero comic book worlds.

4. Lubar, David. **Flip.** New York: Tom Doherty Associates Books, 2003. 304p. $5.98pa. ISBN 0 765 34048 8. [fiction] MJ, CG with high interest for boys. In this humorous exploration of heroism, twins Ryan and Taylor discover disks from another planet that allow them to take on identities of Earth's heroes but bring them into conflict with the school bully and their father.

5. Schmidt, Gary D. **The Wednesday Wars.** New York: Clarion Books, 2007. 264p. $16.00. ISBN-13: 978 0 618 72483 3. [fiction] MJS, CG (*Genre Talks for Teens,* 2009, pages 56 to 59.) Seventh-grader Holling Hoodhood finds a positive direction in the turbulent 1960s when his English teacher challenges him with Shakespeare and sports.

ℭℨℭℨ

Sandell, Lisa Ann. A Map of the Known World.
New York: Scholastic Press, 2009. 304p. $16.99. ISBN-13: 978 0 545 06970 0.
[fiction] JS, G

Themes/Topics: cartography, art, grief, peer pressure, coming of age, friendship

Summary/Description

Cora, a talented cartographer, enters her freshman year following the car crash death of her rebellious older brother. Damian, the boy her parents blame for her brother's death, is in her art class. They become friends, and he shows her the art studio that he and Nate shared. Cora rebels against her already fractured and suffering family and finds new support and friendship with Helen, a sophomore art student. Helen persuades Cora to stage an art show honoring Nate. Damian cooperates. The show pulls together social groups, shows Cora's parents another side of Nate, and helps them heal their family.

Values: Cora realizes that Nate's death was caused by negative incidents and attitudes. With new friends, she discovers her strength, judgment, and talent.

Read Aloud/Reader Response

1. Chapter 1, pages 7 to 10, beginning "Everything fell apart . . ." and ending with the chapter. Cora describes Nate and the day he died.

2. Chapter 3, pages 36 to 36, beginning "I cannot figure out . . ." and ending ". . . a watcher." Cora describes herself as a person not defined by a clique.

3. Chapter 4, pages 56 to 58, beginning "'Cora, before . . .'" and ending ". . . disappointed face." Cora's art teacher presents the London opportunity.
4. Chapter 9, pages 150 to 151, beginning "Finally, he . . ." and ending ". . . believe it." Damian compares Cora's strength and their weaknesses.
5. Chapter 18, page 272, beginning "I wish . . ." and ending with the chapter. Cora reflects on the year.

Booktalk

Fourteen-year-old Cora is starting high school. It will be great, except for one thing—Cora's brother. He died last February. He was one of those dress-all-in-black kids who drove family, friends, and teachers crazy. Anger drove him into a tree. He made Cora the troublemaker's sister, that dead guy's sister. Mom and Dad won't talk to her or each other about it or him. So Cora hides from the world all summer, walks into art class, and sees the boy who killed her brother. He wants to talk to Cora, to be friends. Then he invites her to take a ride. Cora agrees. They travel to a new place to meet a brother she never knew, a place where she could lose track of friends and family. But Cora draws maps, and she figures out where she is by creating a masterpiece, *A Map of the Known World*.

Curriculum Connections

1. (Research, mental health) Using library and community resources, learn more about the grief process. Act as a resource person for the group.
2. (Research, art) Using your library resources, learn more about cartography as an art form. Act as a resource person for the group.
3. (Research, language arts) Using library resources, learn more about semantic or mental maps that guide people's thinking. Act as a resource person for the group.

Related Works

1. Anderson, Laurie Halse. **Speak.** New York: Farrar, Straus and Giroux, 1999. 198p. $16.00. ISBN 0 374 37152 0. [fiction] JS, G (*Booktalks and More*, 2003, pages 75 to 77.) After Melinda Sordino is raped, she withdraws until her art teacher and two students help her speak.
2. Averett, Edward. **The Rhyming Season.** New York: Clarion Books, 2005. 214p. $16.00. ISBN 0 618 46948 6. [fiction] JS, G (*Booktalks and Beyond*, 2007, pages 65 to 68.) After the death of

her basketball-star brother, Brenda Jacobsen discovers her own strength by leading the girls' basketball team to a championship.

3. Koja, Kathe. **Buddha Boy.** New York: Farrar, Straus and Giroux/ Frances Foster Books, 2003. 117p. $16.00. ISBN 0 374 30998 1. [fiction] MJS, CG with high interest for boys. (*Booktalks and Beyond*, 2007, pages 40 to 43.) A new student who is an orphan, a gifted artist, and a student of Buddhist principals confronts school bullies.

4. Schmidt, Gary D. **Trouble.** New York: Clarion Books, 2008. 297p. $16.00. ISBN-13: 978 0 618 92776 1. [fiction] MJS, CG (*Genre Talks for Teens*, 2009, pages 292 to 295.) A family blames a Cambodian refugee for their son's death but discovers that their daughter was responsible.

5. Soto, Gary. **The Afterlife.** New York: Harcourt, 2003. 161p. $16.00. ISBN 0 15 204774 3. [fiction] JS, CG (*Teen Genre Connections*, 2005, pages 294 to 296.) Stabbed to death in a restroom, eighteen-year-old Jesús moves to the after-life, and sees how his family and friends love him.

♋♋

Vivian, Siobhan. **A Little Friendly Advice.**

New York: Scholastic/Push, 2008. 248p. $16.99.
ISBN-13: 978 0 545 00404 6. [fiction] JS, G

Themes/Topics: friends, divorce, family relationships, conduct of life, privacy

Summary/Description

Sixteen-year-old Ruby has three close friends. One friend, Beth, dominates her. On Ruby's sixteenth birthday, Ruby's father, who left years ago, arrives. Encouraged by her friends, she refuses to talk to him. Beth hides a letter the father leaves that states he will be at a local hotel for the week. Ruby finds the letter and waits for Beth to confess. A confrontation comes at Beth's Halloween/birthday party. Beth reveals that she found Ruby's mother with another man on the day that Ruby's dad left and kept that secret also. Ruby confronts the mother, visits the father, and discovers that they both wanted out of the marriage. Ruby confides in her new good-listener boyfriend instead of Beth, and although the girls reconcile, Ruby decides that Beth will not manage her relationships.

Values: Ruby becomes a responsible person independent of her parents' personal decisions and realizes that friendship does not mean ownership.

Read Aloud/Reader Response

1. Chapter 1, pages 7 to 8, beginning "Katherine's only . . ." to ". . . needed some new friends." Ruby introduces Katherine who has decided to come into their group.
2. Chapter 3, pages 26 to 27. In this chapter, Ruby recalls her father leaving.
3. Chapter 17, pages 123 to 130. In this chapter, Ruby and Charlie get acquainted, and Ruby uses her first kiss to irritate her mother.
4. Chapter 19, pages 144 to 148, beginning "When I arrive . . ." and ending with the chapter. Ruby trails her father and finds the box he leaves for her.
5. Chapter 38, pages 247 to 248, beginning "I can't believe . . ." and ending with the chapter. Ruby decides to make a collage of her life instead of hiding it.

Booktalk

Sixteen-year-old Ruby has three of the best friends. And that isn't counting her super mom. Her sweet-sixteen birthday promises to be one of the best days of her life. And then Dad shows up. So sweet sixteen isn't that great, but it might be memorable. Ruby has some other memorable days too. She was in grade school when her dad left her and her mom. That day was memorable. No letters. No phone calls. No contact. No Dad since. Why does he show up now with a sick bouquet and his signature cigar? Ruby doesn't know. She just leaves—with her friends. And her friends are great. They won't let her call him Dad. Who needs him? They can take care of her better than he can. They can help her with what to wear, who to meet, and how to act. They can even screen her boyfriends. Screen her boyfriends? She may be in dangerous territory. Maybe she is old enough to confront a deadbeat dad herself instead of following *A Little Friendly Advice*.

Curriculum Connections

1. (Research, psychology, life skills) Using library resources, learn more about the effects of peer pressure on teen behavior.
2. (Discuss, life skills, language arts) Write your own definition of *friend*. Use specifics from the story to illustrate your definition. Share your definition with the group.
3. (Discuss, life skills) Ruby blames others for her emotional turmoil: her mother, father, and Beth are three of them. What responsibility does she have for that turmoil?

Related Works

1. Beard, Philip. **Dear Zoe.** New York: Viking, 2005. 196p. $21.95. ISBN 0 670 03401 0. [fiction] JS, G (*Booktalks and Beyond,* 2007, pages 14 to 16.) When her younger step-sister is killed, Tess thinks that her mother is having an affair and moves in with her drug-selling biological father, whom her mother married at nineteen.

2. Brooks, Martha. **Mistik Lake.** New York: Farrar, Straus and Giroux/Melanie Kroupa Books, 2007. 207p. $16.00. ISBN-13: 978 0 374 34985 1. [fiction] S, G (*Genre Talks for Teens,* 2009, pages 4 to 6.) In the small town of Mistik Lake, the family's summer retreat, seventeen-year-old Odella unravels family secrets and discovers love.

3. Cooney, Caroline B. **A Friend at Midnight.** Colorado Springs, CO: Waterbrook Press, 2006. 183p. $15.95. ISBN 1 4000 7208 5. [fiction] J, CG with high interest for girls. (*Genre Talks for Teens,* 2009, pages 6 to 9.) Fifteen-year-old Lily is in the middle of a family divided by her absent, manipulative, and self-centered biological father.

4. Hobbs, Valeri. **Tender.** New York: Farrar, Straus and Giroux/Francis Foster Books, 2001. 256p. $18.00. ISBN 0 374 37397 3. [fiction] MJS, G (*Teen Genre Connections,* 2005, pages 48 to 49.) Fifteen-year-old Liv Trager moves to California to live with the distant, hardworking father she doesn't know after the grandmother who raised her dies.

5. Ryan, Pam Muñoz. **Becoming Naomi León.** New York: Scholastic Press, 2004. 256p. $16.95. ISBN 0 439 26969 5. [fiction] MJS, CG (*Booktalks and Beyond,* 2007, pages 249 to 251.) Naomi and her physically challenged brother Owen live with their grandmother, but their alcoholic, abusive mother returns to their lives.

Authority

☙❧

Booth, Coe. Kendra.

New York: Scholastic, 2008. 292p. $16.99. ISBN-13: 978 0 439 92536 5. [fiction] JS, G

Themes/Topics: teen pregnancy, dating, family, conduct of life

Summary/Description

Fourteen-year-old Kendra was born when her mother was fourteen. Kendra's father lives next door. Her grandmother raised her. Her mother went to school. Her mother has completed her doctorate and landed a job but plans her life without Kendra. Kendra reacts by becoming sexually active with a much more experienced boy who also dates her aunt, Kendra's best high school friend. Afraid of another pregnancy, the grandmother sends Kendra to live with her mother. Her aunt/best friend beats her up after school. Her mother talks to her about pregnancy and offers her birth control. The boy persuades her to date him again. Kendra knows that she will be sexually active with this boy but wants to make that her, not his, decision. She persuades her mother to become a permanent part of her life and begins to reconcile with her grandmother and aunt. The language and situations could be considered controversial.

Values: Kendra realizes that romantic relationships may not be lasting and responsibly chooses to use birth control.

Read Aloud/Reader Response

1. Chapter 5, pages 33 to 34, beginning "She looks . . ." and ending with the chapter. In this passage, Kendra describes how her relationship with grandmother has changed.
2. Chapter 7, pages 41 to 45. In this chapter, Kendra's mother disappoints her.
3. Chapter 21, page 127, beginning "When I was . . ." and ending with the chapter. Kendra describes the conflict between her grandmother and mother over Kendra's home.
4. Chapter 27, page 170, beginning "My head is jumping . . ." and ending ". . . just say no." Kendra learns Nashawn is also dating her aunt.
5. Chapter 28, pages 174 to 175, beginning "I'm actually glad . . ." and ending ". . . the undo button." Kendra reacts to her mother's apartment for one.

Booktalk

Fourteen-year-old Kendra would like to get to know her mother, the woman Kendra knows as Renée, the woman who became her mother at fourteen. Nana, Renée's mother, raised Kendra, and since Kendra turned fourteen, Nana doesn't want any boys hanging around. Kendra doesn't understand why Nana worries. Kendra isn't like that. She has a good head. She wants to move in with her mom who just finished school. Then she will get a little respect, a little freedom. But Mom doesn't seem eager to include Kendra. She lets people think that Kendra is her sister, not her teenage daughter. She shares the details of her own dating life instead of helping Kendra figure out hers. And then Kendra meets two boys, good-looking nice boys, boys that other girls would like to claim. Those boys want to claim *Kendra*.

Curriculum Connections

1. (Research, social studies) Using your library resources, learn more about the effects of teenage pregnancy. Share your findings with the discussion group.
2. (React, language arts) Who is your favorite adult in the novel? Be sure to list specific reasons for your choice.
3. (Discuss, language arts) Should Kendra go back to Nashawn? Use details from the novel to support your answer.

Related Works

1. Booth, Coe. **Tyrell.** New York: Scholastic/Push, 2006. 320p. $16.99. ISBN 0 439 83879 7. [fiction] JS, CG with high interest for boys. Fifteen-year-old Tyrell, who has grown up in the projects, unsuccessfully tries to hold his family and his love life together even though his father is in jail and his mother is self-centered and dysfunctional.
2. Flake, Sharon G. **Who Am I without Him? Short Stories about Girls and the Boys in Their Lives.** New York: Hyperion Books for Children/Jump at the Sun, 2004. 168p. $15.99. ISBN 078680693 1. [fiction, short stories] JS, G (*Booktalks and Beyond,* 2007, pages 19 to 21.) Ten short stories explore the female/male relationship.
3. Johnson, Angela. **The First Part Last.** New York: Simon & Shuster Books for Young Readers, 2003. 131p. $15.95. ISBN 0 689 84922 2. [fiction] JS, CG (*Booktalks and Beyond,* 2007, pages 24 to 25.) Bobby tells about fatherhood after his baby's mother dies.
4. Myers, Walter Dean. **145th Street: Short Stories.** New York: Delacorte Press, 2000. 151p. $15.95. ISBN 0 385 32137 6. [short stories] JS, CG (*Booktalks and More,* 2003, pages 91 to 93.) Myers portrays frustration, achievement, and compassion on 145th Street.
5. Myers, Walter Dean. **What They Found: Love on 145th Street.** New York: Wendy Lamb Books, 2007. 243p. $18.99. ISBN-13: 978 0 375 93709 5. [short stories] JS, CG with high interest for boys. (*Genre Talks for Teens,* 2009, pages 51 to 53.) A sequel to *145th Street: Short Stories,* fifteen interrelated stories explore love and friendship.

CRID

Aronson, Marc, and Patty Campbell (eds.).
War Is: Soldiers, Survivors, and Storytellers Talk about War.

Cambridge, MA: Candlewick Press, 2008. 200p. $17.99. ISBN-13: 978 0 7636 3625 8.
[anthology: nonfiction and fiction] S, CG

Themes/Topics: war protest, war service, war correspondence

Summary/Description

Twenty selections divided into four sections explore war from the points of view of protestors, correspondents, soldiers, and military family members. In "What I Believe about War," Patty Campbell declares her anti-war perspective, and Marc Aronson commits to listening to those close to war. "Deciding about War" deals with the hero's example, enlistment, first combat, conscientious objectors, the relationship of religion and war, and war protest. "Experiencing War" spans reactions from World Wars I and II, Vietnam, and Iraq and includes the experience of women in modern warfare. "The Aftermath of War" consists of a one-act play by Rita Williams-Garcia about post-traumatic stress and a post-apocalyptic short story by Margo Lanagan.

Values: The selections address the personal decisions a person confronts within our definitions of authority, common good, duty, justice, and charity.

Read Aloud/Reader Response

1. "The Moment of Combat," pages 27 to 38. Chris Hedges, foreign correspondent for the *New York Times,* explains his opposition to war.
2. "The War Prayer," pages 46 to 49. Mark Twain's bitter satire explores the prayer behind the prayer for victory.
3. "In the Front Lines," pages 63 to 75. In a series of columns about World War II, Ernie Pyle explains the life of the foot soldier. Three of the columns address D day.
4. "Wordsmith at War," in the section "The Government Center—March 4, 2006," pages 118 to 124. Lee Kelley describes a peaceful encounter between the Americans and Iraqis.
5. "Killing Flies," pages 155 to 169. In this one-act play, Rita Williams-Garcia depicts the post-traumatic stress experienced by a woman who has served in modern combat.

Booktalk

War. What is it? Can it end? Even if peace means survival, is it possible? And finally, what are those people like who fight the wars we talk about, and how should we treat them?

The soldiers, survivors, and storytellers in this book talk about those questions. They talk about enlistment, heroism, the real meaning of *tough,* the so-called holy war, and what life is like before, during, and after battle. They talk about a soldier's day that shifts from boredom to life or death in a second. And they talk about the life that soldiers create for survivors. Some of these writers have lived war, some have seen its results, and others draw only from their imaginations. But each will leave you thinking a little more carefully about what *War Is.*

Curriculum Connections

1. (Research, social studies) Choose one of the topics, such as conscientious objection, enlistment, or women in war, dealt with in the selections. Learn more about the topic and act as a resource person for the group.
2. (React, language arts) Which selection was the most powerful for you? Explain your answer with specifics from the essay.
3. (Discuss, social studies) Is a required universal service program, military and nonmilitary, necessary in our country today?

Related Works

1. Beah, Ishamael. **A Long Way Gone: Memoirs of a Boy Soldier.** New York: Farrar, Straus and Giroux/Sarah Crichton Books, 2007. 229p. $22.00. ISBN-13: 978 0 374 10523 5. [nonfiction] JS/A, CG with high interest for boys. (*Genre Talks for Teens,* 2009, pages 98 to 100.) When Ishmael is twelve, his family is killed in a rebel raid, and he begins his journey of physical, emotional, and intellectual survival.
2. Crist-Evans, Craig. **Amaryllis.** Cambridge, MA: Candlewick Press, 2003. 184p. $15.99. ISBN 0 7636 1863 2. [fiction, mixed format] JS, CG (*Booktalks and Beyond,* 2007, pages 205 to 207.) With personal narrative and his brother's letters, fifteen-year-old Jimmy tells about his home life and his brother's service in Vietnam.
3. Holub, Josef. **An Innocent Soldier.** New York: Arthur A. Levine Books, 2005. 240p. $16.99. ISBN 0 439 62771 0. [fiction] JS, CG (*Booktalks and Beyond,* 2007, pages 207 to 210.) Sixteen-year-old Adam Feuchter, after working three years as a farmhand, is falsely conscripted into Napoleon's army in place of his farmer's son, Georg.

4. Staples, Suzanne Fisher. **Under the Persimmon Tree.** New York: Farrar, Straus and Giroux/Frances Foster Books, 2005. 275p. $17.00. ISBN 0 374 38025 2. [fiction] MJS, CG with high interest for girls. (*Booktalks and Beyond,* 2007, pages 236 to 239.) The lives of Najmah, a village girl, and Nusrat, an American married to an American-educated Afghan doctor, intertwine during the Afghan war in 2001.

5. Stassen, J. P. Alexis Siegel (trans.). **Deogratias: A Tale of Rwanda.** New York: First Second, 2006. 78p. $16.95. ISBN-13: 978 1 59643 103 4. [graphic] S/A Deogratias's descent into madness parallels his own country's insane descent into genocide.

ᘓᘐ

Lynch, Janet Nichols. Messed Up.

New York: Holiday House, 2009. 250p. $17.95. ISBN-13: 978 0 8234 2185 5.

[fiction] JS, CG with high interest for boys

Themes/Topics: family, abandoned children, Hispanic Americans, California

Summary/Description

Fifteen-year-old R. D. is repeating eighth grade and waiting to go on to high school through social promotion. He lives with Earl, his grandmother's former boyfriend. Earl dies, and R. D. keeps the death secret to avoid foster care. He attends school regularly, does his home-work, re-thinks his friends, seeks help from adults, and figures out cook-ing, cleaning, and some financing. The death is discovered, and Earl's sister arrives to bury her brother and claim an inheritance. Her lawyer tells R. D. that Earl left him half of the house and made him the insur-ance beneficiary. R. D. signs over the house to the sister but keeps the insurance money. The lawyer helps him claim independence, manage his money, get a job, and graduate from high school. R. D. receives help from the local police, a social worker, his grandmother, and her new husband.

Values: Being responsible for his life after Earl dies, R. D. develops a respect for authority, self-confidence, and integrity. He learns how much Earl cared for him.

Read Aloud/Reader Response

1. Chapter 8, pages 34 to 38, beginning with the chapter and ending "This class is easy." R. D. attends his first day of core class.

2. Chapter 20, pages 88 to 91. In this chapter, R. D. learns to shop on a budget.
3. Chapter 40, pages 182 to 183, beginning "It's time" and ending with the chapter. R. D. calls his grandmother in the middle of the night to find out about his father.
4. Chapter 53, pages 240 to 245. In this chapter, R. D. discovers Miss Trueblood moving out of her classroom, and Miss Trueblood draws the symbols she thinks belong on R. D.'s shield. (See Read Aloud/ Reader Response 1).
5. "Later," pages 246 to 250. In this epilogue, R. D. explains his new life.

Booktalk

Fifteen-year-old R. D. has a good life. His grandma takes care of him, and they have a good place to live with Earl, a guy who takes care of all of them. R. D. doesn't worry about school. He is repeating eighth grade and knows, by the grapevine, that they have to send him to high school when he is sixteen. The icing on the cake is that he has a first-year teacher. He has his eye on the most beautiful girl in the class, and another girl has her eye on him. No worries. Then Grandma leaves town with a trucker. Earl goes down hill and dies. R. D. is alone and underage. That means foster care. No way. He'll keep it secret, cash Earl's disability checks, and live life as usual. Wrong. Usual is gone, and some people wonder what happened to Earl. Hiding the death seemed like a good idea at the time—but R. D. may have to admit that instead of simple, his life plan is just pretty *Messed Up*.

Curriculum Connections

1. (Research, social studies) Using your library resources, learn more about alternative schools available in your state. Share you information with the group.
2. (Discuss, language arts) Why does Lynch open and close with the coat of arms exercise?
3. (Written or Oral Presentation, language arts) Using specifics from the story, describe R. D.'s character. Compare your conclusions with others in the class.

Related Works

1. Booth, Coe. **Tyrell.** New York: Scholastic/Push, 2006. 320p. $16.99. ISBN 0 439 83879 7. [fiction] JS, CG with high interest for boys. Fifteen-year-old Tyrell, who has grown up in the projects, unsuccessfully tries to maintain his family and his love life.

2. Brooks, Kevin. **Martyn Pig.** New York: The Chicken House, 2002. 240p. $10.95. ISBN 0 439 29595 5. [fiction] JS, CG with high interest for boys. (*Booktalks and Beyond,* 2007, pages 114 to 116.) Fifteen-year-old Martyn Pig accidentally kills his abusive father and hides the body so that he won't be sent to his aunt's home or foster care.

3. Gantos, Jack. **Hole in My Life.** New York: Farrar, Straus and Giroux, 2002. 200p. $16.00. ISBN 0 374 39988 3. [nonfiction] JS, CG with high interest for boys. (*Teen Genre Connections*, 2005, pages 1 to 3.) Gantos tells about his jail time for selling drugs. He emphasizes that he did not have the ability to make good decisions in difficult times.

4. Martinez, Victor. **Parrot in the Oven.** New York: Harper Trophy/ Joanna Cotler Books, 1996. 216p. $5.95pa. ISBN 0 06 447186 1. [fiction] JS, CG with high interest for boys. (*Booktalks Plus,* pages 112 to 114.) Manny Hernandez experiences work, school, family, gang, and friendship and decides his family is most important to him.

5. Soto, Gary. **The Afterlife.** New York: Harcourt, 2003. 161p. $16.00. ISBN 0 15 204774 3. [fiction] JS, CG with high interest for boys. (*Teen Genre Connections*, 2005, pages 294 to 296.) Eighteen-year-old Jesús moves from life to the after-life and sees how much his family and friends love him.

❧❧

Monninger, Joseph. **Baby.**

Asheville, NC: Front Street, 2007. 173p. $16.95. ISBN-13: 978 159078 502 7. [fiction]
JS, CG with high interest for girls

Themes/Topics: foster home care, sled dogs, New Hampshire, conduct of life

Summary/Description

Fifteen-year-old Baby is assigned to the Potters, her last chance for foster care. Having lived homeless with her boyfriend and preoccupied with the mother who deserted her, Baby is bitter and confrontational. She bonds with the sled dogs that the Potters raise, but when Bobby arrives, she runs away and, by mistake, takes a puppy with her. She begins to see Bobby differently. He disregards the dog's welfare, uses and sells drugs, sets up Baby's friend for a prostitution sting, and is arrested for dealing coke. Baby returns to the Potters with the puppy. They allow her to race a team. The team breaks through the ice, and Baby heroically rescues herself and the dogs. After another reunion with the imprisoned Bobby and an attempted reunion with her alcoholic mother, she decides to live with the Potters who give her the puppy.

Values: Baby achieves self-respect, responsibility, and integrity when she learns, through her contact with the sled dogs, that her reckless decisions can affect those she loves.

Read Aloud/Reader Response

1. Chapter 5, pages 43 to 44, beginning with the chapter and ending ". . . to be the cause of it." Baby reflects on dogs, plants, and her mother.
2. Chapter 6, pages 54 to 55, beginning "Humans did not . . ." and ending ". . . scares them away." In reflecting on dogs, Baby learns about humans.
3. Chapter 18, pages 129 to 138. In this chapter, Baby returns to the Potters.
4. Chapter 20, pages 148 to 150, beginning "The line between doing . . ." and ending with the chapter. Baby talks to Bobby about her heroic act.
5. Chapter 20, page 157, beginning "Fred told me . . ." and ending ". . . they have grown?" Fred gives Baby the phrase "All understood, all forgiven."

Booktalk

Rough and tough fifteen-year-old Baby is about to get her last chance at foster care before she gets locked up in a juvenile detention center. Her social worker tracked her down at a tattoo parlor in the middle of the night, and she is dumping Baby with a couple old enough to be her grandparents—and their dogs. But the golden-agers are pretty tough too, and the dogs? They are sled dogs and can't wait to run the trails in New Hampshire winters. How did a girl savvy enough to survive on the streets without a mother and father find herself in a kennel? Baby isn't sure, but she knows that she's not staying. She calls Bobby, her boyfriend. He will get her back to the city. And that decision forces Baby to discover that she is no *Baby*.

Curriculum Connections

1. (Research, science, recreation) Using library resources, learn more about the role of animals in rehabilitation and the sport of running sled dogs. Act as a resource person for the group.
2. (Discuss, language arts) Choose a character. Write a short essay about how that character perceives the world. Be sure to use specif-

ics from the story. You might want to title it, "The world according to . . ." Share your short essay with the group.

3. (Compare and Discuss) For both *Baby* and *Snow Falling in Spring*, *The Call of the Wild* by Jack London is an important allusion. After reading all three books, discuss why you think *The Call of the Wild* is important in both stories.

Related Works

1. Koja, Kathe. **The Blue Mirror.** New York: Farrar, Straus and Giroux/Frances Foster Books, 2004. 119p. $16.00. ISBN 0 374 30849 7. [fiction] JS, CG with high interest for girls. Seventeen-year-old Maggy is drawn into the world of stealing and homelessness but finally sees the manipulative leader of the group for what he is.

2. Li, Moying. **Snow Falling in Spring: Coming of Age in China during the Cultural Revolution.** ("Openness and Tolerance," pages 227 to 229.) A twelve-year-old recalls her family's survival during China's Cultural Revolution.

3. London, Jack (text), and Scott McKowen (illus.). **The Call of the Wild and White Fang.** New York: Sterling Publishing, 2004. 312p. (Sterling Unabridged Classics Series) $19.95. ISBN 978 1 4027 1455 9. [classic] JS/A, CG with high interest for boys. Buck, a kidnapped dog, survives the harshest conditions during the Yukon Gold Rush.

4. Nolan, Han. **Born Blue.** New York: Harcourt, 2001. 177p. $17.00. ISBN 0 15 201916 2. [fiction] JS, G (*Teen Genre Connections*, 2005, pages 13 to 15.) After a near drowning caused by her addicted mother's neglect, Janie grows up in foster care, pursues a destructive life pattern, but leaves her own baby with a stable family.

5. Rhodes-Courter, Ashley. **Three Little Words: A Memoir.** New York: Atheneum, 2008. 304p. $17.99. ISBN-13: 971 1 4169 4806 3. [nonfiction] S, CG with high interest for girls. College senior Ashley Rhodes-Courter recounts her early life in a dysfunctional family, her struggles in foster care, and her adoption adjustment.

Balance: Contemporary Books

Contemporary books also deal with teen challenges but focus more on the day-to-day dilemmas of growing adulthood. How does a person organize all the beliefs, duties, and feelings that come with the freedom to choose? Increased freedom means considering the impact decisions have on others. How do these characters deal with that pressure and learn to set priorities? They work toward a balance of humor, hard work, and fair play.

Humor

Bauer, Michael Gerard. **Don't Call Me Ishmael.**

New York: HarperCollins/Greenwillow Books, 2007. 255p. $17.89. ISBN-13: 978 0 06 134835 8. [fiction] MJ, CG with high interest for boys

Themes/Topics: bullies, friendship, love, coming of age

Summary/Description

Fourteen-year-old Ishmael, a class geek, attributes his loser status to his name. He folds under the threats, taunts, and harassment of Barry Bagsley and his gang until an odd new student, James Scobie, stands up to them and declares that removing a tumor from his brain freed him of fear. Scobie cheers the football team to an impossible win and organizes a debating team that includes Ishmael, an overweight science fiction fan, a statistical genius, and a would-be comedian. When James leaves for medical reasons, a formerly timid Ishmael leads the team. The team gains recognition. Ishmael develops a romantic interest, learns to work through problems, appreciates his teammates' talents, and explores the roots of his name in *Moby Dick.* Ishmael, with the help of returning Scobie, believes he can face the still threatening Bagsley.

Value: As Ishmael takes responsibility, he grows stronger and realizes success.

Read Aloud/Reader Response

1. Chapter 6, pages 18 to 19. In this chapter, Ishmael explains why he avoided attention.
2. Chapter 9, pages 29 to 36. In this chapter, Miss Tarango verbally takes on Barry Bagsley.
3. Chapter 14, pages 60 to 65. In this chapter, James Scobie confronts Bagsley.
4. Chapter 19, pages 95 to 102. In this chapter, Scobie inspires the team to win and becomes the untouchable school hero.
5. Chapter 40, pages 202 to 211. In this chapter, Ishmael discovers that a good deed brings him to the attention of the girl he admires.

Booktalk

Fourteen-year-old Ishmael Leseur didn't choose his name. His parents did, while they were laughing. Barry Bagsley enjoys making fun of it. In fact, he enjoys making fun of everything about Ishmael and anybody or anything in the class. Then James Scobie, a new student, arrives. He acts and looks stranger than Ishmael's name. A sure target, he should be shaking. But a scar on Scobie's head shows where he had a tumor removed. When the doctors cut out the tumor, they took out Scobie's capacity for fear. He wants to take Bagsley on! Ishmael is assigned to show Scobie around the school. Whatever Bagsley throws at Scobie will probably land on Ishmael too. Ishmael believes that this is just one more result of the Ishmael Leseur's Syndrome triggered by the sound of Ishmael's first and last names said together. (*Say the two names together.*) How can trouble come so fast to such a peaceful person whose greatest wish is quite simple, just *Don't Call Me Ishmael?*

Curriculum Connections

1. (Research, language arts) Using library resources, learn more about Herman Melville's *Moby Dick* through print or film. Share the information with the group. (see the following Related Work 5)
2. (Research and Discuss, language arts) Using your library's resources, define *sustained allusion.* Explain the definition to the group, and

then discuss how it affects the novel. Consider the quotations from *Moby Dick* that introduce the story's five parts.

3. (Research and Discuss, language arts) Using library resources, define *karma*. Then, with specifics from the story, discuss how karma applies to the novel.

Related Works

1. John, Antony. **Busted: Confessions of an Accidental Player.** Woodbury, MN: Flux, 2008. 240p. $16.95. ISBN 0 7387 1373 2. [fiction] S, CG Senior Kevin Mopsely decides to shed his nerd image and become popular with the school jocks.

2. Garfinkle, D. L. **Storky: How I Lost My Nickname and Won the Girl.** New York: G. P. Putnam's Sons, 2005. 184p. $16.99. ISBN 0 399 24284 8. [fiction] MJ, CG with high interest for boys. (*Booktalks and Beyond*, pages 63 to 65.) High school freshman Michael "Storky" Pomerantz loses his nickname and gains self-respect, real friends, and values.

3. Grant, Vicki. **Pigboy.** Victoria, BC, Canada: Orca Publishers, 2006. 101p. (Orca Currents) $8.95pa. ISBN-13: 978 1 55143 643 2. [fiction] MJ, CG with high interest for boys. (*Genre Talks for Teens*, 2009, pages 103 to 105.) Fourteen-year-old class nerd Dan Hogg becomes a hero when he saves his class from an escaped convict.

4. Koja, Kathe. **Buddha Boy.** New York: Farrar, Straus and Giroux/ Frances Foster Books, 2003. 117p. $16.00. ISBN 0 374 30998 1. [fiction] MJS, CG with high interest for boys. (*Booktalks and Beyond*, 2007, pages 40 to 43.) A new boy in school teaches Justin the power of peaceful resistance against bullies.

5. Melville, Herman. Sophie Furse (text) and Penko Gelev (illus.). **Moby Dick.** Hauppauge, NY: Barron's, 2007. 48p. (Graphic Classics) $15.99. ISBN-13: 978 0 7641 5977 0. [graphic] MJS, CG This graphic retelling presents basic elements of Melville's classic. It also includes supplementary information about Melville, the period, the novel, and whaling. An index is included.

⚜

Freitas, Donna. **The Possibilities of Sainthood.**

New York: Farrar, Straus and Giroux/Frances Foster Books, 2008. 272p. $16.95.
ISBN-13: 978 0 374 36087 0. [fiction] JS, G

Themes/Topics: saints, female family relationships, first kiss, love, conduct of life

Summary/Description

Fifteen-year-old Antonia Lucia Labella strives to get her first kiss and become the Patron Saint of Kissing. She petitions the pope about once a month and studies the saints and their lives. The boy she hopes will kiss her proves to be vain and arrogant. He makes her realize that her longtime friend, Michael, who tried to kiss her two years before is truly her soul mate, and she allows Michael to kiss her at a school dance she is forbidden to attend. When her mother discovers her disobedience, Antonia returns home in disgrace, but with her grandmother's intervention, Antonia's mother relents. Antonia shares her hopes of sainthood with Michael who reveals that the neighborhood already considers her to be a saint.

Value: Antonia's positive attitude and generosity are more important than a title.

Read Aloud/Reader Response

1.   Chapter 1, pages 5 to 7, beginning with the chapter and ending with ". . . my most sacred possessions." Antonia reveals her view of the saints and her own thoughtfulness.
2.   Chapter 3, pages 20 to 21, the list of "The Top Five Ways Italians Express Love." Antonia explains the place of fighting, talking, gesticulating, and eating in Italian life.
3.   Chapter 3, page 27, beginning "I was even named . . ." and ending ". . . by coincidence." Antonia explains her name.
4.   Chapter 4, pages 36 to 37, beginning "I am *not* . . ." and ending ". . . pretty devastating." Antonia explains her relationship to sainthood.
5.   Final letter to the Vatican Committee on Sainthood, pages 270 to 272. Antonia ends her proposals for sainthood and concludes that each of us has a little sainthood within.

Booktalk

Ask the group to share what they know about saints and sainthood.

Fifteen-year-old Antonia Lucia Labella has two ambitions. One, she wants to become a saint. Two, she wants to be kissed. As far as sainthood goes, she wants to be a living saint, not a dead one, and she wants to be the patron of something that the church has overlooked—like fig trees or kissing. No gore for her. She knows that the patron saint of kissing is badly needed because kissing cannot be taken lightly or done with just anyone. As for kissing, the first kiss must be special, romantic, and perhaps lead to marriage several years down the road. So you must be getting the idea that Antonia has high ideals, stiff conditions, and no results. Will she die a virgin like her own patron saint, or will an angel come down from heaven and grant her both sainthood and kissing? In a modern world, never underestimate *The Possibilities of Sainthood*.

Curriculum Connections

1. (Research, language arts) Using library resources, research the life of one saint and share it with the group.
2. (Discuss, language arts) What drives Antonia in her search for saint-hood? Use specifics from the story.
3. (Create, language arts) After reading the story, define *sainthood.* Compare your definition with others from the group.

Related Works

1. Bagdasarian, Adam. **First French Kiss and Other Traumas.** New York: Farrar, Straus and Giroux/Melanie Kroupa Books, 2002. 134p. $16.00. ISBN 0 374 32338 0. [fiction] JS, CG (*Teen Genre Connections,* 2005, pages 73 to 74.) In five groups of essays, a fictional character tells his traumatic and humorous coming-of-age experiences.
2. Carter, Alden. **Love, Football, and Other Contact Sports.** New York: Holiday House, 2006. 261p. $16.95. ISBN 0 8234 1975 4. [short stories] JS, CG with high interest for boys. (*Genre Talks for Teens,* 2009, pages 64 to 66.) These connected short stories center on the dynamic that football players add to high school life.
3. Nye, Naomi Shihab. **Going Going.** New York: Harper Collins/Greenwillow Books, 2005. 232p. $16.89. ISBN 0 06 029366 7. [fiction] JS, G (*Genre Talks for Teens,* 2009, pages 59 to 61.) Sixteen-year-old Florrie realizes that her longtime boyfriend is a better man than the glamorous new boy she desires.
4. Rylant, Cynthia. **God Went to Beauty School.** New York: Harper Tempest, 2003. 56p. $15.89. ISBN 0 06 009434 6. [poetry] JS, CG (*Teen Genre Connections,* 2005, pages 84 and 85.) In twenty-three poems, Rylant characterizes God as an almighty being who discovers from the ordinary challenges of life the pain and beauty in his creation.
5. Zevin, Gabrielle. **Memoirs of a Teenage Amnesiac.** New York: Farrar, Straus and Giroux, 2007. 271p. $17.00. ISBN-13: 978 0 374 34946 2. [fiction] JS, G (*Genre Talks for Teens,* 2009, pages 61 to 64.)

A hit on the head makes high school junior Naomi Paige Porter reevaluate her feelings about the old friend whom she realizes is her soul mate.

CXXD

Johnson, Maureen. Suite Scarlett.

New York: Scholastic/Point, 2008. 353p. $8.99pa.
ISBN-13: 978 0 545 09632 4. [fiction] JS, G

Themes/Topics: New York, historic buildings, hotel life, brothers and sisters, acting, dating

Summary/Description

For her fifteenth birthday, Scarlett Martin receives the Empire Suite in her parents' historic hotel. Each family member over fifteen maintains a suite and serves the guests in it. The glamorous and demanding Mrs. Amberson signs into the suite and hires Scarlett as her personal assistant. The Martins, recovering financially from their youngest daughter's fight with cancer, are pressuring their nineteen-year-old son, who specializes in physical comedy, to abandon acting and attend chef school for the hotel, but he lands a part in a *Hamlet* production and introduces a fellow actor, perhaps a boyfriend, to Scarlett. Mrs. Amberson manages the play and Scarlett's romance. She also uses Scarlett, her brother, and the boyfriend to sabotage another actress's Broadway tryout. The sabotage backfires, and with the skills learned from Mrs. Amberson, Scarlett reconciles the two women and saves the play and hotel. Mrs. Amberson becomes a theatrical agent. Her first client is Scarlett's brother. Her assistant is Scarlett.

Values: Scarlett, with conflict and humor, develops confidence, responsibility, and empathy.

Read Aloud/Reader Response

1. "A Guest Arrives," pages 40 to 49. In this chapter, the dramatic Mrs. Amberson arrives.
2. "The Other Famous Whitehouse," pages 151 to 155, beginning "Scarlett tried to sleep . . ." and ending with the chapter. Mrs. Amberson connects Spencer's theater group with Billy Whitehouse, a famous acting coach.
3. "Lola Sees a Dinosaur," pages 195 to 197, beginning with the chapter and ending ". . . I didn't anymore." Scarlett's older sister breaks up with her rich boyfriend.

4. "The Loneliest Girl in New York," pages 239 to 246, beginning "She sounded serious . . ." and ending with the chapter. Scarlett seeks counseling from Mrs. Amberson.
5. "The Final Battle," pages 296 to 305. In this chapter, Donna and Mrs. Amberson reconcile.

Booktalk

On her fifteenth birthday, Scarlett Martin receives her own suite in her family's New York hotel. Like her older brother and sister before her, she manages it and tends to the guests. She doesn't think she will have much to do, because the shabby art deco landmark hotel is almost ready to close. It looks like a long, boring, and maybe disastrous summer. But a Mrs. Amberson requests the Empire, Scarlett's suite. Mrs. Amberson, a rich, aging actress, might write her autobiography, produce a play, or snoop into the Martins' lives. Suddenly, the suite is managing Scarlett. Her cell phone rings off the hook with Amberson's requests. When Scarlett gets a chance at romance, Mrs. Amberson wants to manage that too. Scarlett's summer becomes a marathon of defending family, defending herself from family, trying to find true love, and secretly pulling off a premiere performance of *Hamlet*. It's just a day's work in the suddenly no-vacancy life of *Suite Scarlett*.

Curriculum Connections

1. (Research, social studies) Using library resources, learn more about a historic building in your town. Make a display about the building for your local library.
2. (Research and Discuss, language arts) Using library resources, learn more about *Hamlet*. How did the choice of that play affect the novel?
3. (Create, life skills) Scarlett's power outfit is a Dior. Create your dream power outfit.

Related Works

1. Cabot, Meg. **Teen Idol.** New York: HarperCollins Publishers, 2004. 293p. $16.89. ISBN 0 06 009617 9. [fiction] MJS, G (*Booktalks and Beyond*, 2007, pages 61 to 63.) Junior Jenny Greenley clarifies her personal friendships and loyalties when she is assigned to escort movie star Luke Striker around her school.
2. Dunton Downer, Leslie, and Alan Riding. **Essential Shakespeare Handbook.** New York: DK Publishing, 2004. 480p. $25.00. ISBN 0 7894 9333 0. [reference] MJS, CG. This reference includes plot

summaries and interpretative material for all thirty-nine plays. Pages 324 to 335 summarize and discuss *Hamlet*.

3. Gratz, Alan. **Something Rotten.** New York: Penguin Group/Dial Books, 2007. 207p. (A Horatio Wilkes Mystery) $16.99. ISBN-13: 978 0 8037 3216 2. [fiction] JS, CG with high interest for boys. (*Genre Talks for Teens*, 2009, pages 130 to 132.) Horatio Wilkes visits his school friend Hamilton Prince in Denmark, Tennessee, to investigate the recent death of Rex Prince, Hamilton's father.

4. Johnson, Maureen. **Scarlett Fever.** New York: Scholastic/ Point, 2010. 352p. $16.99. ISBN-13: 978 439 89928 4. [fiction] JS, G In this sequel, the demanding Mrs. Amberson employs Scarlett as her assistant. Scarlett juggles the job, a challenging high school schedule, a confusing love life, and her family's demands and surprises.

5. Nye, Naomi Shihab. **Going Going.** New York: Harper Collins/ Greenwillow Books, 2005. 232p. $16.89. ISBN 0 06 029366 7. [fiction] JS, G (*Genre Talks for Teens*, 2009, pages 59 to 61.) Sixteen-year-old Florrie persuades her mother, father, and brother to campaign to save old buildings and small business.

ᘓᘔ

Sonnenblick, Jordan. **Zen and the Art of Faking It.**

New York: Scholastic Press, 2007. 272p. $16.99.
ISBN-13: 978 0 439 83707 1. [fiction] MJ, CG

Themes/Topics: identity, friendship, Zen, family crisis

Summary/Description

Fourteen-year-old San Lee, a new eighth-grade student, poses as a Zen Buddhist to fit into to his new school and impress Woody Long, a girl in his social studies class. San's father has moved the family often to avoid arrest. The father is in jail. San and his mother sort out the fallout of the father's lies. San maintains his "Buddha Boy" identity by reading about Zen. His reputation grows with a school project he shares with Woody on Eastern religions. Woody helps him apply Zen to basketball, and they volunteer at the local soup kitchen. San learns about Woody's tumultuous life, and Woody, inspired by San's "beliefs," organizes a charity basketball game for the soup kitchen and clarifies some of her identity problems. San's lies come unraveled. Woody's brother beats him up. Woody leaves San, and his classmates ignore him. With support from his teacher, the librarian, the head of the soup kitchen, and his mother, San faces his lies, confronts his father, and continues volunteering in the soup kitchen. By summer, Woody returns to the soup kitchen, and they renew their friendship.

Value: With his lies, San learns the role honesty plays in friendships.

Read Aloud/Reader Response

1. "the right path," pages 51 to 55, beginning with the chapter and ending ". . . *way in the world.*" San reflects on how his parents' beliefs and actions affect him.
2. "calls and misses," pages 113 to 116, beginning with the chapter and ending ". . . lot of time." San's mother confronts him about lying.
3. "signs and wonders," pages 126 to 136. In this chapter, Peter and San have confrontations in class and on the basketball court.
4. "the revenge of Peter Jones," pages 245 to 247, beginning "Anyway, I decided . . ." and ending ". . . care of my mom." After his lies are discovered, San writes a letter to his dad.
5. "having changed, you pass through," page 264. In this last chapter, San talks about the next school year.

Booktalk

Fourteen-year-old San Lee is starting over. He is used to it. He is "adopted and adapted" from China. His family moved often because Dad is a scam artist. This last time he left a little too late. Now Dad is in a Texas jail. San and his mother are climbing out of debt in Nowheresville, Pennsylvania. Mom tells him to blend in. As the lone Chinese kid, San decides that he had better learn to stand out. The social studies class is starting the unit on Eastern religions, the same topic the social studies class in his old school just finished. Sam has the right face. He'll become the local Zen master, the source of vision and light. Not only is he noticed, but he is noticed by the most interesting girl in the class. Keeping up appearances is harder than he thought. He reads constantly to stay one step ahead in wisdom. The girl's brother suspects San Lee's plan and is willing and able to punch out San's enlightenment. Life's questions become complicated and dangerous when San becomes a student of *Zen and the Art of Faking It*.

Curriculum Connections

1. (Research, social studies) Using library resources, learn more about Zen Buddhism. Act as a resource person for the group.
2. (React, language arts) San's false role brings trouble. Does it bring about good things also? Cite specifics from the story to support your answer.

3. (Discuss, language arts) Evaluate the advice that San gives in the novel.

Related Works

1. Baroni, Ph.D., Helen J. **The Illustrated Encyclopedia of Zen Buddhism.** New York: The Rosen Publishing Group, 2002. 426p. $95.00. ISBN 0 8239 2240 5. [reference] MJS, CG This reference provides a history of Zen and the vocabulary to understand further discussions about it.
2. Ikeda, DaiSaku. **The Way of Youth: Buddhist Common Sense for Handling Life's Questions.** Santa Monica, CA: Middleway Press, 2000. 188p. $14.95. ISBN 0 9674697 08. [nonfiction] JS, CG This book applies Buddhist principles to friendship, ownership, individuality, parents, teachers, and self-discipline.
3. Koja, Kathe. **Buddha Boy.** New York: Farrar, Straus and Giroux/ Frances Foster Books, 2003. 117p. $16.00. ISBN 0 374 30998 1. [fiction] MJS, CG (*Booktalks and Beyond*, 2007, pages 40 to 43.) Jinsen uses Buddhist principles to confront bullies.
4. Muth, Joh. **Zen Shorts.** New York: Scholastic Press, 2005. 36p. $17.99. ISBN-13: 978 0 439 33911 7. [fiction, picture book] CMJS/A, CG Stillwater, the panda, uses three Zen stories to give three siblings a different perspective on the world.
5. Simmons, Michael. **Pool Boy.** Brookfield, CT: Roaring Brook Press/A Neal Porter Book, 2003. 164p. $23.90. ISBN 0 7613 2924 2. [fiction] JS, CG with high interest for boys. (*Booktalks and Beyond*, 2007, pages 54 to 56.) After his father is sent to jail, fifteen-year-old Brett works for the family's former pool man and changes his view of life.

ლქ♪ლ

Spinelli, Jerry. Smiles to Go.
New York: Harper Collins/Joanna Cotler Books, 2008. 248p. $16.99.
ISBN-13: 978 0 06 028133 5. [fiction] JS, CG

Themes/Topics: brothers and sisters, friendship,
self-actualization, first love, skateboarding

Summary/Description

Intellectually gifted and emotionally controlling ninth-grader William Tuppence sees his life changing for the worst when Mi-Su, the girl he considers a best buddy, kisses the "live-in-the-moment" BT, his other best friend. Will intellectualizes his feelings and plans every move in a romantic relationship with Mi-Su to prove he is more worthy than BT. He also contends with his four-year-old sister Tabby who gets his attention through negative behavior and relates better to laid-back BT. Will excludes his distracting sister from his school chess match. She retaliates by attempting to ride his skateboard down Dead Man's Hill, a feat that only BT completed successfully. Her life-threatening accident and recovery prove to Will that he loves her, that she loves him, and that both his friends support him. He vows to give her attention, live more in the moment, and accept his friends rather than controlling them.

Values: William learns that love and trust are more important than control.

Read Aloud/Reader Response

1. "Unsmashable," pages 1 to 6. In this introduction, Will explains his relationship with the proton.
2. "PD19," pages 41 to 44. In this chapter, BT demonstrates his scatterbrained but appealing character and presents his revision of Robert Frost's poem, "Stopping by Woods on a Snowy Evening," the revision that provides the book's title.
3. "PD30," pages 66 to 67, beginning "Like a song on . . ." and ending ". . . flying away . . ." Will contemplates that everything is changing and leaving.
4. "PD148," pages 121 to 125. The chapter demonstrates Will's angry and rigid behavior.
5. "September 2," pages 241 to 248. Will clarifies his thinking and escorts Tabitha down the aisle in kindergarten.

Booktalk

William Jay Tuppence knows that the world will never disappear and that he will always be a part of it in some form—until the day he doesn't. That is the day his good friend, Mi-Su, tells him that someone smashed the proton, a piece of matter thought to be unsmashable. Before that event, William had permanence. Now chaos surrounds him. He is trying to figure out how to turn his best friend into his girlfriend, but she is busy with other people who want the same thing. He would like to win another chess trophy, but his crazy little sister won't leave him alone long enough to work out his strategy. And then there is another friend, BT, who doesn't have a grip on anything and really doesn't care. Will isn't going to get any permanence or reassurance hanging around him. Will is trying to hold the world together. BT, with some other very annoying people, is all about just packing up some *Smiles to Go*.

Curriculum Connections

1. (Research, language arts) Using library resources, find examples of carpe diem literature. Share the examples that you find either through group discussion, a bibliography, or a display.
2. (Discuss, language arts) How does carpe diem apply to *Smiles to Go*? Use specifics.
3. (Discuss, language arts) Which characters make the best choices? Be specific.

Related Works

1. Cooney, Caroline B. **A Friend at Midnight.** Colorado Springs, CO: Waterbrook Press, 2006. 183p. $15.95. ISBN 1 4000 7208 5. [fiction] J, CG with high interest for girls. (*Genre Talks for Teens*, 2009, pages 6 to 9.) Fifteen-year-old Lily sees her family careening out of control when her father abandons her little brother who asks her for help but won't discuss the incident.
2. Green, John. **An Abundance of Katherines.** New York: Dutton Books, 2006. 215p. $16.99. ISBN 0 525 47688 1. [fiction] JS, G (*Genre Talks for Teens*, pages 44 to 46.) Dumped by the nineteenth Katherine he has dated, Colin Singleton embarks on a road trip with his best friend, the humorous, overweight Hassan who embraces life emotionally. Colin wants to develop a mathematical formula that will predict the length of romantic relationships and prove his worth in the world.
3. Green John. **Looking for Alaska.** New York: Dutton Books, 2005. 224p. $15.99. ISBN 0 525 47506 0. [fiction] S, CG (*Booktalks and Beyond*, 2007, pages 37 to 40.) Sixteen-year-old Miles Halter, bored and isolated in his local high school, attends his father's alma mater to seek "a Great Perhaps" and finds a brilliant, beautiful, but completely unfocused girl who upends his life.
4. Sonnenblick, Jordan. **Drums, Girls and Dangerous Pie.** New York: Scholastic Press, 2005. 288p. $16.99. ISBN 0 439 75519 0. [fiction] MJS, CG Thirteen-year-old Steven, a talented drummer, learns to handle his own conflicts and emotions as his family copes with his four-year-old brother's battle with leukemia.
5. Spinelli, Jerry. **Stargirl.** New York: Alfred A. Knopf, 2000. 186p. $15.95. ISBN 0 679 88637 0. [fiction] MJ, CG (*Booktalks and More*, pages 8 to 10.) Leo Borlock recalls the live-in-the-moment Stargirl from his high school life.

Hard Work

ℭℌℭ

Cabot, Meg. Airhead.

New York: Scholastic/Point, 2008. 352p. $16.99.
ISBN-13: 978 0 545 04052 5. [fiction] JS, G

Themes/Topics: modeling, geeks, stereotypes,
friendship, identity

Summary/Description

In this first book of a series, seventeen-year-old intellectual tomboy Emerson Watts scorns appearance and worldly fame but accompanies her star-struck fourteen-year-old sister to a celebrity-filled, megastore opening. A screen falls on Emerson's head and kills her at the same time that Nikki Howard, the company's top model, dies of a brain aneurism. The doctors transplant Emerson's brain into Nikki's body, and from Nikki's best friend, she begins to learn about Nikki's rags-to-riches life and the challenges of modeling and looking good. The new Nikki-Emerson tries to balance her celebrity life with family relationships and her challenging academic classes while reconnecting with her rebel best friend who saw her as his best buddy but never quite a girlfriend.

Value: Emerson Watts develops respect and acceptance for a life different than her own.

Read Aloud/Reader Response

1. Chapter 13, pages 169 to 170, beginning "My jaw dropped . . ." and ending "'. . . Nikki Howard.'" Emerson begins to comprehend her new identity.

2. Chapter 15, pages 187 to 198. In this chapter, Emerson opens herself to the worlds of cheerleading, through Frida, and modeling, through Lulu.

3. Chapter 18, pages 232 to 236, beginning "I got back in my place . . ." and ending ". . . before I could say another word." Nikki-Emerson tries to confront Mr. Stark.

4. Chapter 21, pages 287 to 290, beginning "'Oh, my God . . .'" and ending ". . . even *more* romantic." Nikki, with Frida, ponders the new Christopher.

5. Chapter 22, page 301, beginning "Modeling isn't easy . . ." and ending ". . . all your heart." Emerson realizes how difficult modeling is.

Booktalk

Emerson Watts, seventeen-year-old geek and tomboy, is a social outcast—by choice. She doesn't understand her fourteen-year-old sister's fascination with celebrities, cheerleading, and the girly world in general. Her best friend is a boy—not a boyfriend—and they share a world of virtual reality games. She agrees to take her star-struck sister Frida to a celebrity-filled store opening. All the beautiful people are there, including the model Nikki Howard, the most beautiful and glamorous girl she and her boy buddy have ever seen. Emerson stares like everyone else. More important, she notices that her unromantically inclined boy friend stares too. Then wham! A big screen falls and smashes Emerson's head. She wakes up in the hospital a month later. Emerson is a new person in a new world. Her parents cry when they look at her. Her sister just stares, and her best friend never visits. Two people she doesn't know try to kidnap her. Emerson, the great intellectual, can't seem to put her brain pieces together. Is this a dream, a reaction to the trauma? Or did one trip to the celebrity world transform Emerson the intellectual into Emerson the *Airhead*?

Curriculum Connections

1. (Research, language arts) Using library resources, investigate the relationship between appearance and *success*. Act as a resource person for the group.
2. (React, language arts) Rate the title from 1 to 10. Compare your rating with the ratings of others in the group.
3. (Discuss, language arts) Who is the new Nikki-Emerson?

Related Works

1. Anderson, Laurie Halse. **Prom.** New York: Viking Press, 2005. 215p. $16.99. ISBN 0 670 05974 9. [fiction] JS, G (*Booktalks and Beyond,* 2007, pages 56 to 58.) Eighteen-year-old Ashley Hannigan discovers her administrative talents when she agrees to help with the prom, an event she previously scorned.
2. Cabot, Meg. **Being Nikki.** New York: Scholastic/Point, 2009. 352 p. $16.99. ISBN-13: 978 0 545 04056 3. [fiction] JS, G In her new world of school and modeling, Nikki-Emerson deals with feelings for best friend Christopher and British Gabriel Luna.
3. Cabot, Meg. **Runaway.** New York: Scholastic/Point, 2010. 320p. $16.99. ISBN-13: 978 0 545 04060 0. [fiction] JS, G This third book wraps up the complications of the first two as frustrated Emerson discovers Nikki's secret and seeks Christopher's help to expose the truth.

4. Shull, Megan. **Amazing Grace.** New York: Hyperion, 2005. 247p. $15.99. ISBN 078685690 4. [fiction] JS, G Grace, a teenage tennis star, model, cover girl, and spokesperson, seeks a more grounded life that allows her to keep the things that are important to her.
5. Zevin, Gabrielle. **Memoirs of a Teenage Amnesiac.** New York: Farrar, Straus and Giroux, 2007. 271p. $17.00. ISBN-13: 978 0 374 34946 2. [fiction] JS, G (*Genre Talks for Teens,* 2007, pages 61 to 64.) After an amnesia-producing fall, high school junior Naomi Page Porter reevaluates her relationships with her friends and family.

ॐ

Harmon, Michael. **The Last Exit to Normal.**
New York: Alfred A. Knopf, 2008. 273p.
ISBN-13: 978 0 375 94098 9. [fiction] JS, CG with high interest for boys

Themes/Topics: fathers and sons, homosexuality, interpersonal relations, child abuse, coming of age, Montana

Summary/Description

Seventeen-year-old Ben Campbell rebels against his father's coming out of the closet and his mother's subsequent departure. The father and his partner move Ben to the rural Montana home of the partner's feisty and demanding mother where Ben earns respect by working hard and saving a man's life. He tries to help an eight-year-old neighbor boy, also deserted by his mother and abused by his father. Dealing with his anger over his father's sexual orientation, the break-up of his family, and the harassment of the local bullies, Ben moves out, supports himself, and learns enough about town history to foil a mentally ill teenager who tries to burn down the neighbor boy's house with the boy trapped inside.

Value: Ben realizes he is responsible for himself and the consequences of his actions.

Read Aloud/Reader Response

1. Chapter 1, pages 1 to 2, beginning with the chapter and ending ". . . warm climates." Ben introduces himself and his family situation.
2. Chapter 7, pages 59 to 65, beginning with the chapter and ending "I will, too." Ben and his father fight over the father's homosexuality.
3. Chapter 13, pages 135 to 137, beginning "He shrugged . . ." and ending ". . . gay father." Edward talks about the relationship with his own father.

4. Chapter 14, pages 138 to 141, beginning with the chapter and ending ". . . himself to me." Ben sees his father as dodging responsibility for his actions.
5. "Epilogue," pages 271 to 273. The epilogue describes the results of each character's actions.

Booktalk

Read the opening paragraph of chapter 1.

That life philosopher is seventeen-year-old Ben Campbell. His dad moved Ben to Butte, Montana, because Ben went to the store to get toilet paper and ended up driving the get-away car for a store robbery. Things just seem to happen to Ben. But the biggest thing that happened to Ben was his dad announcing that he was gay and then moving in Edward as Ben's new mom. Or dad? Ben notices that his eight-year-old Montana neighbor looks like a victim too. His dad is a preacher willing to beat sin out of anyone he can, and he finds lots of sin to beat out of his son. Ben decides to change things, even though everyone tells him not to try. Life is a dangerous and crazy ride, even in Butte, Montana, but with or without a decoder card, Ben Campbell is still looking for *The Last Exit to Normal*.

Curriculum Connections

1. (Research, social studies) Using library resources, learn more about the structure and stability of families with gay parents. Share the information that you find with the group.
2. (React, language arts) What do you think is the most important issue in the story? Be sure to use specifics from the novel to support your opinion.
3. (Discuss, language arts) Who do you think is the most important character in Ben's development? Be sure to use specifics from the novel to support what you say.

Related Works

1. Alexie, Sherman (text), and Ellen Forney (illus.). **The Absolutely True Diary of a Part-Time Indian.** New York: Little, Brown & Co., 2007. 228p. $16.99. ISBN-13: 978 0 316 01368 0. [fiction] JS, CG with high interest for boys. (*Genre Talks for Teens*, 2009, pages 269 to 272.) Arnold Spirit decides to challenge his heritage and attend a prosperous white school.
2. Anderson, Laurie Halse. **Twisted.** New York: Viking Press, 2007. 250p. $16.99. ISBN-13: 978 0 670 06101 3. [fiction] JS, CG with

high interest for boys. (*Genre Talks for Teens,* 2009, pages 1 to 4.) Senior Tyler Miller struggles to achieve independence from his upwardly mobile parents.

3. Curtis, Christopher Paul. **Bucking the Sarge.** New York: Wendy Lamb Books, 2004. $15.95. ISBN 0 385 32307 7. [fiction] MJS, CG (*Booktalks and Beyond,* 2007, pages 9 to 12.) Fourteen-year-old Luther T. Farrell breaks free of his dominating and dishonest mother with the help of the aged Chester X.

4. Flake, Sharon G. **Bang!** New York: Hyperion Books for Children/ Jump at the Sun, 2005. 298p. $16.99. ISBN 078681844 1. [fiction] MJS, CG with high interest for boys. (*Genre Talks for Teens,* 2009, pages 11 to 14.) Grieving over the death of another son, the father throws thirteen-year-old Mann out into the world to survive.

5. Simmons, Michael. **Pool Boy.** Brookfield, CT: Roaring Brook Press/A Neal Porter Book, 2003. 164p. $23.90. ISBN 0 7613 1914 2. [fiction] JS, CG with high interest for boys. (*Booktalks and Beyond,* 2007, pages 54 to 56.) After his father is convicted of insider trading, fifteen-year-old Brett works for the family's former pool man and learns the satisfaction of hard work and good personal relationships.

෴

Lockhart, E. **The Disreputable History of Frankie Landau-Banks.**

New York: Hyperion, 2008. 342p. $16.99.

ISBN-13: 978 078683818 9. [fiction] JS, CG with high interest for girls

Themes/Topics: private schools, gender roles, conduct of life, pranks

Summary/Description

Frankie Landau-Banks, a member of the 2010 graduating class of a highly competitive boarding school, is marginalized by the popular and privileged senior boys who form a secret society, the Loyal Order of the Basset Hounds. Seen as a harmless date for one of the members, she wants to be a member herself and control the club. Following the clues in the club oath, she finds the group's "disreputable history" and launches a series of daring pranks in the name of the group leader. The authorities threaten to expel the leader, until Frankie confesses. Neither she nor the leader is expelled. Frankie is ostracized by the group, but their disapproval will not change the way she approaches power.

Value: Frankie demands equal opportunity and recognition for equal work and ability.

Read Aloud/Reader Response

1. "A Piece of Evidence," pages 1 to 3. This chapter is Frankie's confession.
2. "A Chance Encounter That Would Prove Seminal," pages 8 to 13, beginning with the chapter and ending "Inconsequential." This passage communicates how Frankie is viewed.
3. "Alabaster," pages 22 to 25. This chapter describes the school.
4. "The Panopticon," pages 52 to 56. Frankie learns about the panopticon, a building where she feels a person's feelings can be watched.
5. "Star," pages 168 to 170. This chapter describes Star's rejection from the group.

Booktalk

In her freshman year, Frankie Landau-Banks is her father's "Bunny Rabbit." She is a geek who dates geeks at Alabaster Preparatory Academy, a very competitive and exclusive boarding school. Her older sister, a senior, protects her. The sister graduates. A new year means a new, independent Frankie. The new Frankie has a head-turning figure, an attitude, and a popular senior boyfriend. Frankie doesn't need protection. She is *in*, where every girl as Alabaster would love to be. But is she where Frankie wants to be? This *in* place in the Alabaster world is a little space where girlfriends learn to be sweet, show some intellectual interest, and wait patiently for boyfriends to finish in-group, secret society projects. If a girl doesn't keep her place, she can become invisible. Frankie likes the in-group people, but she doesn't like their in-group minds. She will change their secret society, their thinking, and their gender-role game. She is willing to lie, cheat, and steal to get the job done. So to get all the way into the in-group, Frankie goes way out on a limb. The story is all recorded in *The Disreputable History of Frankie Landau-Banks.*

Curriculum Connections

1. (Research, language arts) Using library resources, learn more about pranks and secret school societies. See the author's acknowledgments at the end of the book. Share your information with the group.
2. (React, language arts) Do you agree with Frankie's decision to infiltrate the secret society?
3. (React, social studies and language arts) The Alabaster Preparatory Academy is supposed to be the incubator for the in-group or leader-

ship of our society. After reading the novel, how do you feel about that idea?

Related Works

1. Anderson, Laurie Halse. **Prom.** New York: Viking, 2005. 215p. $16.99. ISBN 0 670 05974 9. [fiction] JS, G (See full booktalk in *Booktalks and Beyond,* 2007, pages 56 to 58.) When the adviser steals the prom funds Ashley decides to help her best friend plan a prom in the school gym and discovers her power as an organizer.

2. Flinn, Alex. **Breaking Point.** New York: Harper Tempest, 2002. 240p. $6.99pa. ISBN 006 447371 6. [fiction] JS, CG with high interest for boys. (See full booktalk in *Booktalks and Beyond,* 2007, pages 12 to 14.) Paul, a lonely computer nerd, enrolls in an exclusive school where a charismatic and manipulative student offers Paul friendship if Paul breaks into the school and changes a low grade.

3. Green, John. **Looking for Alaska.** New York: Dutton Books, 2005. 224p. $15.99. ISBN 0 525 47506 0. [fiction] S, CG (See full booktalk in *Booktalks and Beyond,* 2007, pages 37 to 40.) Sixteen-year-old Miles Halter attends his father's alma mater, Culver Creek, and finds three friends, including the brilliant, beautiful, and emotionally damaged Alaska.

4. Moriarty, Jaclyn. **The Year of Secret Assignments.** New York: Arthur A. Levine Books, 2004. 352p. $16.95. ISBN 0 439 49881 3. [fiction] JS, JS (See full booktalk in *Teen Genre Connections,* 2005, pages 81 to 83.) Three high school friends in a private girls' school acquire pen pals from a school stereotyped as a juvenile-delinquent haven.

5. Prose, Francine. **Bullyville.** New York: HarperTeen, 2007. 260p. $16.99. ISBN 975 0 06 057497 0. [fiction] MJ, CG with high appeal for boys. (*Genre Talks for Teens,* 2010, pages 16 to 19.) Thirteen-year-old Bart Rangely receives a scholarship to an exclusive boys' school in his New Jersey town and faces the in-group bullies.

ʦʨ

Vivian, Siobhan. **Same Difference.**
New York: Scholastic/Push, 2009. 287p. $18.99.
ISBN-13: 978 0 545 00407 7. [fiction] JS, G

Themes/Topics: friendship, identity, family,
conduct of life, art

Summary/Description

During a college summer art institute, sixteen-year-old Emily discovers her talent, which has been stifled by "fitting in" to her affluent family and friends. A dependent friendship with a less talented, but more determined and vocal female art student fuels Emily's transformation. Emily's attraction to the nineteen-year-old teaching assistant who eventually loses his job because of their relationship complicates her journey. Emily discovers that her new friend hides poverty and fear behind her artsy, cool façade and that the teaching assistant has developed a personality to fit the art world. She eventually accepts that personas are part of life and setbacks mean new beginnings.

Value: Emily learns to respect her own talents and the feelings of friends and family as she evaluates life's rewards and failures.

Read Aloud/Reader Response

1. Chapter 7, pages 66 to 69. In this chapter, Fiona challenges Emily's "fake" smile.
2. Chapter 9, pages 78 to 79, beginning "It's creepy . . ." and ending with the chapter. After Fiona calls her fake, Emily considers Fiona's judgment.
3. Chapter 11, pages 94 to 97, beginning "'I'm not sure . . .'" and ending with the chapter. Emily and Fiona talk about Emily's confusing personality.
4. Chapter 13, page 112, beginning "Rick is not . . ." and ending "Except not . . ." Emily challenges Meg about Rick.
5. Chapter 35, page 260, beginning "I want to talk . . ." and ending ". . . back up again." Mr. Frank counsels Emily never to hide her potential.

Booktalk

Ask the group why they think that people travel or seek out new experiences.

Sixteen-year-old Emily is about to experience a new life. She is accepted in a summer art class. Not such a big deal compared to something like, say, a trip around the world? Oh yes it is. Because she will learn to draw the real tree, not the one she has in her head or has read about. She will be required to add her attitude to her talent instead of listening for someone else's. And all that looking and reacting could change her world and her life. She might see and draw the real people instead of the ones in her head. And she might start to see the real Emily instead of the one she is supposed to be, the one everyone else has in *their* heads. This summer won't be filled with the popular group she hangs out with at Starbucks. This summer she is going to meet the out-group she ignores. This summer won't mean hanging with her best friend Meg and Meg's hunk of a boyfriend. This summer might mean finding her own boyfriend. Big journey? Big changes? Yes, if Emily can see the whole picture. Otherwise, it is all going to be a summer of the *Same Difference.*

Curriculum Connections

1. (Research, language arts) Define the word *persona.* Find examples of its application to the world of art and literature.
2. (Research, language arts, art) Duchamp and his art are central allusions in the novel. Using library resources, learn more about Duchamp, find examples of his work, and act as a resource person for the group.
3. (Discuss, language arts) Has Emily changed? Use specifics from the story to support your answer.

Related Works

1. Anderson, Laurie Halse. **Prom.** New York: Viking Press, 2005. 215p. $16.99. ISBN 0 670 05974 9. [fiction] JS, G (*Booktalks and Beyond,* pages 56 to 58.) Eighteen-year-old Ashley Hannigan ignores the prom until she is pulled into running the event and discovers that she may be college material.
2. Averett, Edward. **The Rhyming Season.** New York: Clarion Books, 2005. 214p. $16.00. ISBN 0 618 46948 6. [fiction] JS, G (*Booktalks and Beyond,* 2007, pages 65 to 68.) Senior Brenda Jacobsen develops a whole new view of life when an eccentric English teacher coaches the girls' basketball coach.
3. Dessen, Sarah. **Just Listen.** New York: Penguin Group/Speak, 2006. 371p. $8.99pa. ISBN-13: 978 0 14 241097 4. [fiction] JS, G (*Genre Talks for Teens,* pages 24 to 27.) Shunned by her peer group and struggling with family problems, Annabel Green meets an outcast who teaches her how to express her opinions and trust her choices.
4. Marchetta, Melina. **Saving Francesca.** New York: Alfred A. Knopf, 2004. 243p. $17.99. ISBN 0 375 92982 7. [fiction] JS, G (*Booktalks and Beyond,* 2007, pages 52 to 54.) Sixteen-year-old Francesca, a new student at a formerly all-boys school, finds new friends with people who were considered part of her old school's out-group.

5.   Muharrar, Aisha. **More Than a Label.** Minneapolis, MN: Free Spirit Publishing, 2002. 144p. $13.95pa. ISBN 1 57542 110 0. [nonfiction] JS, CG Muharrar distinguishes between labels and slurs and explains how each is peer pressure. She provides extensive references for dealing with bullying and peer acceptance.

෬෭

Wolff, Virginia Euwer. **This Full House.**

New York: HarperCollins/HarperTeen/The Bowen Press, 2009. 476p.

(*Make Lemonade* trilogy) $17.99.

ISBN-13: 978 0 06 158304 9. [novel in verse] JS, CG with high interest for girls

Themes/Topics: conduct of life, interpersonal relations, science, teen pregnancy, mother/child relationships

Summary/Description

In this third book of the *Make Lemonade* trilogy, LaVaughn enters the Women in Science program, her path to college. The program leader, Dr. Moore, reminds her of her abandoned friend, Jolly, who grew up in foster care. With the help of Patrick, the intellectually gifted boy she previously ignored, LaVaughn matches the DNA of the two women. Jeopardizing her chances for her college education, she tells the truth to both women who react bitterly but eventually reconnect at Jolly's GED graduation. She also deals with her childhood friend's pregnancy and her feelings for Patrick, who was abandoned at birth and raised by nuns in an orphanage. At the end of the novel, she receives her college acceptance with a scholarship and realizes that she has deep feelings for Patrick.

Value: LaVaughn demonstrates her respect for family, friendship, education, and honesty.

Read Aloud/Reader Response

The entire book is an excellent read aloud. Some poems form mini dramas that focus on elements of the related plots. The selections below center on LaVaughn's goals and conflicts.

1.   Part 1, poem 6, page 14. LaVaughn describes her struggle to be in charge.
2.   Part one, poem 20, pages 69 to 78. LaVaughn's trip to the art museum brings together her desire for college, her feelings for Jody, and her interest for and regret about Patrick.

3. Part 1, poem 38, pages 145 to 150. LaVaughn writes her thank-you note for the computer.
4. Part 2, poem 42, pages 168 to 173. LaVaughn meets with the "Guidance Man" and Dr. Moore to get her letters of recommendation.
5. Part 3, poem 99, pages 414 to 424. LaVaughn releases her emotion in the shower.

Booktalk

Hold up Make Lemonade *and* True Believer. *Ask how many have read the books.*

These are the first two books in the *Make Lemonade* trilogy. In them, LaVaughn got a job and lost love. Always she had a college goal. As a senior, she has a serious chance for that goal. She qualifies for the Women in Science program that will give her skills and recommendations. But LaVaughn is her own worst enemy. She loves so much and wants to help those she loves. She still helps the girl who first hired her to babysit, Jolly. She makes sure that Jolly and her two children are making it, even when Jolly doesn't want her help. LaVaughn's friend from her Head Start days is pregnant, and LaVaughn has to help her. But another baby bothers her more, a baby that could destroy her chances for school, a baby that no one else knows about. What should she do? To whom should she turn? And if she makes the wrong decisions, can she and the people she loves ever live with the consequences? How many people can a girl from the projects care for in *This* (already) *Full House*?

Curriculum Connections

1. (Research, social studies) Using library resources, learn more about health and life statistics for single mothers. Act as a resource person for the group.
2. (Research, social studies) Using library resources, learn more about the success statistics of foster care. Act as a resource person for the group.
3. (Create, language arts) Using positive and negative examples from the novel, define character.

Related Works

1. Fleischman, Paul. **Breakout.** Chicago: Cricket Books/A Marcato Book, 2003. 124p. $15.95. ISBN 0 8126 2696 6. [fiction] JS, CG with high interest for girls. In alternating chapters, seventeen-year-old

Del, while stuck in a traffic jam, reflects on her foster home life and the imminent performance of her one woman show.

2. Frost, Helen. **Keesha's House.** New York: Farrar, Straus and Giroux/Frances Foster Books, 2003. 116p. $16.00. ISBN 0 374 34064 1. [novel in verse] JS, CG (*Booktalks and Beyond,* 2007, pages 21 to 24.) Joe, accepted into this house when he was twelve by a lady named Aunt Annie, offers refuge to troubled teens.

3. Nolan, Han. **Born Blue.** New York: Harcourt, 2001. 177p. $17.00. ISBN 0 15 201916 2. [fiction] JS, S (*Teen Genre Connections,* 2005, pages 13 to 15.) Janie, a damaged foster child, leaves her illegitimate daughter with a caring family.

4. Wolff, Virginia Euwer. **Make Lemonade.** New York: Henry Holt, 1993. 208p. (*Make Lemonade* trilogy) $15.95. ISBN 0 8050 2288 7. [novel in verse] JS, CG with high interest for girls. In this first book, fourteen-year-old LaVaughn takes a babysitting job and decides going to college is a better choice than single motherhood.

5. Wolff, Virginia Euwer. **True Believer.** New York: Atheneum, 2001. 264p. (*Make Lemonade* trilogy) $17.00. ISBN 0 689 82827 6. [novel in verse] JS, CG with high interest for girls. (*Teen Genre Connections,* 2005, pages 26 to 28.) In this second book, romance teaches fifteen-year-old LaVaughn to continue her education and accept people for who they are.

Fair Play

ध्यु

Coy, John. **Box Out.**
New York: Scholastic Press, 2008. 289p. $16.99.
ISBN-13: 978 0 439 87032 0. [fiction] JS, CG with high interest for boys

Themes/Topics: basketball, religious freedom,
small town life, prejudice, conduct of life

Summary/Description

When sophomore Liam Bergstrom is called up to varsity, he realizes that Darius Buckner, the best player on the team, is harassed because he refuses to pray with the team and meet with the Horizon Athletic Fellowship, a Christian athletic group with a Protestant focus. Darius quits the team. Liam questions the prayer and plays less. He contacts an agency that deals with separation of church and state. The agency sends the school a letter stating that no teacher can force prayer in public school. He quits the team and becomes close friends with Darius who plays pick-up on the college court. They practice with the girls' team, which is preparing for their championship game. He experiences a supportive and goal-directed coaching style that encourages him to think for himself. The girls lose the championship game because of questionable referee calls. The varsity team, coming off a poor season, challenges Darius, Liam, and three starters on the girls' team to a game. Then Liam, Darius, and the girls win.

Values: Liam demonstrates integrity and independence when he challenges the prayer and learns about true friendship.

Read Aloud/Reader Response

1. Chapter 4, pages 31 to 32, beginning with the chapter and ending ". . . he'd made his free throws." The seniors trash Darius after he quits the team. Liam does not defend him.
2. Chapter 8, pages 72 to 78, beginning "Thursday morning . . ." and ending with the chapter. Liam attends a meeting of the Horizon Athletic Fellowship.
3. Chapter 15, pages 142 to 145, beginning "He exhales, jumps, and launches . . ." and ending with the chapter. Basketball principles apply to life.
4. Chapter 22, pages 206 to 207, beginning with the chapter and ending with ". . . love and humility." Liam contemplates love.
5. Chapter 25, pages 238 to 241, beginning with the chapter and ending with "*My road.*" Passages from Whitman show Liam's commitment to independence.

Booktalk

Ask how many people in the group know what a box out is in basketball. If no one knows, read the definition of box out on the inside cover.

Liam Bergstrom gets called up to the varsity team as a sophomore. He is great on box out and has a trophy girlfriend—even if she is spending part of the year in France. Life is good, and if Liam can compete with the seniors, it will stay that way. But the perfect life is cracking. His varsity coach wants his team to do just as he says, on and off the court. If they don't, they pay. Everyone keeps the coach happy, except the team's best player. Liam's girlfriend seems to be getting carried away with France, especially one particular Frenchman. Liam can cave into the coach's demands, wait for his girlfriend to be All-American again, and keep the good life in this small town. He has lived here just two years, and he is still learning their rules. But doing what someone else wants you to do instead of what you feel is right gets old fast. Is Liam going to play the old game or improve it? It depends on his controlling the *Box Out*.

Curriculum Connections

1. (Research, social studies) Using library resources, find out more about the separation of church and state. Act as a resource person for the group.
2. (Discuss, language arts) Does the game of basketball teach Liam about life?
3. (Create, language arts) Liam chooses his own journey by reading Walt Whitman. Choose a poet that you feel focuses your life. Share the significant passages with the group.

Related Works

1. Averett, Edward. **The Rhyming Season.** New York: Clarion Books, 2005. 214p. $16.00. ISBN 0 618 46948 6. [fiction] JS, G (*Booktalks and Beyond,* 2007, pages 65 to 68.) Senior Brenda Jacobsen improves more than basketball skills when an English teacher, who requires the players to memorize poetry, becomes the new coach.
2. Coy, John. **Crackback.** New York: Scholastic Press, 2005. 208p. $16.99. ISBN 0 439 69733 6. [fiction] JS, CG with high interest for boys. Pressured by his coach, teammates, and father to perform well in football, junior Miles Manning considers taking steroids.
3. Krech, Bob. **Rebound.** Tarrytown, NY: Marshall Cavendish, 2006. 271p. $16.99. ISBN-13: 978 0 7614 5319 2. [fiction] JS, CG with high interest for boys. (*Genre Talks for Teens,* 2010, pages 74 to 76.) Ray Wisniewski makes the school's African American basketball team, faces deep prejudice, and revises his criteria for friendship and integrity.
4. Myers, Walter Dean. **Game.** New York: HarperTeen, 2008. 218p. $17.99. ISBN-13: 978 0 06 058295 1. [fiction] MJS, CG with high interest for boys. (*Genre Talks for Teens,* 2009, pages 71 to 74.) Harlem high school senior, a star basketball player who rejects coaching, finds his star spot threatened by a Czech immigrant.
5. Waltman, Kevin. **Learning the Game.** New York: Scholastic Press, 2005. 224p. $16.95. ISBN 0 439 73109 7. [fiction] JS, CG with high interest for boys. (*Booktalks and Beyond,* 2007, pages 33 to 35.) Practicing for his senior season on the local court, Nate Gilman decides if he will cave into the team bully or follow his conscience.

❦

Deuker, Carl. **Gym Candy.**

New York: Houghton Mifflin Harcourt/Graphia, 2007. 313p. $8.99pa.
ISBN-13: 978 0 547 07631 7. [fiction] JS, CG with high interest for boys

Themes/Topics: football, fathers and sons, high schools, steroids, family life, Washington State

Summary/Description

Mick Johnson is a year older than his classmates because his father, an unsuccessful professional football player, wants him to have the physical edge over his classmates. As a ninth-grader, he is an outstanding player but needs more strength to star in high school varsity. When his father arranges a gym membership, Mick encounters a trainer who offers him nonaddictive steroids. Mick accepts the offer, accelerates his use, sets records, and wins games, until his best friend discovers the drugs and turns him in to the coach. Although Mick seems compliant in rehab, he sometimes perceives his friend as a "Judas" and realizes that he may still use the drugs to win.

Values: Mick's lack of self-respect makes him want to prove himself, even if it means sacrificing friendship and integrity. For him, winning is addictive.

Read Aloud/Reader Response

1. Part 1, chapter 4, pages 14 to 17. In this chapter, Mick describes the thrill of football.
2. Part 2, chapter 11, pages 80 to 82. Mick experiences failure.
3. Part 3, chapter 1, pages 91 to 92, beginning "In the hallway . . ." and ending with the chapter. Mick turns the coach's advice into an insult.
4. Part 4, chapter 1, page 161, beginning "Peter went . . ." and ending with the page. Peter warns Mick about the drug side effects.
5. Epilogue, pages 312 to 313, beginning "Before all . . ." and ending with the novel. Mick realizes that his drive to win may be his addiction.

Booktalk

Hold up a large gold star. Ask what the group associates with it.

Stars mean a great deal to us. We work hard for them when we start school. They show we're special. Some of us become stars. Mick Johnson is raised to be a star, a football star. (*Read chapter 1, beginning with the chapter and ending "Your first touchdown!"*) His dad holds him back in school a year to give him that competitive edge in sports. In ninth grade, he makes varsity. But just being on the varsity team isn't enough for Mick. He wants to be the varsity star. His age doesn't give him an edge anymore, and he has to get that edge back. He drinks protein shakes and works out at a gym. It's slow progress, but then he gets an offer. A friendly trainer helps him get bigger and stronger faster. First some pills, then some injections. Sure, he will get a little depressed, maybe a little angrier than usual. But he will get what he has to have—winning. And isn't fame's gold star worth the price of a little *Gym Candy*?

Curriculum Connections

1. (Research, biology, mental health) Using library resources, learn more about the effect of steroids on the body. Act as a resource person for the group.
2. (Research, mental health) Using library resources, learn more about the principles of team work. Act as a resource person for the group, and be prepared to discuss how your research affects your feelings about Mick and his father.
3. (React, mental health) Who do you feel is responsible for Mick's steroid use? Be sure to use specifics from the novel to support your opinion.

Related Works

1. Coy, John. **Crackback.** New York: Scholastic Press, 2005. 208p. $16.99. ISBN 0 439 69733 6. [fiction] JS, CG with high interest for boys. Pressured by his coach, teammates, and father to perform well in football, junior Miles Manning considers taking steroids.
2. Freedman, Jeri. **Steroids: High-Risk Performance Drugs.** New York: Rosen Publishing, 2009. 64p. $29.95. ISBN-13: 978 1 4358 5013 2. [nonfiction] MJS, CG Freedman describes steroids and explains the legal uses and the dangers of abuse.
3. Green, Tim. **Baseball Great.** New York: HarperCollins Publishers, 2009. 250p. $16.99. ISBN-13: 978 0 06 162686 9. [fiction] MJ, B A seventh-grader on an all-star baseball team is offered gym candy to enhance his performance and decides to expose the sources.
4. Myers, Walter Dean. **Game.** New York: HarperTeen, 2008. 218p. $17.99. ISBN-13: 978 0 06 058295 1. [fiction] MJS, CG with high interest for boys. (*Genre Talks for Teens*, 2009, pages 71 to 74.) A star basketball player who rejects coaching finds his star spot threatened when a Czech immigrant joins the Harlem team.

5. Waltman, Kevin. **Learning the Game.** New York: Scholastic Press, 2005. 224p. $16.95. ISBN 0 439 73109 7. [fiction] JS, CG with high interest for boys. (*Booktalks and Beyond*, 2007, pages 33 to 35.) Nate Gilman comes from an affluent family but helps his team rob a college fraternity. His decision to confess teaches him about true loyalty, friendship, and responsibility.

❦❦

Murdock, Catherine Gilbert. **Dairy Queen Trilogy.**

Boston, MA: Houghton Mifflin Co. [fiction] JS, CG with high interest for girls

Themes/Topics: football, farming, interpersonal relationships, sexual identity, family, coming of age, conduct of life

Dairy Queen.

2006. 275p. $16.00. ISBN-13: 978 0 618 68307 9.

Summary/Description

In her sophomore year, fifteen-year-old D. J. Schwenk runs her family's farm while her father recovers from hip surgery. She fails English. The novel, D. J.'s explanation of her summer and the dynamics of her family and friends, satisfies D. J.'s writing requirement for sophomore English. This summer, Brian Nelson, the rich quarterback from the rival school's football team is assigned to work on the Schwenk farm to learn a work ethic. He and his friends insult D. J. with cow jokes, but she grows to like Brian and becomes his football trainer. D. J. considers the truth of those jokes and notices that many people in the community, like cows, simply live up to everyone else's expectations. She breaks out of those expectations and tries out for the football team. D. J.'s relationship with Brian crushes her best friend, Amber, who assumed that she and D. J. were a lesbian couple. Her "secret" decision to try out for football infuriates Brian. D. J. eventually plays against him. Her team wins. Brian later asks her to date him.

Values: D. J.'s work ethic and maturity won't be complete until she can examine and express her feelings.

Read Aloud/Reader Response

1. Chapter 2, pages 13 to 15, beginning "As cut up . . ." and ending with the chapter. D. J. explains part of the family history.

2. Chapter 6, pages 50 to 51, beginning "That evening at . . ." and ending with the chapter. D. J. realizes that she is a poor coach for Brian.

3. Chapter 15, pages 118 to 129. In this chapter, D. J. decides to take control of her life.

4. Chapter 20, pages 170 to 171, beginning "There's another thing . . ." and ending with the chapter. D. J. considers homosexual stereotypes.

5. Chapter 31, pages 274 and 275. D. J. reflects on her summer.

Booktalk

Fifteen-year-old D. J. Schwenk runs her family's farm. She is too busy to worry about that English course she failed, or about quitting the girls' basketball team, or about the nasty remarks that guys make about her size. She is too busy to think about why her older brothers left home, why her younger brother won't talk, why her mother works all the time, why her best friend is suddenly absent, if or when her father will recover enough to run the farm, or if or when she will have a chance to leave Red Bend, Wisconsin. D. J. has work to do, and if there is one thing that any Schwenk knows how to do, it's work. They work hard on the farm, on the basketball court, and on the football field. They don't waste time talking about how they feel. And now D. J. has another job. The new farmhand is the quarterback from her high school's rival football team. He is a rich boy with an easy life, and his coach wants him to learn to work hard. What better school than the Schwenk farm? The problem is that D. J. knows that she not only can work harder than the pretty boy but also play harder, football that is. Should she let him in on those Schwenk family secrets that sent her brothers to two Big Ten schools? What the soon-to-be-star-quarterback does know how to do is talk. Talk? To a Schwenk? He's got to be kidding. But one word leads to another. Talking starts D. J. thinking, thinking about everything. And that is really hard work. All that thinking comes down to one big question. Will she spend her life doing the things she wants to do or spend her life doing what everyone else expects her to do—ruling those cows and holding on to her title, the *Dairy Queen*?

The Off Season.

2007. 277p. $16.00. ISBN-13: 978 0 618 68.

Summary/Description

*T*he *Off Season* begins with the Labor Day mentioned in the conclusion of *Dairy Queen*. Eleventh-grader D. J. Schwenk starts her junior year as a linebacker for Red Bend High School, but her football injury and her oldest brother's spinal cord injury interrupt her season. As she helps her brother regain his will to live, she deals with her feelings about her best friend's lesbian relationship with an older partner, the sporadic attentions of Brian Nelson, her younger brother's seemingly delinquent behavior, her father's off-the-wall ideas about how to keep the farm afloat, her mother's emotional collapse, and her personal fame as perhaps the first girl linebacker in northern Wisconsin. She proves her emotional as well as physical strength by helping her father maintain the farm, accepting her friend in spite of peer pressure, supporting the family through crises, celebrating their successes, and breaking up with Brian whose popularity and "easy life" keep him from accepting her and standing up for her in front of his friends.

Values: D. J. loves unconditionally and draws on a sense of self-respect that allows her to pursue her own talents and break up with Brian who doesn't seem to really respect her.

Read Aloud/Reader Response

1. Chapter 1, pages 4 to 6, beginning "Then there's Curtis . . ." and ending with the chapter. This passage introduces Curtis, reveals D. J.'s values, and anticipates the complicated adult problems that she faces.
2. Chapter 15, pages 139 to 152. In this chapter, D. J. demonstrates her emotional strength.
3. Chapter 17, pages 173 to 177, beginning "Charlie and Bill," and ending with the chapter. The passage focuses on D. J.'s relationship with Bill.
4. Chapter 27, pages 257 to 258, beginning "Maybe that's what . . ." and ending ". . . like Brian." In her college visit, D. J. encounters people who are accepted for who they are and realizes how immature Brian is.
5. Chapter 28, pages 266 to 267, beginning "'Do you know . . .'" and ending ". . . couldn't be broken." D. J. convinces Win to ignore what people will say about his being crippled.

Booktalk

Hold up the book Dairy Queen.

Remember D. J., "the Dairy Queen"? D. J. Schwenk, all six feet and more of her, is in the eleventh grade now, and her life is getting more complicated by the minute. She can't believe that the knockout gorgeous quarterback, Brian Nelson, who worked on the Schwenk farm last summer, is interested in her. The rivalry between their schools shouldn't be too big of an obstacle to their relationship except that D. J. is the first female linebacker in her high school's history—maybe in all of northern Wisconsin history. That fact makes dating a little more high profile than either one of them would like. Then there is her best friend Amber who has to leave town to be herself. That leaves D. J. alone. But the most complications come from her family. Her two older brothers play staring roles in the Big Ten, but they don't come home. When he isn't cutting school, her little brother hides his six-foot, two-inch frame behind little kids, the only people he can talk to. Her father works twenty-four/seven trying to save his farm, and her mother's back is collapsing at the worst possible times. What do these people's lives have to do with D. J.? Everything. D. J., a close-my-mouth-and-keep-flying-under-the-radar-kind-of-girl is part of everyone else's problems and has no answers. She might not even know the questions. She is a Schwenk. How can she know how to talk about anything? But she is willing to work as hard as she can to stay in any game, even if it's *The Off Season.*

Front and Center.

2009. 254p. $16.00. ISBN-13: 978 0 618 95982 8.

Summary/Description

This last novel in the *Dairy Queen* trilogy starts after five months of D. J. caring for Win. She returns to school in time for girls' basketball, and faces her own life complications. Her good friend Beaner wants to date her. A reformed Brian Nelson wants to get back together. Colleges try to recruit her, and her team and coach pressure her to be point guard. With the help of family and friends, she finally expresses her choices. Brian and she reconcile, and she decides to join Aaron and her brother Bill at the University of Minnesota.

Values: As in the first two novels, D. J. develops inner strength and her identity as she takes responsibility for her talents and feelings and helps others develop their talents, but in this last novel, she learns truly to accept people as they are.

Read Aloud/Reader Response

1. Chapter 11, pages 159 to 160, beginning "At least practice . . ." and ending ". . . already was?" Ashley gives advice on shyness.
2. Chapter 13, page 199, beginning "And—poof" and ending "'. . . everyone does.'" Mother tells D. J. that her feelings are part of growing up.

3. Chapter 14, pages 213 to 214, beginning "Which one . . ." and ending with the chapter. Brian makes the case for Division I schools.
4. Chapter 15, pages 220 to 222, beginning "Bill walked us . . ." and ending with the chapter. Bill talks to D. J. about fear.
5. Chapter 16, pages 252 to 254, beginning "So. Meeting Brian's . . ." and ending with the novel. D. J. describes Win's gratitude to her and her gratitude to him.

Booktalk

Hold up Dairy Queen *and* The Off Season.

In these two books, you got acquainted with D. J. She saved her family's farm, and she saved her brother's life. Now she can concentrate on basketball. After five months, she is back at school and glad because life with family got way too complicated. Now D. J. has a personal problem. She is getting picked. Not picked on and made fun of, but picked. Longtime friend Beaner wants to be her boyfriend. Brian Nelson has something to say about that even though he has no chance of getting the title ever again. Then Division I, II, and III schools are sending her letters, a whole bag full. They want her to call and visit when they get a chance. Right. Then the team keeps putting those number one signs on her locker. They want her to be point guard. Forget that because point guards have to talk. D. J. doesn't talk. And big brother Win has decided to take her on as his own personal makeover project. D. J. loves being a "plain old background" person. Hard work, no pressure. But it just doesn't look like that kind of year. This year D. J. is picked, selected, and groomed. This year D. J. and her decisions are all *Front and Center.*

Curriculum Connections

1. (Research and Follow-Up, language arts) Using library resources, learn about one communication technique that you think might improve your own communication. Use that technique and keep a journal about how its use affects you.
2. (Discuss, language arts) How is communication related to respect in the novels? Be sure to use specific examples. How is communication related to respect in real life? Be sure to cite specific examples.
3. (Discuss, language arts) Hard times give D. J. good times. After reading this statement, choose a number from one to five, with the number one meaning highly disagree and the number five meaning highly agree. Compare your number with the number choices of

others in the group. Be sure to support your choice with specifics from the novel.

Related Works

1. Averett, Edward. **The Rhyming Season.** New York: Clarion Books, 2005. 214p. $16.00. ISBN 0 618 46948 6. [fiction] JS, G (*Booktalks and Beyond,* 2007, pages 65 to 68.) When an eccentric English teacher becomes the new girls' basketball coach, senior Brenda Jacobsen sorts out her relationship to sports and life.

2. Clarke, Judith. **One Whole and Perfect Day.** Honesdale, PA: Front Street, 2006. 250p. $16.95. ISBN-13: 978 1 932425 95 6. [fiction] JS, CG with high appeal for girls. (*Genre Talks for Teens,* 2009, pages 41 to 44.) Lily, the sensible one in her eccentric family, hopes for one perfect day of togetherness even though that day requires healing the conflict between her irascible, prejudiced grandfather and her aimless older brother.

3. Covey, Sean. **The 6 Most Important Decisions You'll Ever Make: A Guide for Teens.** New York: Simon & Shuster/Fireside Books, 2006. 319p. $15.95. ISBN-13: 978 0 7432 6504 1. [nonfiction] JS Using the seven habits philosophy, Covey addresses the issues of school, friends, parents, dating and sex, addictions, and self-worth. Each chapter concludes with a "Baby Steps" application section for reader application. "Help Desk," at the end of the book, lists applicable Web sites for each chapter. A bibliography lists the references for each chapter.

4. Muharrar, Aisha. Elizabeth Verdick (ed.). **More Than a Label: Why What You Wear or Who You're with Doesn't Define Who You Are.** Minneapolis, MN: Free Spirit Publishing, 2002. 144p. $13.95. ISBN 1 57542 110 0. [nonfiction] MJS, CG Muharrar defines labeling, explains how labels make people feel, and suggests ways to deal with them.

5. Smith, Sherri L. **Lucy the Giant.** New York: Delacorte Press, 2002. 217p. $15.95. ISBN 0 385 72940 5. [fiction] MJS, G (*Teen Genre Connections,* 2005, pages 121 to 123.) Lucy Otswego, fifteen years old and more than six feet tall, lives in Sitka, Alaska, where she regularly carries her father home from drunken binges and is pitied by adults and blocked by peers.

6. Swanson, Julie A. **Going for the Record.** Grand Rapids, MI: Eerdmans Books for Young Readers, 2004. 217p. $8.00pa. ISBN 0 8028 5273 4. [fiction] JS, G (*Teen Genre Connections,* 2005, pages 68 to 70.) Seventeen-year-old Leah Weiczynkowski re-thinks her relationship with Olympic-level soccer when her father develops cancer.

CRED

Weaver, Will. **Saturday Night Dirt.**

New York: Farrar, Straus and Giroux, 2008. 163p. (Motor Novels) $14.95.
ISBN-13: 978 0 374 35060 4. [fiction] JS, CG with high interest for boys

Themes/Topics: stock car racing, interpersonal relations,
success, conduct of life

Summary/Description

Short chapters designated by the characters' names are divided by
times in the evening. Seventeen-year-old Trace Bonham, a talented
racer and mechanic whose father pressures him to drive, is being sabo-
taged by their jealous mechanic. Seventeen-year-old Melody Walters
runs her injured father's struggling Headwaters Speedway. She is
hoping that bad weather elsewhere draws drivers to their track. Patrick
Fletcher has a crush on Mel and sings with her in the choir. He does
odd jobs at the track. Beau Carlson, a scrappy five feet five, wants to
defeat Amber, his rival, who has a crush on him. Sonny and Leonard are
Native Americans. Sonny's car is his ticket off the reservation. Leonard
wants to stay on the reservation but goes to the Speedway to see Tudy,
a Native American girl who works in her step-father's barbecue wagon.
By the end of the night, the dating relationships have started to form,
and Trace will try out for a promotional team.

Values: All the teens work hard for self-knowledge and recognition.

Read Aloud/Reader Response

1. "Saturday Noon," "Trace," pages 3 to 4, beginning with the chapter
    and ending "'. . . for tonight.'" Trace exchanges words with Larry,
    the mechanic.
2. "Saturday Noon," "Patrick," pages 18 to 19. In this section, Patrick
    wants to wear the clothes that will attract Mel, who runs the track
    for her father.
3. "Saturday, 6:00 P.M.," "Amber," pages 97 to 99, beginning "With a
    thumbs up . . ." and ending ". . . end of hot laps." Amber drives her
    hot laps.
4. "Saturday, 8:00 P.M.," "Trace," pages 125 to 126, beginning "Seeing
    a half car . . ." and ending ". . . the longest?" Trace makes his move
    to win the race.
5. "Saturday, 8:00 P.M.," "Amber," pages 134 to 135, beginning "Look-
    ing forward . . ." and ending ". . . wrecked No. 192." Amber sees
    Beau's car fly apart and moves to protect him.

Booktalk

It's Saturday night. The place to be is Headwaters Speedway. Trace Bonham is the track favorite. His father supplied him with a Street Stock Chevy. Now Trace has to make sure he can get it to run. Plenty of drivers are ready to take him on. The independent Amber knows cars as well as her brothers who crew for her. Beau Kim drives a bag of borrowed bolts, but his will to win may keep the hardware together. Then there are the older regulars who want to prove themselves on and off the track just as much as the teenagers. And Melody, known as "Mel," welcomes them all. She runs the track for her father, a legendary driver whose career ended with a speedway wreck. Tonight everyone competes. With the good weather, Headwaters is drawing the big-time stock car racers. But wrecks can happen anywhere and to anyone—especially when everyone is willing to go for broke on *Saturday Night Dirt.*

Curriculum Connections

1. (Research, language arts) Using your library resources, learn more about the origin of stock car racing. Act as a resource person for the group.
2. (Analyze, language arts) Weaver changes the format in the subsequent Motor Novels. (See the following Related Works 2 and 5.) Why do you think he makes that choice?
3. (Create, language arts) Using all the books that you can find in your library about car racing, create a display that you feel will draw interest.

Related Works

1. Hobbs, Valerie. **Sonny's War.** New York: Farrar, Straus and Giroux/ Frances Foster Books, 2002. 215p. $16.00. ISBN 0 374 37136 9. [fiction] JS, CG (*Teen Genre Connections,* 2005, pages 230 to 233.) A Vietnam veteran, wounded, angry, and addicted, turns to daredevil car racing.
2. Weaver, Will. **Checkered Flag Cheater.** New York: Farrar, Straus and Giroux, 2010. 198p. $16.99. ISBN-13: 978 0 374 35062 8. [fiction] JS, CG with high interest for boys. After Mel discovers the other girlfriends and Trace discovers how an illegal engine allows him to win, Trace leaves his racing team and hopes to reconnect with Mel.
3. Weaver, Will. **Full Service**. New York: Farrar, Straus and Giroux, 2005. 232p. $17.00. ISBN 0 374 32485 9. [fiction] JS, CG (*Booktalks and Beyond,* 2007, pages 257 to 259.) Fifteen-year-old Paul Sutton

learns about life and his own beliefs when he takes a job in a local gas station.

4. Weaver, Will. "If You Give a Kid a Ride: Stock Cars, Novels and Mentoring." *VOYA*. (August, 2009): 192–195. Weaver describes the background of the Motor Novels series, which includes his own hands-on experience with the Farrar, Straus and Giroux stock car driven by Skyler Smith and the blog address related to the novels (http://www.motornovels.com).

5. Weaver, Will. **Super Stock Rookie.** New York: Farrar, Straus and Giroux, 2009. 197p. (Motor Novels) $14.95. ISBN-13: 978 0 374 35061 1. [fiction] JS, CG with high interest for boys. Questions about his winning and the deterioration of his personal life make Trace question his success.

Courage: Action, Adventure, and Survival Novels

In action, adventure, and survival books, characters faced with crisis discover the courage to persevere to save themselves and the generosity to help others. *The Hunger Games* and *Catching Fire* fit in both perseverance and generosity and illustrate the genre's central lesson: to be a hero or heroine to others, a person must first save himself or herself.

Perseverance

𝕮𝕺

Allen, Justin. **Year of the Horse.**

New York: The Overlook Press, 2009. 320p. $18.95.
ISBN-13: 978 1 59020 273 9. [fiction] JS, CG with high interest for boys

Themes/Topics: western America, post–Civil War period, ethnic groups, mysticism, good vs. evil, gold mining, prejudice, father/daughter relationships, conduct of life, coming of age

Summary/Description

Fourteen-year-old Lu, the child of Chinese immigrants, is pressed into service by his grandfather and Jack Straw, a mysterious gunslinger, to help an unlikely gang steal a gold mine from a mystical villain in the Wild West. The group represents America. Henry Jesus is a former slave and Union soldier. Chino is a Mexican outlaw from California with no country. John MacLemore, the expedition's financier, is a former Confederate, and MacLemore's teenage daughter is the independent woman spawned by the West. The many encounters on the journey teach Lu his strengths. MacLemore dies. Henry and Chino pursue the man who caused his death and discover that he is Old Scratch, a messenger of the devil who destroys people with their own fears. Lu, who acquired truth bullets on the journey, helps save the day, and Jack Straw explains their experience. Each person uses his or her share of the gold to fulfill a dream. Lu, with Straw, returns home to learn to read from his grandfather.

Values: Lu's perseverance and open mind allow him to survive and develop insight and wisdom to build his future.

Read Aloud/Reader Response

1. Chapter 5, pages 63 to 68, beginning "They found . . ." and ending ". . . on the second verse." The song reveals the prejudices and hate of the time.
2. Chapter 13, pages 177 to 178, beginning "And here I can . . ." and ending ". . . he didn't show it." MacLemore shows his prejudices against women and Lu.
3. Chapter 19, pages 254 to 255, beginning "What sort of tools . . ." and ending ". . . and there's always . . ." Strong reacts to Lu's identity and tries to turn him against Chino.
4. Chapter 21, pages 298 to 309, beginning "The sun was setting . . ." and ending with the chapter. These pages describe the shoot-out between Jack Straw and friends and Phillip Traum and his defenses.
5. Chapter 22, page 317, beginning "When I was with . . ." and ending "I guess . . ." Jack Straw helps Lu define an American.

Booktalk

Ask how many people have heard of the Civil War, the Wild West, and Ghost Riders.

This book has all three plus some gold. Fourteen-year-old Lu is the child of Chinese immigrants. His grandfather is a mystic, famous for cures and potions. One day a stranger comes into Lu's life. He too is a mystic, but he is a gunfighter. Lu's grandfather decides that Lu will go with this gunfighter—to blow something up. Who is this man? How does his grandfather know him? What is Lu supposed to blow up? How is he supposed to do it? But there is no time for questions and no one willing to answer them. The next morning, Lu is on his way with the gunslinger, a former Union soldier and slave, and a Mexican outlaw. They meet the wealthy Mr. MacLemore who is financing the trip and his lovely teenage daughter who prefers men's pants over women's dresses. What is their goal? Stealing a gold mine. Who has it? A mysterious, supernatural villain who kills everyone who tries. But before Lu faces that battle, there are wild animals, deserts, canyons, mountains, supernatural storms, Indians, distrustful settlers, and his own terror. Can he and his companions make it? All questions will be answered in the *Year of the Horse*.

Curriculum Connections

1. (Research, social studies, language arts) Using library resources learn more about the astrology associated with the Year of the Horse. Discuss how it applies to Lu.
2. (Analyze and Discuss, language arts) Read the prologue on pages 7 and 8. The author makes several declarations. List each major opinion you find. Agree or disagree with each, and support your reaction with specifics from the text.
3. (React, language arts) Does this adventure story have any larger application or meaning?

Related Works

1. Ferris, Jean. **Much Ado about Grubstake.** New York: Harcourt Children's Books, 2006. 272p. $17.00. ISBN 0 15 205706 4. [fiction] MJ, CG (*Booktalks and Beyond*, 2007, pages 126 to 128.) In 1888, Arley, a sixteen-year-old orphan, mothers a group of dysfunctional, unsuccessful miners at her Grubstake, Colorado, boarding house and with the help of a young geologist discovers a valuable ore vein and thwarts a plot to steal it.
2. Hardman, Ric Lynden. **Sunshine Rider: The First Vegetarian Western.** New York: Laurel-Leaf Books, 1998. 343p. $4.99pa. ISBN 0 440 22812 3. [fiction] MJS, CG with high interest for boys. A comic cattalo and colorful human characters force Wylie Jackson into manhood when he signs up for a cattle drive with the father he never met.
3. Hite, Sid. **Stick and Whittle.** New York: Scholastic Press, 2000. 208p. $16.95. ISBN 0 439 09828 9. [fiction] MJS, CG with high interest for boys. In this 1872 setting, the least likely heroes save the day, get the girls, bag the money, and discover true friendship.
4. Karr, Kathleen. **The Great Turkey Walk.** New York: Sunburst, 2000. 197p. $4.95pa. ISBN 0 374 42798 4. [fiction] MJ, CG (*Booktalks and More*, 2003, pages 77 to 80.) In 1860, fifteen-year-old orphan Simon Green drives a flock of turkeys to Denver and finds love and his own self-worth in the process.

5. Wadsworth, Ginger. **Words West: Voices of Young Pioneers.** New York: Clarion Books, 2003. 191p. $18.00. ISBN 0 618 23475 6. [nonfiction] MJS, CG (*Teen Genre Connections,* 2005, pages 104 to 106.) Fourteen chapters use the words of children and young adults to describe the opening of the West, preparations for leaving home, the dangerous travel conditions, work, entertainment, and the fulfillment of the promise.

ය්ඩ

Cadnum, Michael. **Peril on the Sea.**

New York: Farrar, Straus and Giroux, 2009. 245p. $16.95.
ISBN-13: 978 0 374 35823 5. [fiction] JS, CG

Themes/Topics: pirates, armada, 1588, Great Britain, Elizabeth I, conduct of life

Summary/Description

Brandon Fletcher, a notorious English pirate rescues eighteen-year-old Sherwin Morris. Morris offers to write favorable accounts of the captain's adventures, but Fletcher focuses on profit more than patriotism or heroism. When the ship is on shore for repairs, Sherwin meets sixteen-year-old Katharine Westing and her father. A local lord is pressuring them to pay their sizable debts to him, if not with money, then with marriage to Katharine. The Westings have invested in a ship's cargo and hire Fletcher to find and seize the ship before the lord does. Katharine joins the crew to safeguard their investment. Both Sherwin and Katherine grasp the difference between war's romance and reality. They locate the Westings' cargo. Fletcher is knighted, and the queen purchases the cargo at a generous price. Sherwin and Katharine look forward to a life together.

Values: Sherwin and Katharine choose love and loyalty over fame and riches

Read Aloud/Reader Response

1. "Inferno," chapter 4, pages 12 to 14. In this chapter, Sherwin is about to drown.
2. "Last Breath," chapter 12, pages 66 to 67, beginning with "There was a . . ." and ending with ". . . defense of his country." Sherwin signs on with the pirates.

3. "Hazard and Death," chapter 13, page 77, beginning "LATER, as Sherwin . . ." and ending with the chapter. Sherwin embraces the adventure of war.

4. "Hazard and Death," chapter 14, pages 80 to 82, beginning "Bartholomew's undertakings . . ." and ending "'. . . no such command.'" Bartholomew explains his former job as a toad eater and his loyalty to Captain Fletcher.

5. "Armada," chapter 32, pages 190 to 194. This chapter describes the sea battle.

Booktalk

Hold up a pirate hat, sword, or flag. Ask the group what they associate with those items.

Movies show what ancient pirates looked like and what wonderfully brave things they did. Were they generous and courageous, or did they just have good press agents? Eighteen-year-old Sherwin Morris thinks that behind every deserving famous man with a sword is a hardworking writer with a pen. (*You may wish to hold up a pen and a sword also.*) He decides to witness the blood, guts, and glory and make pirates legends. They will pay him well. After Sherwin's first job blows up, he is fished out of the ocean by the notorious Captain Brandon Fletcher, a treasure chest of material. Wrong. Pirate captains are businessmen. That's how they get rich. They are cowards. That's how they stay alive. Sherwin has heroic writer's block. Then he meets the beautiful Katharine Westing who hires Captain Fletcher. She goes to sea also, not to write about powerful men, but to steal a ship and keep from marrying a powerful man. This is 1588. The Spanish armada and the English navy are at war. Sherwin and Katharine are in the middle. Staying alive is a full-time job when they come face-to-face with *Peril on the Sea.*

Curriculum Connections

1. (Research, social studies) Using your library resources, learn more about Queen Elizabeth's sixteenth-century pirates and the English/Spanish conflict. Act as a resource person during the discussion.

2. (Analyze, language arts) Examining the characters and their reactions to events, how do you think that Cadnum would define *heroism*? Use specifics from the story for support.

3. (Discuss, language arts) Why do you think Cadnum includes the battle with the pig?

Related Works

1. Aronson, Marc. **Sir Walter Ralegh and the Quest for El Dorado.** New York: Clarion Books, 2000. 222p. $20.00. ISBN 0 395 84827 X. [nonfiction] JS, CG (*Booktalks and More*, 2003, pages 232 to 235.) Ralegh is characterized as a modern man who lived each day as a drama and realized that his support from Queen Elizabeth depended upon the profits that he could give her.

2. Meyer, L. A. **Bloody Jack: Being and Account of the Curious Adventures of Mary "Jacky" Faber, Ship's Boy.** New York: Harcourt, 2002. 278p. $17.00. ISBN 0 15 216721 5. [fiction] JS, CG (*Teen Genre Connections*, 2005, pages 118 to 121.) A eighteenth-century street orphan helps the British navy fight pirates.

3. Rees, Celia. **Pirates!** New York: Bloomsbury, 2003. 380p. $16.95. ISBN 1 58234 816 2. [fiction] MJS, G (*Booktalks and Beyond*, 2007, pages 95 to 97.) Nancy, an English girl of the eighteenth century, becomes a pirate to stop her marriage to a diabolical Brazilian plantation owner.

4. Reuter, Bjarne. Tiina Nunnally (trans.). **The Ring of the Slave Prince.** New York: Dutton Children's Books, 2003. 373p. $22.99. ISBN 0 525 47146 4. [fiction] MJ, CG (*Booktalks and Beyond*, 2007, pages 97 to 100.) In the seventeenth century, fourteen-year-old Tom O'Connor returns a slave boy to his rightful throne, fights pirates, and blocks his sister's marriage to a former officer of the Spanish Inquisition.

5. Thomas, Jane Resh. **Behind the Mask: The Life of Queen Elizabeth I.** New York: Clarion Books, 1998. 196p. $19.00. ISBN 0 395 69120 6. [nonfiction] JS, CG (*Booktalks and More*, 2003, pages 247 to 249.) Resh explains how Elizabeth shapes and is shaped by her times. Queen Elizabeth's life is presented in full-color portraits.

      ℭℑℭ

Collins, Suzanne. **Hunger Games Trilogy.**
New York: Scholastic Press.
[fiction] JS, CG

Themes/Topics: interpersonal relationships, reality television, family, love, futuristic societies, morality of war

The Hunger Games.

2008. 374p. $17.99. ISBN-13: 978 0 439 02348 1.

Summary/Description

The nation of Panem is located in the ruins of North American. The "shining" and indulged national Capitol is surrounded by twelve outlying districts. To discourage another rebellion, the Capitol requires each district to send one boy and one girl between the ages of twelve and eighteen to participate in the annual Hunger Games, a fight to the death on live TV in a government-manipulated environment. Sixteen-year-old Katniss Everdeen takes the place of her twelve-year-old sister whose name is drawn. Katniss has cared for her mother and sister since her father died in a mine explosion when she was eleven. She hunts and forages with eighteen-year-old Gale, who loves her. Peeta Mellark, who gave her bread when she was a starving child and who has loved her from afar, is the boy chosen for the games. Their support teams present them in matching costumes, and Peeta's story about his love for Katniss wins them audience support as star-crossed lovers. During the games, Katniss accepts that role, and they are both allowed to live when they threaten a double suicide instead of a fight to the death.

Value: Katniss and Peeta epitomize the power of love over force.

Read Aloud/Reader Response

1. Chapter 3, pages 42 to 44, beginning "At the last minute . . ." and ending ". . . flying through the trees." Katniss reflects on the mockingjay.
2. Chapter 4, pages 49 to 52, beginning "So I'm . . ." and ending ". . . in months, full." Katniss remembers how her survival skills relate to Peeta.
3. Chapter 5, pages 70 to 72, beginning "The crowd's initial . . ." and ending ". . . outshone them all." Katniss and Peeta wow the audience with their costumes.
4. Chapter 17, pages 222 to 224, beginning with the chapter and ending ". . . teeth from chattering." Katniss reacts after blowing up the supplies.
5. Chapter 18, pages 234 to 238, beginning "Sing" and ending "Good and safe." When Rue dies, Katniss acts in defiance.

Booktalk

Ask how many in the group watch reality television. Ask them about their favorite show.

The futuristic Capitol of Panem has figured out the ultimate reality show. (*Read the passage explaining the Hunger Games: chapter 1, pages 18 to 19, beginning "Just as the town . . ." and ending ". . . battle starvation."*) That is the reality game. When sixteen-year-old Katniss's twelve-year-old sister is chosen to compete, she takes her place. Everyone in the arena will have to kill Katniss to live, and she will have to kill all of the other contestants to survive. Katniss hunts to keep her family alive. How much harder could it be to kill humans? For the masterminds at the distant Capitol, it isn't hard at all. But humans bring love and hate to a fight as well as brains, two dangerous elements for any person or government to control or kill in *The Hunger Games.*

Catching Fire.

2009. 400p. $17.99. ISBN-13: 978 0 439 02349 8.

Summary/Description

Breaking the rules to win the annual Hunger Games gives Katniss and Peeta safety and plenty for themselves and their families but also makes them the face of a rebellion. The Capitol uses the seventy-fifth games as an opportunity to place them back in the arena with other winners. Katniss may lose Peeta, Gale, and her family as the authorities threaten her with their deaths. In the games, Katniss recognizes and accepts alliances that she does not understand are conspiratorial in order to keep Peeta alive. One of the conspirators explodes the game dome. Katniss survives, finds Gale by her side, meets some of the conspirators, and learns that the Capitol has captured Peeta and that the district that they represent is obliterated, but her mother and sister are safe.

Values: Both Katniss and Peeta value love, loyalty, and duty over material gain.

Read Aloud/Reader Response

1. Chapter 2, pages 23 to 24, beginning "I didn't mean . . ." and ending ". . . with him each Sunday." Katniss discovers that the president considers her dangerous.
2. Chapter 4, pages 60 to 62, beginning "A wave . . ." and ending with the chapter. Katniss speaks in Rue's district and sees the power and danger of revolution.

3. Chapter 7, pages 91 to 92, beginning "I stepped in closer" and ending ". . . to take me." Katniss reviews the origins of the mockingjay and how it ties her to Rue.
4. Chapter 13, pages 186 to 187, beginning "Since I don't plan . . ." and ending with the chapter. The revised reaping has no celebration.
5. Chapter 24, pages 351 to 352, beginning "A double deal" and ending "Me." Peeta shows his love for Katniss, and she realizes her love for him.

Booktalk

Hold up both The Hunger Games *and* Catching Fire.

In *The Hunger Games*, Katniss, in her flaming costume, became an immediate television favorite. She survived. She should be worrying about who to marry and how to decorate the beautiful house awarded by the Capitol. Not so lucky. (*Show picture on the book's cover.*) Katniss and her mockingjay pin are symbols, the sparks of a rebellion that she doesn't even know about. Just by being Katniss, she has inspired others to question the government, to reach out and help others. How does the Capitol deal with the heat? They decide to extinguish the fire. This is the seventy-fifth anniversary of the Hunger Games, and the rules change, big-time. All former champions are in the name pool. The strongest of the strong will destroy each other. Death will prove the government's power. For Katniss destruction is a certainty because she is determined to die to save another. But Katniss can't make that decision. Another player is in the games, a player that Katniss can't see and the government can't find. That player is using the rules to change the world, and that player is going to use Katniss's spark to make sure that the world is *Catching Fire.*

Mockingjay.

2010. 390p. $17.99. ISBN-13: 978 0 439 02351.

Summary/Description

After District 12 is destroyed, Katniss agrees to be the rebels' *Mockingjay* even though she realizes that the authorities may be manipulating her. Gale is one of her protectors, and President Snow is using a brainwashed Peeta in newscasts against her. Katniss becomes involved in the battleground and media wars. Gale develops battle plans based on his hunting experience. The rebels rescue high-profile prisoners that include Peeta, who is programmed to kill Katniss. Katniss joins a sharpshooter unit to destroy the Capitol. A supposedly rehabilitated Peeta is assigned to the unit, and suspicion grows that Katniss is set up as a martyr. Peeta slowly recovers and convinces Katniss of her value to the people over either government. Given the opportunity to kill the captured President Snow, she kills the rebel leader instead and chooses Peeta over Gale, because Peeta proves himself to be fully committed to peace, and Gale is focused on battle plans, one of which probably killed Katniss's sister.

Value: When Katniss chooses Peeta over Gale, she chooses peace over love.

Read Aloud/Reader Response

1. Chapter 2, pages 21 to 26, beginning "Caesar settles himself . . ." and ending "'. . . regularly scheduled programming.'" Katniss views Peeta's first interview.
2. Chapter 8, pages 185 to 186, beginning "At first, my screen . . ." and ending ". . . my lifetime, anyway." Katniss sees her "IF WE BURN . . ." film clip.
3. Chapter 9, pages 121 to 127, beginning "Cheese sandwiches . . ." and ending "'. . . back to town.'" Katniss explains "The Hanging Tree."
4. Chapter 11, pages 153 to 154, beginning "Inside the bunker . . ." and ending ". . . begin to break." Katniss figures out how Snow seeks to break her.
5. Chapter 23, pages 328 to 329, beginning "We change bandages . . ." to the end of the chapter. Peeta and Gale discuss which of them Katniss will choose.

Booktalk

Hold up all three of the books in the trilogy.

Here is the saga of Katniss Everdeen, the girl who volunteered for the Hunger Games to save her sister, then risked her life again to save the boy she loved. Her district is destroyed, her family is in hiding, and her beloved Peeta is President Snow's tortured captive. Now she has another battle. Katniss is a national hero, and without ever knowing it, the face of the rebellion. She has an opportunity to destroy a country she hates, but can she do it fighting for a group she can't trust? Do these rebels want peace or just the enemy's power? Will Katniss be a living hero or a convenient martyr for their cause? She decides to face the risks and her heart's confusion. After all, her other love, the ever loyal Gale, is by her side. Even as the body count mounts, she is determined to take down the government. She will kill the evil Snow. She will be the larger-than-life heroine called the *Mockingjay*!

Curriculum Connections

1. (Research, language arts) Using your library resources, learn more about the power of propaganda to change people's thinking. Act as a resource person during the discussion.
2. (Discuss, language arts) In the novels, what are the most powerful weapons? Be specific.
3. (Create) Choose a set of characters and present them in a graphic format, or choose a scene and re-create it in a graphic format.

Related Works

1. Anderson, M. T. **Feed.** Cambridge, MA: Candlewick Press, 2003. 235p. $16.99. ISBN 0 7636 1726 1. [fiction] JS, CG with strong interest for boys. (*Teen Genre Connections*, 2005, pages 201 to 203.) Bored Titus and his teenage friends party on the moon as the feed, a chip implanted in the brain by corporations, controls their news, advertising, and emotional reactions until a rebellious thinker comes into Titus's life.
2. Armstrong, Jennifer, and Nancy Butcher. **Fire Us Trilogy.** New York: HarperCollins Publishers. [fiction] MJS, CG (*Teen Genre Connections*, 2005, pages 204 to 208.)

    The Kindling: Book One. 2002. 224p. $15.89. ISBN 0 06 029411 6. After an adult-killing virus (fire us) sweeps the United States, eight orphans band together to form a family and find the president.

    The Keepers of the Flame: Book Two. 2002. 231p. $17.89. ISBN 0 06 029412 4. The travelers from *Book One* discover a cult-like community, the Keepers, that attempts to control them. The group escapes with some of the residents and continues to Washington.

    The Kiln: Book Three. 2003. 193p. $15.99. ISBN 0 06 008050. The group discovers that the president used the virus to purify the country and that as they reach adulthood, they will be susceptible to it. One group member sacrifices her life to destroy the president forever, and the family journeys away from all adults to build a new home.

3. Hautman, Pete. **Rash.** New York: Simon & Shuster Books for Young Readers, 2006. 249p. $15.95. ISBN-13: 978 0 689 86801 6. [fiction] JS, CG with high interest for boys. (*Genre Talks for Teens,*

2009, pages 169 to 172.) Bo Marsten rebels against his antiseptic, non-violent society and is sentenced to a Canadian pizza factory. His artificial intelligence science project frees him into the polar-bear-filled tundra, where he struggles to survive.

☙❧

Hemphill, Helen. **The Adventurous Deeds of Deadwood Jones.**
Ashville, NC: Front Street, 2008. 228p. $16.95.
ISBN-13: 978 1 59078 637 6. [fiction] MJ, CG

Themes/Topics: cowboys, cattle drives, African Americans, race relations, cousins, 1860–1890

Summary/Description

Accused of stealing a horse, fourteen-year-old Prometheus Jones, with his eleven-year-old cousin Omer, leaves Tennessee and joins a cattle drive. Prometheus seeks his father who was sold. The boys encounter prejudice from the crew but make friends with Rio, a young Mexican, and Old Woman, the drive's African American cook. Prometheus proves his skills. He helps friendly Pawnee and enables the drive to avoid hostile Sioux. Omer dies in a river crossing. When the drive arrives in Deadwood, Prometheus enters a "Champion of the West" contest and confronts the sons of his mother's former slave owner who slandered him in Tennessee. Prometheus wins, but the brothers call him a horse thief. Sentenced to hang, he tricks one brother into recanting his testimony. The brother reveals that Prometheus's father died in the Civil War. Prometheus's fellow cattlemen help him head to Texas before another trial.

Values: Prometheus's journey confirms honesty, integrity, and loyalty.

Read Aloud/Reader Response

1. Chapter 1, pages 11 to 23. This chapter establishes Prometheus's skill, Omer's hope, and the Dill brothers' bitterness and prejudice.
2. Chapter 5, pages 48 to 56. This chapter begins Nack's contentious relationship with Prometheus.
3. Chapter 7, pages 70 to 73, beginning "I hand the ropes . . ." and ending "'. . . part Pawnee to them now.'" Prometheus bonds with the Pawnee scouts.
4. Chapter 16, pages 149 to 162. In this chapter, Omer drowns.

5.   Chapter 19, pages 176 to 178, beginning with the chapter and ending ". . . to a happy life . . ." Rio counsels Prometheus to direct his grief in positive ways.

Booktalk

Fourteen-year-old Prometheus Jones is lucky. His parents were slaves, but he was born free. Most people are not surprised when his raffle ticket wins him a horse, but the Dill brothers are bitter. Prometheus broke a horse for them. They didn't want to pay him. So they gave him a raffle ticket—until it won. Now they say the ticket and the horse are stolen. The raffle crowd becomes an angry mob. Prometheus and his cousin Omer know they better relocate. But where? Prometheus heads for Texas. His mother claimed, before she died, that the father Prometheus never met was sold there. Now is a good time to find him. Prometheus can talk to horses like nobody else, and his shooting skills are gifted. Omer figures that there must be a mansion in Texas with their name on it. They join a cattle drive out of Texas heading for Deadwood in the Dakota Territory. The cows, cowboys, and Indians may be just as dangerous as the crowd that they left in Tennessee, but the cousins aren't backing down. They're going to Texas, and their experiences will fill a book called *The Adventurous Deeds of Deadwood Jones*.

Curriculum Connections

1.   (Research, language arts) Using your library resources, learn more about the meaning of Prometheus. Act as a resource person for your group.
2.   (Research, language arts and social studies) The "Author's Note" refers to Nat Love. Using your library resources, learn more about Love and other African American cowboys. Act as a resource person for your group.
3.   (React, language arts) Is Prometheus lucky? Use specifics to support your opinion.

Related Works

1.   Ferris, Jean. **Much Ado about Grubstake.** New York: Harcourt Children's Books, 2006. 272p. $17.00. ISBN 0 15 205706 4. [fiction] MJ, CG with high interest for girls. (*Booktalks and Beyond*, 2007, pages 126 to 128.) In 1888, Arley, a sixteen-year-old orphan, maintains a boarding house in Grubstake, Colorado, and fantasizes through dime novels called Penny Dreadfuls.

2.   Karr, Kathleen. **The Great Turkey Walk.** New York: Simbirst, 2000. 197p. $4.95pa. ISBN 0 374 42789 4. [fiction] MJ, CG with high interest for boys. (*Booktalks and More,* 2003, pages 77 to 80.) In 1860, fifteen-year-old orphan Simon Green drives a flock of turkeys to Denver and, on the journey, finds love and self-worth.

3.   Paulsen, Gary. **The Legend of Bass Reeves: Being the True and Fictional Account of the Most Valiant Marshal in the West.** New York: Wendy Lamb Books, 2006. 137p. $17.99. ISBN-13: 978 0 38590 898 6. [fiction] JS, CG with high interest for boys. Beginning in 1834 when Bass Reeves is ten and ending with Reeves's death in 1909, the historical novel describes the life of one of the fiercest lawmen of the Indian Territory.

4.   Peck, Robert Newton. **Cowboy Ghost.** New York: HarperCollins Children's Books, 1999. 200p. $15.95. ISBN 0 06 028168 5. [fiction] MJ, CG with high interest for boys. (*Booktalks Plus,* 2001, pages 15 to 16.) In 1924, sixteen-year-old unseasoned Titus Timothy MacRobertson becomes a man when his older brother and the foreman die on a cattle drive, and he takes over.

5.   Wadsworth, Ginger. **Words West: Voices of Young Pioneers.** New York: Clarion Books, 2003. 191p. $18.00. ISBN 0 618 23475 6. [nonfiction] MJS, CG (*Teen Genre Connections,* 2005, pages 104 to 106.) Fourteen chapters use the words of children and young adults to describe the opening of the West.

ᘓᘓ

Smith, Alexander Gordon. **Lockdown: Escape from Furnace.**

New York: Farrar, Straus and Giroux, 2009. 273p. $14.99.
ISBN-13: 978 0 374 32491 9. [fiction] MJS, CG with high interest for boys

Themes/Topics: prisons, unjust sentencing, escapes, gangs, human experimentation, interpersonal relationships

Summary/Description

Alex Sawyer graduates from playground bully to domestic robberies, breaks into a setup crime scene, and is framed for the murder of his accomplice. Sentenced to Furnace Penitentiary, which is buried a mile below the earth's surface, he is trapped in a world ruled by a demonic warden, human-like creatures in gas masks, and giants in black suits who use terror, guns, hard labor, gang violence, howling beasts, and syringes to terrify and subdue the inmates. He lives minute by minute until he meets inevitable violent death or tries a seemingly suicidal escape. He and an unlikely group of conspirators plan the break. This first book in the *Escape from Furnace* series ends with Alex jumping to his freedom and resolving to return for his roommate whom he believes has been taken for human experimentation.

Value: From a life built on negatives, Alex learns loyalty.

Read Aloud/Reader Response

1. "Denial and Damnation," pages 36 to 39, beginning "My trial was . . ." and ending "I didn't do it." Alex describes the trial and sentencing.
2. "The Descent," pages 55 to 59, beginning "The guards came . . ." and ending with the chapter. The warden welcomes them to Furnace.
3. "Darkness Falls," pages 78 to 81, beginning with the chapter and ending "It was my reflection." Alex describes the horror of night in the furnace and experiences the recurring dream about his family for the first time.
4. "Slop," pages 135 to 138, beginning "Unlike the rest of Furnace . . ." and ending ". . . the boiling oil." Alex describes food preparation.
5. "Break," pages 261 to 273. This chapter describes the escape.

Booktalk

For the booktalk, read aloud "No Way Out," which appears on pages 3 to 5.

This passage is a first-person account of living in *Furnace*. At the end of the chapter, Alex tells the reader that the rest of the book will explain how he came to this point.

Curriculum Connections

1. (Research, social studies) Using your library resources, learn about laws for trying young people as juveniles or adults. Act as a resource person for the group.
2. (Create, language arts, art) Using a graphic format, draw the characters or a scene described. Compare your work with that of others who have also used a graphic format.
3. (Discuss, language arts) Discuss the meaning of the word *innocent* in relation to the story.

Related Works

1. Brooks, Kevin. **Being.** New York: Scholastic/Chicken House, 2007. 336p. $16.99. ISBN 0 439 89973 7. [fiction] JS, CG with high interest for boys. (*Genre Talks for Teens,* 2009, pages 85 to 87.) When sixteen-year-old Robert Smith, supposedly an orphan, undergoes a routine endoscopy, he discovers that his body is a maze of wires and chemicals. He draws on new strength, escapes from the hospital, and seeks his identity.

2. Farmer, Nancy. **The House of the Scorpion.** New York: Atheneum Books for Young Readers/A Richard Jackson Book, 2002. 380p. $17.95. ISBN 0 689 85222 3. [fiction] JS, CG with high interest for boys. (*Teen Genre Connections,* 2005, pages 208 to 210.) The clone of a notorious drug lord avoids being farmed for body parts, escapes, and returns to take over and reform the country.

3. Hautman, Pete. **Rash.** New York: Simon & Shuster Books for Young Readers, 2006. 349p $15.95. ISBN-13: 978 0 689 86801 6. [fiction] JS, CG with high interest for boys. (*Genre Talks for Teens,* 2009, pages 169 to 172.) Bo Marsten has issues with self-control and lives in an antiseptic, non-violent society where he is unjustly assigned to a Canadian tundra pizza factory surrounded by polar bears and ruled by an abusive factory manager who releases him to the tundra to die.

4. Patterson, James. **Maximum Ride: The Angel Experiment.** New York: Warner Vision Books, 2005. 440p. $6.99pa. ISBN 0 445 61779 2. [fiction] JS, CG with high interest for boys. (*Booktalks and Beyond,* 2007, pages 181 to 183.) Fourteen-year-old Maximum Ride (Max) leads a six-member "family" made up of children, who have been injected by the government with bird DNA and raised in cages.

5. Sleator, William. **Hell Phone.** New York: Amulet Books, 2006. 237p. $16.95. ISBN 0 8109 5479 6. [fiction] MJ, CG with high interest for boys. (*Genre Talks for Teens,* 2009, pages 164 to 166.) A used cell phone with a connection to hell sets up seventeen-year-old Nick Gordon for a murder conviction. Executed, he goes to hell and tries to escape.

Sleator, William. Test.

New York: Amulet Books, 2008. 298p. $16.95.
ISBN-13: 978 0 8109 9356 3. [fiction] MJS, CG

Themes/Topics: educational tests, political corruption, immigrants, conspiracies

Summary/Description

Seventeen-year-old Ann studies boring paragraph exercises to pass a standardized test that will determine whether she lives in luxury and privilege or battles snarled traffic and pollution. She befriends a Third World immigrant who wears the same logo as a motorcycle rider who threatens her and learns that the logo represents a mega-monopoly whose owner uses the test and the people most threatened by it to build his business interests and fortune. The two take him on with the help of a rogue substitute English teacher who prefers discussion to multiple choice. The three contact the press and organize a student boycott. The boycott gains national attention, exposes the crime, ruins the exploitive businessman, and brings the trio success too.

Values: The three protestors show honesty, loyalty, and integrity.

Read Aloud/Reader Response

1. Chapter 4, pages 44 to 48, beginning "She wasn't as blunt . . ." and ending with the chapter. Ann introduces herself to Lep and finds common ground.
2. Chapter 5, pages 49 to 63. This chapter demonstrates the corruption of Lep's boss, Tony.
3. Chapter 9, pages 93 to 115. In this chapter, the self-indulgent and manipulative Elise visits Grand Diamond to flirt with Tony.
4. Chapter 24, pages 269 to 290. This chapter describes the protest.
5. Chapter 25, pages 291 to 298. This chapter describes the result of the protest.

Booktalk

Ask the group how they feel about standardized tests.

Seventeen-year-old Ann Forrest shares those feelings, but in Ann's world, pass and fail are big-time. If Ann doesn't pass the tests, she won't go to college. She won't get a good job or clean air or practical transportation from any point A to point B. Ann's short life will go nowhere. If that doesn't depress her, she has a man on a motorcycle following her. He looks like he will hurt her. He wears a strange logo on his jacket. (*Read the first sentence on the top of page 2. It begins, "The red logo was egg-shaped . . ."*) Then Ann notices that the new boy in class, a Third World alien, wears the same logo. He does much better on the practice tests than Ann—even though he can barely speak English. How is that possible? What is happening to Ann and around Ann is not standard, but her reaction to those events may be her ultimate *Test*.

Curriculum Connections

1. (Research, social studies) Using your library resources, learn more about how standardized tests are composed. Act as a resource person during discussion.
2. (Research, language arts) Locate the short story "The Machine Stops" by E. M. Forster. Read the short story, and discuss the conclusions of Ann's English class.
3. (Create) Using a graphic format, portray one scene from the story.

Related Works

1. Anderson, M. T. **Feed.** Cambridge, MA: Candlewick Press, 2003. 235p. $16.99. ISBN 0 7636 1726 1. [fiction] JS, CG (*Teen Genre Connections*, 2005, pages 201 to 203.) Titus and Violet realize that a commercial feed implanted into teenage brains and standardizing thought is deteriorating America physically, emotionally, and intellectually.
2. Farmer, Nancy. **The House of the Scorpion.** New York: Atheneum Books for Young Readers/A Richard Jackson Book, 2002. 380p. $17.95. ISBN 0 689 85222 3. [fiction] JS, CG (*Teen Genre Connections*, 2005, pages 208 to 210.) Matteo Alacrán, a clone, is to provide body parts for his creator, the ruler of a corrupt drug world.
3. Forster, E. M. "The Machine Stops" Many Books. Available: http://manybooks.net/titles/forstereother07machine_stops.html (Accessed June, 2010). This site offers a free download of this 1909 short story, which depicts a society dependent upon a machine. The story is alluded to in chapter 10 of *Test*.
4. Huxley, Aldous. **Brave New World.** New York: Perennial Classics, 1998. $11.95pa. ISBN 0 06 092987 1. [fiction] JS/A Originally published in 1932, this novel depicts a future society built on pleasure, instant gratification, and a rigid class structure determined by scientifically produced intelligence.
5. Philbrick, Rodman. **The Last Book in the Universe.** New York: The Blue Sky Press, 2000. 224p. $16.95. ISBN 0 439 08758 9. [fiction] MJS, CG (*Booktalks and More*, 2003, pages 146 to 148.) In a world where mind probes have replaced books and gangs rule, a young, epileptic Urb (city dweller) befriends a writer and becomes the last book.

Generosity

ভ্যত্

Gleitzman, Morris. **Once.**

New York: Henry Holt & Co., 2010. 163p. $16.99.
ISBN-13: 978 0 8050 9026 0. [fiction] MJS, CG

Themes/Topics: Holocaust, Jews, Poland, orphans,
World War II, 1939–1945

Summary/Description

Living in a Polish Catholic orphanage for three years and eight months where he is told that Hitler is his savior, Felix fantasizes about his Jewish bookseller parents returning to take him home. He runs away to find them. As he struggles to survive, he learns about prejudice against Jews and Hitler's diabolical cruelty. In the countryside, he discovers an executed couple and their left-for-dead daughter Zelda. He and Zelda are caught up in a forced march to a Jewish ghetto. A Jewish dentist who shelters and hides other children in a cellar saves them, but Nazis find them and place them on death camp trains. Felix discovers rotten boards in the train car. Despite the machine-gun guards on top of the train, Zelda, Felix, and another girl jump from the train. Zelda and Felix survive.

Values: Felix rejects the lies of his parents, the orphanage, and government, as well as his own fantasies, and embraces the stark truths and deep loyalties that have helped him survive.

Read Aloud/Reader Response

1. Pages 24 to 28, beginning "I wait till . . ." and ending with the chapter. Felix leaves the orphanage.
2. Pages 46 to 49, beginning "They've stopped chasing . . ." and ending ". . . I don't." Felix flees an angry crowd and is invited to join the Nazi/Jew game.
3. Pages 69 to 71, beginning "Why do these people . . ." and ending with the chapter. Zelda and Felix are caught up in a forced march, and Felix fears that people hate him as a Jew.
4. Pages 91 to 98. In this chapter, Felix can't tell a story and ponders adult stories, or lies.
5. Pages 121 to 122. In this chapter, Barney gives Felix a pair of good boots.

Booktalk

Felix's parents left him in a Catholic orphanage three years and eight months ago. They are Jewish booksellers in World War II Germany. He writes stories about their fantastic adventures. Felix knows that he can find them because he has God, Jesus, the Virgin Mary, the pope, and Adolf Hitler to help him. He runs away. But the outside world doesn't look like the one he heard about in the orphanage. New people live in their apartment. Townspeople chase him away. Hungry and thirsty crowds, at gunpoint, march on the roads. Then he meets Zelda. In fact, he saves her life, and they find a good home in a cellar. Still, no parents. Are they safe? Are they in America? Are they alive? Felix, the story boy, wants a nonfiction answer just *Once.*

Curriculum Connections

1. (Research, social studies) Using library resources, learn more about Jewish children hiding during World War II. Share your information with the group.
2. (Discuss, language arts) Are stories important? Support your answer with specifics.
3. (Discuss, language arts) How is the title significant?

Related Works

1. konigsburg, e. l. **The Mysterious Edge of the Heroic World.** New York: Atheneum Books for Young Readers/Ginee Seo Books, 2007. 244p. $16.99. ISBN-13: 978 1 4169 4972 5. [fiction] M, CG (*Genre Talks for Teens,* 2009, pages 146 to 149.) Amedeo discovers valuable art and a World War II sacrifice when helping a wealthy woman downsize her house.
2. Nir, Yehuda. **The Lost Childhood.** New York: Scholastic Press, 2002. 288p. $16.95. ISBN 0 439 16389 7. [fiction] JS, CG with high interest for boys. After his father is killed in a mass execution, Yehuda and his family hide in the open as Catholics.
3. Opdyke, Irene Gut, with Jennifer Armstrong. **In My Hands: Memories of a Holocaust Rescuer.** New York: Alfred A. Knopf, 1999. $18.00. ISBN 0 679 89181 1. [nonfiction] JS, CG (*Booktalks and More,* 2003, pages 255 to 257.) Opdyke helped Polish Jews and eventually joined the Resistance.
4. Spinelli, Jerry. **Milkweed.** New York: Alfred A. Knopf, 2003. 208p. $15.95. ISBN 0 375 81374 8. [fiction] JS, CG (*Teen Genre*

Connections, pages 240 to 243.) An eight-year-old-gypsy narrates his survival journey in occupied Poland and the post-war United States.

5. Zusak, Markus. **The Book Thief.** New York: Alfred A. Knopf, 2006. 552p. $21.90. ISBN 0 375 93100 7, [fiction] JS, CG with high interest for girls. (*Genre Talks for Teens,* pages 241 to 243.) Death tells the story of Liesel Meminger, the daughter of a Communist, who survives the war in a German foster home.

ᘓᘔ

Myers, Walter Dean. **Sunrise over Fallujah.**
New York: Scholastic Press, 2008. 304p. $17.99. ISBN-13: 978 0 439 91624 0.

[fiction] JS, CG with high interest for boys

Themes/Topics: invasion of Iraq, military life, friendship, love

Summary/Description

Private Robin Perry (aka "Birdy") relates his experiences as a member of a Civil Affairs Unit in the Iraq invasion. Robin's unit faces roadside bombs, sniper fire, and rape as they reach out to a besieged population dealing with violence and death. Many Muslims see the Americans as infidels who should be killed, and some American units create conflicts to manipulate tribal leaders. When the unit is disbanded, Robin professes his love to a fellow soldier, but she says that no one should decide about romance in the heat of combat. Robin writes letters to his Uncle Richie, the main character in Myer's *Fallen Angels.*

Values: In the name of patriotism and the common good, Robin enlists, bonds with his fellow soldiers, and then questions authority as he sees intolerance and hate on both sides.

Read Aloud/Reader Response

1. Pages 85 to 86. Birdy's letter to his parents gives his first impressions of his mission.
2. Pages 121 to 122, beginning "Hey, Jamil . . ." and ending ". . . keeping it?" The Americans question Jamil about what he wants out of the war.
3. Pages 212 to 214, beginning "Coles came over to see me . . ." and ending with the chapter. Birdy reflects on killing and dying.

4. Page 244, beginning "My name is . . ." and ending ". . . what I'm talking about." Lieutenant Colonel John Kelly explains the situation in the war.
5. Pages 280 to 282. In his final letter to Uncle Richie, Birdy realizes how war has changed him and separated him from his previous American attitudes and life.

Booktalk

Private Robin Perry is from Harlem. His uncle Richie fought in Vietnam, a long and bitter war. (*Hold up the book* Fallen Angels.) Now Robin is going to fight in Iraq. His war will be good, clean, purposeful, heroic, and short. That's what he believes before he meets people. Some are admirable, some are confusing, and some are willing to kill him. Those are the Americans. Then there are the people he is there to save. Most of them wonder why he *is* there. To take out Saddam? Yes, Saddam Hussein is an evil ruler. He kills his people and destroys their land. Don't Americans do the same? Will one bad government replace another? They wonder. Or is it the oil, not suffering, that brings the infidels? Birdy wonders too, and he finds that new questions, fear, and pain come with every *Sunrise over Fallujah*. (*Hold up the book.*)

Curriculum Connections

1. (Research, social studies) Using library resources, learn more about Saddam Hussein's rule and the United States role in Iraq. Act as a resource person for the group.
2. (Research, social studies) Using library resources, find out more about Islamic beliefs. Act as a resource person for the group.
3. (React, language arts) Name one thing in the novel that surprised you. Compare your reaction with that of others in the group.

Related Works

1. Keller, Julia. **Back Home**. New York: Egmont, 2009. 194p. $15.99. ISBN-13: 978 1 60684 005 4. [fiction] JS, CG Thirteen-year-old Rachel Browning and her family cope with her father's return from Iraq where he suffered brain trauma and lost an arm and a leg.
2. McCormick, Patricia. **Purple Heart**. New York: Harper Collins Publishers/Balzar & Bray, 2009. 199p. $16.99. ISBN-13: 978 0 06 173090 0. [fiction] JS, CG with high interest for boys. When eighteen-year-old Matt Duffy wakes up in the hospital, he is awarded a purple heart but doubts that he is worthy of it.

3. Myers, Walter Dean. **Fallen Angels.** New York: Scholastic, 2008. 309p. (Anniversary Edition) $6.99pa. ISBN-13: 978 0 545 05576 5. Fighting as a teenager, Robin's uncle realizes the horror of the Vietnam War and questions its purpose.

4. Myers, Walter Dean. **What They Found: Love on 145th Street.** New York: Wendy Lamb Books, 2007. 243p. $18.99. ISBN-13: 978 0 375 93709 5. [related short stories] JS, CG with high interest for boys. (*Genre Talks for Teens,* 2009, pages 51 to 53.) A sequel to *145th Street: Short Stories,* these fifteen interrelated stories explore love and friendship. The last story, "Combat Zone," centers on a corporal finding love in war.

5. Siddiqui, Haroon. **Being Muslim.** Toronto, ON, Canada: Anansi Press/Groundwood Books, 2006. 160p. (Groundwood Guide). $9.95pa. ISBN-13: 978 0 88899 786 9. [nonfiction] JS, CG Siddiqui explains the politics affecting the faithful, the situation of European Muslims, Muslim beliefs, the role of women, the relationship between jihad and terrorism, and the future of the movement. He includes source notes, a list of readings, and an index.

$C_{\zeta}^{0}\zeta^{0}$

Pratchett, Terry. **Nation.**

New York: HarperCollins Publishers, 2008. 367p. $17.89.
ISBN-13: 978 0 06 143302 3. [fiction] MJS, CG with high interest for boys

Themes/Topics: disasters, grief, friendship, trust, religious belief, identity, coming of age

Summary/Description

A shipwreck and a tidal wave place a young girl who is a member of a British-style royal family and an island boy who has completed his manhood trials on the same devastated island in the fictional Great Pelagic Ocean. As they support each other, cope with destruction and death, care for refugees, and battle pirates, they bond and examine their beliefs. Inspired by island voices, the girl discovers that the island's ancient civilization pioneered scientific advances. When she is rescued by her father, now the country's king, she persuades him to grant the island's independence as they share knowledge with her country's scholars. She leaves the island and eventually becomes queen of her country. The boy stays and leads his new *Nation.*

Values: In their survival, the girl and boy realize tolerance, bravery, responsibility, and integrity.

Read Aloud/Reader Response

1. "How Imo Made the World, in the Time When Things Were Otherwise and the Moon was Different," pages 1 and 2. This passage is *Nation's* mythology.
2. Chapter 2, pages 40 to 43, beginning "Granddad Nawi . . ." and ending ". . . world had emptied." Mau recalls Granddad Nawi, a dissenter in the community.
3. Chapter 3, pages 71 to 73, beginning "Mau was just . . ." and ending "Does not happen!" Mau saves Ermintrude from drowning and declares that he has stopped death.
4. Chapter 4, pages 75 to 84, beginning with the chapter and ending ". . . was he frightened of?" The passage reveals Ermintrude's background and character.
5. Chapter 14, pages 312 to 321. This chapter describes the duel between Mau and Cox.

Booktalk

Mau has just finished his test of manhood and looks forward to his village's celebration. Ermintrude is on a ship. She has royal privileges and few responsibilities. After all, 138 people have to die before she will be queen. But a huge wave brings these two very different worlds together on one small island. To Ermintrude, Mau is a savage. To Mau, Ermintrude is a ghost haunting what is left of his island home. Different voices tell them how to live. Ermintrude's voices speak about social etiquette and empire. Mau's voices offer him protection from angry and vindictive gods. But the loudest voice in both of their heads is survival. They listen. Then others survivors come, some whose lives and plans have been destroyed, and some who plan more destruction. And there are island secrets, secrets that can change the world. Mau and Ermintrude are suddenly two unlikely leaders—in charge of it all. In charge of a *Nation*.

Curriculum Connections

1. (Research, social studies) Using your library resources, learn about the relationship between one civilization and its mythology. Act as a resource person for the group.
2. (Discuss, language arts) Do Mau and Ermintrude maintain their standards? Use specific support.
3. (Discuss, language arts) What roles do religion and belief play in the novel? Use specific support.

Related Works

1. Colfer, Eoin. **Airman.** New York: Hyperion Books for Children, 2008. 412p. $17.99. ISBN-13: 978 142310750 7. [fiction] MJS, CG with high interest for boys. (*Genre Talks for Teens,* 2009, pages 116 to 119.) Intervening in a plot to kill the king, Conor is declared dead but sent to the kingdom's prison island. He becomes a hero.

2. McCaughrean, Geraldine. **The Kite Rider.** New York: HarperCollins Publishers, 2001. 272p. $15.95. ISBN 0 06 623874 9. [fiction] MJS, CG with high interest for boys. (*Booktalks and Beyond,* 2007, pages 105 to 107.) Twelve-year-old Haoyou sees his father die, takes revenge, earns his living as a kite flyer, and returns home to save his family.

3. McNamee, Eoin. **The Navigator: Chosen to Save the World.** New York: Random House/Wendy Lamb Books, 2006. 342p. $15.99. ISBN-13: 978 0 375 83910 8. [fiction] MJS, CG with high interest for boys. (*Genre Talks for Teens,* 2009, pages 180 to 182.) Lonely Owen encounters a time shift and becomes the key player in world survival.

4. Meyer, L. A. **Bloody Jack: Being and Account of the Curious Adventures of Mary "Jacky" Faber, Ship's Boy.** New York: Harcourt, 2002. 278p. $17.00. ISBN 0 15 216721 5. [fiction] JS, G (*Teen Genre Connections,* 2005, pages 118 to 121.) Mary (Jacky) Faber, orphaned in 1797, finds a job on a ship as a ship's boy. She kills a man, battles pirates, and falls in love.

5. Oppel, Kenneth. **Airborn.** New York: Eos, 2004. 355p. $17.89. ISBN 0 06 053181 9. [fiction] MJS, CG with high interest for boys. (*Booktalks and Beyond,* 2007, pages 107 to 110.) Fifteen-year-old Matt Cruse, a cabin boy, rescues dying Benjamin Molloy who tells about beautiful, winged creatures. One year later, Matt joins Molloy's granddaughter, Kate, in retracing her grandfather's journey.

❧❧

Sedgwick, Marcus. Revolver.

New York: Roaring Brook Press, 2010. 204p. $16.99.
ISBN-13: 978 1 59643 592 6. [fiction] JS, CG with high interest for boys

Themes/Topics: Colt Revolver, faith,
family relationships, gold rush,
Arctic wilderness, survival, 1899–1910

Summary/Description

Fourteen-year-old Sig guards his father's frozen corpse while his sister and step-mother go for help. A huge man, Gunther Wolff, appears claiming that the father owes him a share of a stolen horde of gold from the Alaskan gold rush days ten years before. While Wolff threatens and beats him, Sig decides whether to seek help in the family's ancient Colt Revolver or his mother's religious advice. His sister returns, is also threatened, and accuses Wolff of their mother's brutal murder. Sig persuades him that the path to the gold might be in papers the father left on the Arctic ice. They retrieve the papers. In the cabin, Sig baits Wolff into firing the family revolver with new ammunition. It explodes taking half of Wolff's hand. He furiously pursues Sig and Anna into the snow but sinks. The step-mother arrives with reinforcements who pull Wolff out and turn him over to the authorities. The map to the gold is in the mother's Bible. The story combines three time periods: 1899–1900, the Alaskan gold rush; 1910, the father's death; and 1967, seventy-two-year-old Sig reflecting on the significance of his experience.

Values: Drawing on his family's advice about spiritual values and physical survival, Sig crafts his own solution when confronting his terror and saves both his sister and himself.

Read Aloud/Reader Response

1. Chapter 3, pages 14 to 16, beginning "The horror of seeing . . ." and ending with the chapter. Sig visualizes his father's death.
2. Chapter 10, page 51, beginning with the chapter and ending ". . . anything at all." The paragraph expresses what Sig's parents tried to teach.
3. Chapter 18, pages 88 to 95, beginning "Sig turned . . ." and ending ". . . heavy it was." Sig recalls the birthday on which he received the revolver.
4. Chapter 33, pages 173 to 174, beginning "The Bible . . ." and ending with the chapter. Sig recalls his father repairing the Bible.
5. "Postscript," pages 198 to 200, beginning "Just then . . ." and ending ". . . with him." Anna and Sig discuss his decision to give Wolff the gun.

Booktalk

Fourteen-year-old Sig sits in his family's Arctic cabin with his father's corpse. His father fell through the ice and froze to death a few hours ago. There's a knock on the door. Sig opens it and sees a man. (*Read aloud page 34, beginning "The man was . . ." and ending ". . . his left hand."*) Is he here to help? No. He wants gold. He claims that he made a deal with Sig's father ten years ago during the Alaskan gold rush. Sig and his family have scraped a living from the wilderness. Sig has never seen a horde of gold, but his father told him that even dead men tell stories. Will the father's story be about gold, murder, betrayal, or survival? Will its central character be Sig, the giant stranger, or the *Revolver*?

Curriculum Connections

1. (Research, social studies) Using your library resources, learn more about life during the Alaskan gold rush. Act as a resource person during discussion.

2. (Research, social studies) Using your library resources, learn more about the invention of the Colt Revolver and its role in the West. Act as a resource person during discussion.

3. (Discuss, language arts) What is the most powerful weapon in the novel?

Related Works

1. Bastedo, Jamie. **On Thin Ice.** Calgary, AB, Canada: Fitzhenry & Whiteside Co./Red Deer Press, 2006. 348p. $10.95pa. ISBN 0 88995 337 6. [fiction] JS, CG with high interest for girls. (*Genre Talks for Teens*, 2009, pages 262 to 264.) As sixteen-year-old Ashley helps her family battle unusual storms and catastrophic environmental events caused by global warming in the Far North, she accepts her Inuk powers.

2. Haas, Jessie. **Chase.** New York: HarperCollins, 2007. 250p. $17.89. ISBN-13: 978 0 06 112851 6. [fiction] MJS, CG with high interest for boys. (*Genre Talks for Teens*, 2009, pages 90 to 93.) Fifteen-year-old Pim witnesses a murder by the "Sleepers," an Irish underground organization, escapes, and helps both of his pursuers stay alive.

3. Heneghan, James. **Safe House.** Victoria, BC, Canada: Orca Book Publishers, 2006. 151p. $7.95pa. ISBN-13: 978 1 55143 640 1. [fiction] MJS, CG with high interest for boys. (*Genre Talks for Teens*, 2009, pages 93 to 95.) Twelve-year-old Liam Fogarty sees the face of the triggerman who guns down his defenseless parents and eludes the man by using memories of his parents and his circus skills.

4. McCaughrean, Geraldine. **The White Darkness.** New York: HarperTempest, 2005. 373p. $17.89. ISBN-13: 978 0 06 089036 0. [fiction] JS, CG (*Genre Talks for Teens*, 2009, pages 105 to 108.) After

her obsessed uncle takes her into the Antarctic wilderness, fourteen-year-old Sym survives by talking to the deceased Captain Oates.

5. Pullman, Philip. **Once upon a Time in the North.** New York: Alfred A. Knopf, 2008. 96p. $12.99. ISBN-13: 978 0 375 84510 9. [fiction] JS, CG with high interest for boys. Lee Scoresby and Iorek Byrnison from *His Dark Materials* defeat corruption in the frozen Arctic.

ॐॐ

Smith, Roland. Peak.

New York: Harcourt, 2007. 246p. $17.00. ISBN-13: 978 0 15 202417 8.
[fiction] MJS, CG with high interest for boys

Themes/Topics: mountaineering, Mount Everest, China/Tibet relations, family, coming of age, conduct of life, writing

Summary/Description

Fourteen-year-old Peak Marcello tags New York buildings with his blue mountain trademark until he is arrested and threatened with incarceration until eighteen. His biological father, Joshua Wood, whom Peak hasn't seen for seven years, volunteers to take him to Thailand. The court grants the request, and Peak's school allows him to finish his school requirements by completing a coherent, written story. Josh takes Peak to Mount Everest rather than Thailand. Peak's story chronicles the survival challenges, the relationships he develops, and his realizations about his mother, step-father, twin sisters, and Josh. Peak or the climber's son, Sun-jo, might be the youngest person to climb Everest. Peak puts aside his ambitions and helps Sun-jo attain that goal so that the boy can provide a better life for himself, his mother, and his sisters. A map of the climb introduces the story.

Values: Peak develops responsibility, fairness, and generosity.

Read Aloud/Reader Response

The entire book is suitable for a read aloud. Below are just a few suggestions.

1. "The Twins," pages 26 to 27, beginning with the chapter and ending "I said." Peak and his mother talk about his leaving with Josh.
2. "Peak Experience," pages 74 to 75, beginning "You could . . ." and ending ". . . my whole life." Peak suspects that he is part of his father's commercial plan.

3. "ABC," pages 109 to 110, beginning "AT FIRST IT APPEARED . . ." and ending ". . . on sharp rocks." Peak reacts to the attitude toward the privileged reporter and the porters.
4. "Family History," pages 182 to 183, beginning "Mom sighed" and ending ". . . flap opened." Peak's mother talks to him about climbing.
5. "Denouement," page 246, beginning, "Here they come . . ." and ending with the novel. Peak writes the denouement for his assignment.

Booktalk

Read "The Hook," pages 3 to 6.

The moron is Peak Marcello. He is fourteen, lives in New York, and tags high buildings for fun. Both his parents are climbers. Can you tell by the name? But nobody knows where the tagging came from. His latest stunt may be the last. You noticed the police? A judge gets involved and also the father he hasn't seen for seven years. Peak is leaving New York, avoiding jail, and doing a real climb—Mount Everest. Dad thought it would be a great surprise, a take-your-son-to-work project. Downside? Both of them could die. Peak has the guts and attitude to climb a New York building. Does he have enough left over to live up to his name and reach Everest's *Peak*?

Curriculum Connections

1. (Research, social studies) Using your library resources, learn about successful and unsuccessful Everest climbs. Act as a resource person for the group.
2. (Research, language arts) Using your library resources, learn more about telling a story. During the discussion, point out various techniques that Roland Smith has used.
3. (Discuss and React, language arts) Do you see Josh Wood in a favorable or unfavorable light? Explain your reaction with details from the story.

Related Works

1. Atkins, Jeannine (text), and Dusan Petricic (illus.) **How High Can We Climb?** New York: Farrar, Straus and Giroux, 2005. 224p. $17.00. ISBN 0 374 33503 6. [nonfiction] MJ, G Twelve accounts of women explorers include the story of Ann Bancroft, who reached both the North Pole and South Pole and crossed Antarctica on foot with Liv Arnesen.

2. Lekuton, Joseph Lemasolai. **Facing the Lion: Growing Up Maasai on the African Savanna.** Washington, DC: National Geographic, 2003. 123p. $15.95. ISBN 0 7922 5125 3. [nonfiction] MJS, CG with high interest for boys. (*Booktalks and Beyond*, 2007, pages 234 to 236.) Joseph Lekuton describes how his nomadic life as a Maasai prepared him to meet the challenges of an industrial society.

3. McCaughrean, Geraldine. **The White Darkness.** New York: HarperTempest, 2005. 373p. $17.89. ISBN-13: 978 0 06 089036 0. [fiction] JS, CG (*Genre Talks for Teens*, 2009, pages 105 to 108.) Fourteen-year-old Sym's uncle changes a surprise tourist trip to the Antarctic into a maniacal search for a mythical city inside the earth.

4. Mikaelsen, Ben. **Touching Spirit Bear.** New York: HarperCollins Publishers, 2001. 241p. $15.95. ISBN 0 380 97744 3. [fiction] MJS, CG with high interest for boys. (*Booktalks and More*, 2003, pages 80 to 82.) Fifteen-year-old Cole Mathews chooses to face the natural elements rather than take jail time.

5. Sullivan, Paul. **Maata's Journal.** New York: Atheneum Books for Young Readers, 2003. 240p. $16.95. ISBN 0 689 83463 2. [fiction] JS, G Seventeen-year-old Maata, an Inuit, records her survival in an Arctic expedition from April to July of 1924.

✿✿

Uehashi, Nahoko. Cathy Hirono (trans.). **Moribito: Guardian of the Spirit.**

New York: Scholastic/Arthur A. Levine Books, 2008. 256p. $17.99.
ISBN-13: 978 0 545 00542 5. [fiction] JS, CG with high interest for girls

Themes/Topics: martial arts, loyalty, fate, conduct of life

Summary/Description

When thirty-year-old Balsa saves the Second Prince from drowning, the Second Queen, Mikado's second wife, hires her to protect his life. A spirit possesses him that can bring drought to the country and kill the boy. The Mikado, the boy's father, given false information from his Star Readers, decides to kill his son. Balsa stages a fire, leaves with the prince, eludes the assassins, and brings him to healers who examine the spirit. Balsa, the healers, and the assassins defeat the monster who wishes to devour the spirit. When the First Prince dies unexpectedly, the Second Prince returns home to become, someday, the Mikado. The book contains a "List of Characters" and a "List of Places and Terms."

Values: Balsa acts on responsibility and bravery.

Read Aloud/Reader Response

1. Part 2, chapter 3, pages 105 to 112. In this chapter, the skills of Balsa and the wisdom of Torogai become clear.
2. Part 2, chapter 4, pages 113 to 115, beginning with the chapter and ending ". . . avoided his eyes." Chagum explores the relationship between Balsa and Tanda.
3. Part 3, chapter 1, pages 146 to 154, beginning "In the days . . ." and ending ". . . I'm just living." Chagum wonders about his fate and learns that Balsa was trapped by fate also.
4. Part 3, chapter 3, pages 174 to 178, beginning "From that day on . . ." and ending ". . . of budding leaves." Balsa explains her anger and what she learned from Chagum.
5. Part 3, chapter 9, pages 236 to 245. In this chapter about destiny, personal choice, responsibility, and bravery are central issues.

Booktalk

Thirty-year-old Balsa is a fighter and protects anyone who needs it. One day she saves a boy from drowning. He is the Second Prince. His mother calls her to the palace for thanks but wants more. The near drowning is the second accident to almost take his life. The egg of the Water Spirit possesses the boy. He must carry it safely to its home in the distant sea. If he fails, he will lose his life, and his land will be overcome with drought. Inept counselors advise the Mikado, his father, to kill the boy. Are the riches the queen offers worth facing supernatural forces and the king's deadly assassins? Of course not. But Balsa is a fighter, a protector. She must follow her fate and help the prince follow his. By forces beyond their choice and understanding, they are both the *Moribito: Guardian of the Spirit.*

Curriculum Connections

1. (Research, social studies) The novel is a fantasy set in the Japan of the Middle Ages. Learn more about Japanese government and life in the Middle Ages. Act as a resource person for your group.
2. (Discuss, language arts) What do the *Moribito* stories say about the conduct of life?

3. (Discuss, language arts) Should the *Moribito* stories be included in the school curriculum? Use specifics to support your opinion.

Related Works

1. Bass, L. G. **Sign of the Qin: Book One.** New York: Hyperion Books for Children, 2004. 383p. (Outlaws of the Moonshadow Marsh) $17.99. ISBN 078681918 9. [fiction] MJS, CG with high interest for boys. (*Booktalks and Beyond,* 2007, pages 147 to 150.) A tattooed monk saves the Starlord who will return justice to the land.

2. Hearn, Lian. **Across the Nightingale Floor: The Sword of the Warrior, Episode 1.** New York: Firebird, 2002. 193p. (Tales of the Otori) $6.50pa. ISBN 0 14 240324 5. [fiction] JS, CG with high interest for boys. Tomasu discovers that he is descended from the Tribe, a group of assassins. The *Tales* focus on justice in a fantasy feudal Japan.

3. Levin, Judith. **Japanese Mythology.** New York: Rosen Central, 2008. 64p. (Mythology Around the World) $29.95. ISBN-13: 978 1 4042 0736 3. [nonfiction] MJS, CG Levin briefly discusses the relationship between Japanese history and mythology, relates particular myths, and characterizes specific gods. The bibliography, list for further reading, and suggested Web sites provide additional sources.

4. Seto, Andy (author), and Wang Du Lu (story). Wayne Moyung and Stephen Ip (trans.). **Crouching Tiger, Hidden Dragon.** Fremont, CA: ComicsOne, 2002. 89p. $13.95pa. ISBN 1 58899 999 8. [graphic] JS, CG with high interest for boys. This volume establishes the relationships between two feuding families, highly trained in the art of kung fu, and the allies who will be drawn in to their conflict.

5. Uehashi, Nahoko. Cathy Hirono (trans.). **Moribito II: Guardian of the Darkness.** Scholastic/Arthur A. Levine Books, 2009. 272p. $17.99. ISBN-13: 978 0 545 10295 7. Relying on truth and loyalty, Balsa clears her uncle's name and thwarts the plot to steal the precious stones from the Mountain King.

ദ്യു

Wood, Don. Into the Volcano.
Scholastic/Blue Sky Press, 2008. 176p. $18.99.
ISBN-13: 978 0 439 72671 9. [graphic] MJS, CG

Themes/Topics: family, volcanoes, brothers

Summary/Description

Duffy and Sumo Pugg travel to Kocalaha, their mother's homeland, with their cousin Come-and-Go to visit Aunt Lulu whom they have never met. They are being used to draw their mother out of her hiding place where she has discovered magic beads extracted from terminal green magma. The aunt and nephew think that she is hoarding the beads, and the mother thinks that someone is trying to steal her discovery. Come-and-Go takes the boys into an active volcano. Duffy and Sumo escape. Brave Duffy falls and is trapped. Cowardly Sumo overcomes his fears, accidentally finds their mother, and saves Duffy. All explorers get out safely with magic beads, and Sumo has new courage. The mother negotiates a favorable settlement with her family and vows to give her sons more time and attention.

Values: The story focuses on trust, bravery, and family.

Read Aloud/Reader Response

1. Chapter 5, page 39. The frames on this page show the conflict and difference between Duffy and Sumo.
2. Chapter 9, pages 64 to 70. The danger brings out the brothers' conflict.
3. Chapter 13, pages 98 to 108. Duffy falls. Sumo fails to save him.
4. Chapter 15, pages 117 to 122. In trying to save Duffy, Sumo confronts Death.
5. Chapter 21, pages 164 to 165. Sumo and Come-and-Go discuss the island, family differences, and the good result of the adventure: Sumo's transformation.

Booktalk

Duffy and Sumo are called out of class at school. They are going on a surprise vacation. A cousin that they have never met will take them to the Island of Kocalaha. (*Point to the picture of Come-and-Go on the cover. Show the map that introduces the story. Note the features such as the Valley of Ghosts and the volcano.*) Definitely, it is not Disneyland. On the island, they will visit their rich aunt whom they have never met and who lives in a Winnebago. (*Show the pictures of the aunt and the Winnebago on pages 16 and 17.*) Their driver is a man named "Mango Jo," a member of the witness protection program. (*Show the picture of "Mango Jo" on page 12.*) Things don't look good, and they get worse: spiders, lava tubes, and an active volcano. Time to go home? Time to call Mom and Dad? Duffy and Sumo think so. But their aunt and cousin have other ideas. Their new relatives won't let them contact anyone. For some reason, they think that an active volcano is a must-see tourist attraction. (*Show frames on pages 46 and 47.*) Duffy and Sumo want to leave, but the only way out seems to be *Into the Volcano*.

Curriculum Connections

1. (Research, science) Using library resources, learn more about volcanoes. Act as a resource person for the group.
2. (React, language arts) Is one brother a winner and the other a loser? Explain your answer by referring to specifics in the novel.
3. (Create, art, language arts) Make up a page of graphic panels and dialogue that illustrates the attitude difference between you and a family member or a friend.

Related Works

1. Allende, Isabel. Margaret Sayers Peden (trans.). **City of the Beasts.** New York: HarperCollins, 2002. 406p. $21.89. ISBN 0 06 050917 1. [fiction] MJ, CG with high interest for boys. (*Teen Genre Connections*, 2005, pages 87 to 90.) Fifteen-year-old Alex Cold reluctantly accompanies his grandmother to the Amazon and saves a native tribe.
2. Grant, Vicki. **Pigboy.** Victoria, BC, Canada: Orca Book Publishers, 2006. 101p. (Orca Currents). $8.95pa. ISBN-13: 978 1 55143 643 2. [fiction] MJ, CG with high interest for boys. (*Genre Talks for Teens*, 2009, pages 103 to 105.) Nerd and target fourteen-year-old Dan Hogg heroically saves his class and teacher from an escaped convict.
3. Hobbs, Will. **Wild Man Island.** New York: HarperCollins Publishers, 2002. 184p. $15.95. ISBN 0 688 17473 6. [fiction] MJ, CG with high interest for boys. (*Teen Genre Connections*, 2005, pages 92 to 94.) Fourteen-year-old Andy Galloway searches for where his father died and bonds with an archeologist who confirms the father's theories.
4. Lekuton, Joseph Lemasolai. **Facing the Lion: Growing up Maasai on the African Savanna.** Washington, DC: National Geographic, 2003. 123p. $15.95. ISBN 0 7922 5125 3. [nonfiction] MJS, CG with high interest for boys. (*Booktalks and Beyond*, 2007, pages 234 to 236.) A confrontation with a lion teaches Joseph Lekuton to confront the other lions in his life.

5. Sala, Richard. **Cat Burglar Black.** New York: First Second, 2009. 126p. ISBN-13: 978 1 59643 144 7. [graphic] MJS, G When K. Westree is sent to a mysterious boarding school owned by an aunt that she never knew, she is drawn into a secret society and mysteries surrounding her father.

Problem Solving: Mystery and Suspense Novels

We think of mysteries and suspense as exciting, edge-of-the-seat stories, but their foundation, problem solving, is one of the most important skills and values of everyday life. Do we solve our problems because we have a moral voice that tells us things could be a little better? Is untying the knots just what we consistently do and love? Or are we pulled into a troubling puzzle because of loyalty to friend, family, or country?

Conscience

ℭℨℨℭ

Blundell, Judy. **What I Saw and How I Lied.**
New York: Scholastic Press, 2008. 288p. $16.99.
ISBN-13: 978 0 439 90346 2. [fiction] JS, G

Themes/Topics: post World War II, conduct of life, coming of age, love, prejudice

Summary/Description

In 1947, fifteen-year-old Evie enjoys her glamorous mother, new step-father, and financially comfortable life. After a mysterious phone call, the step-father takes the family to Palm Beach, Florida. They meet the Graysons, a wealthy New York Jewish couple with whom the step-father wants to do business, and Peter Coleridge, a twenty-five-year-old veteran with whom Evie falls in love. Evie discovers that her family's wealth comes from goods stolen from Jews. Peter, an accomplice, called for his cut, and followed them to Palm Beach. The hotel management discovers that the Graysons are Jewish and forces them to leave. Evie's family stays. Peter dies on a fishing trip with the father. The father and mother go to trial for murder, and during the trial, Evie realizes that Peter and her mother used her to hide their affair. Evie lies in her testimony and saves her parents. When the family returns to New York, Evie takes the money her step-father was saving for a house and gives it to Mrs. Grayson so that she may help Jews struggling after the Holocaust.

Value: Evie seeks justice for the Graysons and the Jews persecuted during World War II.

Read Aloud/Reader Response

1. Chapter 6, pages 36 to 42. In this chapter, Evie dresses up for the dance and takes her first steps to glamour and adulthood.
2. Chapter 9, pages 61 to 66, beginning with the chapter and ending ". . . into Joe's shoulder." Evie recalls Joe coming into their lives and how much she wanted a father.
3. Chapter 16, pages 116 to 118, beginning "Afterward we stopped . . ." and ending ". . . said pointedly." Peter, Evie, and her mother talk about prejudice and hard times.
4. Chapter 21, pages 156 to 160. In this chapter, Evie and Mrs. Grayson talk after the Grayson's are asked to leave the hotel.
5. Chapter 33, pages 251 to 265. Evie gives her testimony.

Booktalk

It's 1947. Evie is fifteen, almost sixteen. Her dad deserted them when Evie was a baby. Her mom and she made it together, right through the Depression. Then Mom met Joe Spooner. He is the father that Evie wanted. When Pearl Harbor came along, Joe married her mom before he shipped overseas. They wait out the war and get the happy ending. Joe comes home, starts a business, saves for a house, and gives Evie and her mom presents they dreamed about. Then the phone rings, a wrong number Joe says, but he piles them in the car, and they are on their way to Palm Beach. It's not exactly the peak season. Only a few people are there. One is worth the trip, gorgeous Peter Coleridge. He served with Joe. Peter, twenty-five, can't stop looking at Evie. Joe doesn't like him hanging around, but Evie's mom chaperones. Life is good until it isn't, until Peter is dead, until Edie unravels family lies and secrets. Will she someday look back and think about how she helped justice, or will she be haunted by her story *What I Saw and How I Lied*?

Curriculum Connections

1. (Research, social studies) Using your library resources, find out more about restitution to the Jews after World War II. You may start with sources that Blundell listed in the "Acknowledgments." Act as a resource person during the discussion.
2. (Research, language arts) Several times in the novel, the word *shyster* is used. Research the etymology of the word and discuss how it applies to this novel.
3. (React, language arts) Make two lists: the good guys and the bad guys. Compare with others the lists and specifics from the novel that helped you make them.

Related Works

1. Chotjewitz, David. Doris Orgel (trans.). **Daniel Half Human.** New York: Simon Pulse, 2004. 325p. $5.99pa. ISBN-13: 978 0689 857485. [fiction] JS, CG (*Booktalks and Beyond,* 2007, pages 191 to 194.) In 1945, Daniel's flashbacks chronicle how his mother's Jewish blood separated him from the German society and his best friend, Armin.
2. Kerr, M. E. **Slap Your Sides.** New York: HarperCollins, 2001. 198p. $15.95. ISBN 0 06 029481 7. [fiction] MJS, CG (*Teen Genre Connections,* 2005, pages 233 to 235.) Kerr presents views of World War II that range from conscientious objection to jingoism.
3. konigsburg, e. l. **The Mysterious Edge of the Heroic World.** New York: Atheneum Books for Young Readers/Ginee Seo Books, 2007. 244p. $16.99. ISBN-13: 978 1 4169 4972 5. [fiction] M, CG (*Genre Talks for Teens,* 2009, pages 146 to 149.) A piece of "decadent" art that Nazis seized for the safe passage of the recently deceased father of the one boy's Jewish godfather reveals a small part of the Holocaust.
4. Pressler, Mirjam. Eric J. Macki (trans.). **Let Sleeping Dogs Lie.** Asheville, NC: Front Street, 2007. 207p. $16.95. ISBN-13: 978 1 932425 84 0. [fiction] S, G (*Genre Talks for Teens,* 2009, pages 233 to 235.) Eighteen-year-old Johanna believes that her grandfather's business belonged to a Jewish family that lost it during the Holocaust.
5. Whelan, Gloria. **Summer of the War.** New York: HarperCollins Children's Books, 2006. $15.99. ISBN-13: 978 0 06 008072 3. [fiction] MJ, G (*Genre Talks for Teens,* 2009, pages 238 to 240.) Fourteen-year-old Mirabelle's 1942 summer vacation teaches her that difference doesn't mean threat.

CR๊ED

Brooks, Kevin. Black Rabbit Summer.

New York: Scholastic/Chicken House, 2008. 496p. $17.99.
ISBN-13: 978 0 545 05752 3. [fiction] JS, CG with high interest for boys

Themes/Topics: friendship, homosexuality, gangs, missing persons

Summary/Description

After an alcohol-and-drugged-filled reunion with childhood friends, sixteen-year-old Pete Boland unravels the resulting mystery of two missing persons: a troubled and bullied member of the reunion and a teenage celebrity. The police find the celebrity's naked body and suspect Raymond, the missing boy, of killing her. Pete discovers that the celebrity blackmailed his gay friend and the friend's secret partner, a local bully, to kidnap her and extort her parents for money. Another drug-crazed group member stumbled into the plan and accidentally killed her. The three disposed of the body and tried to stop Pete's investigation by implicating him in her death. Eventually, the killer hangs himself. Raymond is never found.

Value: Pete discovers the importance of personal integrity in the face of peer pressure.

Read Aloud/Reader Response

1. Chapter 2, pages 21 and 22, beginning with the chapter and ending ". . . route to each other." The passage describes the route Raymond and Pete use to contact each other.
2. Chapter 4, pages 54 to 55, beginning with the chapter and ending "*Kid's stuff.*" The passage describes the hideout.
3. Chapter 7, pages 111 to 112, beginning "'You don't really . . .'" and ending ". . . make sense." Raymond reflects on the relationship of meaning and time. Pete recalls that conversation on page 282 when he is watching the film at the police station.
4. Chapter 24, pages 366 to 370, beginning "She stared back at me for a while . . ." and ending ". . . to think about." Pete talks to the fortune teller.
5. Chapter 28, pages 437 to 438, beginning "I was trying very hard . . ." and ending ". . . waste of time." Pete reflects on the difference between hanging out and being friends.

Booktalk

Sixteen-year-old Pete Boland's old gang invites him to a reunion in their hideout. He doesn't have anything else to do, so he goes. They pass around the drinks and drugs, but things are a little different than he remembered. The jokester isn't as funny. The girlfriend, even when Pete is drinking, isn't as appealing, and his best friend, Raymond, is a lot weirder. They decide to go to the fair. The evening gets worse. Raymond disappears. So does a celebrity. The police look for the celebrity. They think Raymond had something to do with her disappearance. Pete starts his own search. The events of that drug-clouded evening are almost impossible to see, but slowly, secrets of love, rejection, abuse, and mutilation appear. And those secrets change lives one *Black Rabbit Summer*.

Curriculum Connections

1. (Research, social studies) Using your library resources, learn more about procedures in missing persons' investigations. Act as a resource person for the group.
2. (React, language arts) How are settings important to this story?
3. (Create, language arts) What do you think happened to Raymond? Compare your conclusions with those of others in the group. Be sure to use specifics.

Related Works

1. Brooks, Kevin. **Candy.** New York: The Chicken House, 2005. 364p. $16.95. ISBN 0 439 68327 0. [fiction] JS, CG (*Genre Talks for Teens*, 2009, pages 127 to 130.) A young man endangers his family for a girl, a drug addict and prostitute.
2. Brooks, Kevin. **Lucas: A Story of Love and Hate.** New York: The Chicken House, 2002. 432p. $16.95. ISBN 0 439 45698 3. [fiction] JS, CG with high interest for boys. (*Booktalks and Beyond*, 2007, pages 4 to 6.) Sixteen-year-old Caitlin McCann helps Lucas, a stranger with no friends, family, or last name.
3. Brooks, Kevin. **Martyn Pig.** New York: The Chicken House, 2002. 240p. $10.95. ISBN 0 439 29595 5. [fiction] JS, CG (*Booktalks and Beyond*, 2007, pages 114 to 116.) Fifteen-year-old Martyn Pig accidentally kills his abusive father and hides the body.
4. Brooks, Kevin. **Road of the Dead.** New York: Scholastic/The Chicken House, 2006. 352p. $16.99. ISBN 0 439 78623 1. [fiction] JS, CG with high interest for boys. (*Genre Talks for Teens*, 2009,

pages 157 to 159.) Two brothers try to retrieve their sister's body, discover that her beating, rape, and murder were the result of a land-grabbing scheme, and fight the perpetrators who want to drive them away or kill them.

5. Cormier, Robert. **Tenderness.** New York: Bantam Doubleday Dell Publishing Group, 1997. 229p. $16.95. ISBN 0 385 32286 0. [fiction] JS, CG with high interest for boys. (*Booktalks Plus,* 2001, pages 64 to 66.) A serial killer gets away with murder but is convicted of killing his girlfriend, a crime he did not commit.

ᘓᘔ

Dowd, Siobhan. **Bog Child.**

New York: Random House/A David Fickling Book, 2008. 322p. $16.99.
ISBN-13: 978 0 285 75169 8. [fiction] S, CG with high interest for boys

Themes/Topics: Ireland, political prisoners, bog bodies, family life, terrorism, coming of age

Summary/Description

As eighteen-year-old Fergus studies for medical school entrance exams, he is distracted by his imprisoned brother's hunger strike, his dangerous job as a courier for Sinn Fein, and strange dreams sent to him by an ancient murdered girl he finds buried in the bog. Manipulated by a local man who has known both boys since their childhood, Fergus's brother, Joe, refuses to eat until he is declared a political prisoner instead of a common criminal. Joe slips into a coma, and the parents start him on treatment to save his life. A former friend recruits Fergus as a courier with the false promise that he can get Joe to eat. The bog girl's stories about her life and death reveal similar prejudice and violence of her ancient time. Ultimately, Fergus passes his exams and leaves his violent town to start a healing journey.

Values: Fergus learns the importance of tolerance, peace, and independent thinking.

Read Aloud/Reader Response

1. Chapter 13, pages 91 to 92, beginning "He nodded." and ending with the chapter. Fergus considers history a warning.
2. Chapter 17, pages 117 to 118, beginning "Dear Margaret Thatcher, . . ." and ending "From a sincere citizen." Fergus writes Margaret Thatcher a letter, which he does not mail.

3. Chapter 32, page 220, beginning "She was out . . ." and ending with the chapter. Fergus wonders if Joe thought about the effects of his actions on the family.
4. Chapter 42, pages 293 to 294. In this chapter, Fergus uses the sins-of-omission argument on his father for the drip in Joe's arm.
5. Chapter 47, pages 318 to 322. In this chapter, Fergus leaves for school.

Booktalk

Smart and handsome eighteen-year-old Fergus lives in Ireland during the 1980s. He has a great future in medicine. He can leave his small-town life for success, even fame. But Fergus's shining future might turn black. His older brother Joe is in prison for terrorism. Like many of his fellow prisoners, he starves himself a little each day to get public support. The prime minister stands firm and says everyone has a choice. Fergus has choices too. Fergus is a runner. If he runs for the terrorists, they will persuade his brother to eat again. He makes the pick-up and the drop, and wonders how many innocent people the package will kill. Then there are two girls. One is a new girl in town who loves dangerous choices. The other is a dead one Fergus finds in the peat bog. She was murdered thousands of years ago. Should he act on the advice of the living all around him or the haunting truth of the *Bog Child*?

Curriculum Connections

1. (Research, social studies) Using library resources, learn more about Sinn Fein. Act as a resource person for the group.
2. (Research, social studies) Using library resources, learn more about the bog people. Act as a resource person for the group.
3. (Discuss, language arts) Why does Dowd include the bog child in the story?

Related Works

1. Bradley, Kimberly Brubaker. **For Freedom: The Story of a French Spy.** New York: Delacorte Press, 2003. 181p. $17.99. ISBN 0 385 90087 2. [fiction] MJ, G (*Booktalks and Beyond*, 2007, pages 123 to 125.) During the German occupation, fifteen-year-old Suzanne Good becomes a courier for the French Underground.
2. Cooney, Caroline B. **Code Orange.** New York: Delacorte Press, 2005. 200p. $15.95. ISBN 0 385 90277 8. [fiction] MJS, CG with high interest for boys. (*Booktalks and Beyond*, 2007, pages 116 to

118.) Mitty Blake thinks he has infected himself with smallpox and draws the attention of terrorists when he posts his concerns on the Internet.

3. Cooney, Caroline B. **The Terrorist.** New York: Scholastic, 1997. 198p. $15.95. ISBN 0 590 22853 6. [fiction] MJS, CG (*Booktalks Plus,* 2001, pages 135 to 138.) Living in London for a year, naïve Laura Williams tries to find the terrorist who killed her brother.
4. Deuker, Carl. **Runner.** New York: Houghton Mifflin Co., 2005. 216p. $16.00. ISBN 0 618 54298 1. [fiction] JS, CG with high interest for boys. (*Booktalks and Beyond,* 2007, pages 70 to 73.) Chance Taylor agrees to deliver packages to a marina locker for $200 per week, and he finds himself entangled in a deadly terrorist plot.
5. Heneghan, James. **Safe House.** Victoria, BC, Canada: Orca Book Publishers, 2006. 151p. $7.95pa. ISBN-13: 978 1 55143 640 1. [fiction] MJS, CG with high interest for boys. (*Genre Talks for Teens,* 2009, pages 93 to 95.) When twelve-year-old Liam Fogarty witnesses his parents gunned down by Protestant terrorists, he flees the triggerman.

ʊʒ ʂʊ

Northrop, Michael. Gentlemen.
New York: Scholastic Press, 2009. 234p. $16.99.
ISBN-13: 978 0 545 09749 9. [fiction] JS, CG with high interest for boys

Themes/Topics: guilt, missing persons, teachers, friendship, crime, labels, conduct of life

Summary/Description

"Micheal," Mixer, and Bones suspect that their remedial English teacher, Mr. Haberman, killed their fourth-most-troublesome group member, Tommy. The plot of *Crime and Punishment,* along with Mr. Haberman's presentation, reinforces their suspicions. They confront him at his home. Bones beats Haberman senseless even after he explains why their suspicions are groundless. Micheal sees Bones's anger coming from his hate and fear of failing English rather than a desire for justice but watches the beating because Bones is his friend. The next day, the police find Tommy who used his time away to come out of the closet. The three who confronted Haberman are arrested. Micheal testifies against Bones. Bones is sentenced as an adult. Micheal and Mixer are sent to juvenile detention. In detention, Micheal reads *Crime and Punishment* and writes Haberman who encourages Micheal to see the incident and his incarceration as the first chapter in his life.

Value: Micheal realizes that each person has responsibility for his action or lack of action.

Read Aloud/Reader Response

1. Chapter 1, pages 26 to 29, beginning "What is a crime?" and ending ". . . the barrel anyway?" Mr. Haberman makes his initial *Crime and Punishment* presentation.
2. Chapter 10, pages 112 to 118. Micheal reflects on Tommy.
3. Chapter 18, pages 183 to 186. Bones beats Haberman, and the others watch.
4. Chapter 25, page 231, beginning "You know why . . ." and ending ". . . seven to ten years, bitch." Micheal tells why he testified against Bones.
5. Chapter 26, pages 232 to 234. Micheal writes to Haberman, and Haberman replies.

Booktalk

"Micheal" hangs with three other losers, Tommy, Mixer, and Bones, in math and English for dummies. Micheal is a chip off the old block. His dad didn't even spell Micheal's name right on the birth certificate. It's "eal" instead of "ael." But their English teacher, Mr. Haberman, thinks that the class isn't that dumb. He calls them gentlemen and ladies. He thinks that they can read *Crime and Punishment*. (*Hold it up*.) A huge book filled with names like . . . (*Read some of the names*.) Just before the class starts the book, Tommy throws a desk across the room in math and gets thrown out of school—not that unusual for Tommy. Then he disappears. It has happened before. At the same time, Mr. Haberman talks about the crime in the book. He brings a barrel to class with something jointed in it. He talks about crimes close to what might have happened to Tommy. (*Hold up* Crime and Punishment *again*.) So does Haberman think that these losers are smart enough to read a big book like this but so dumb that they won't know that Tommy's body is in the barrel? Mr. Haberman is about to learn something from his *Gentlemen*.

Curriculum Connections

1. (Research and Discuss, language arts) Using your library resources, research what constitutes a classic and discuss how the sustained allusion to *Crime and Punishment* affects the novel.

2. (Research and Apply, language arts) Using your library resources, define *unreliable narrator.* Rate Micheal's reliability as a narrator on a scale of 1 to 10. Compare your rating with the ratings of others in the group. Support your rating with specifics.

3. (Discuss, language arts) How do crime, punishment, and resurrection apply to the novel?

Related Works

1. Brooks, Kevin. **Martyn Pig.** New York: The Chicken House, 2002. 240p. $10.95. ISBN 0 439 29595 5. [fiction] JS, CG with high interest for boys. (*Booktalks and Beyond,* pages 114 to 116.) Fifteen-year-old Martyn Pig conspires with an older neighborhood girl to hide his father's body. The girl betrays him and steals his inheritance money.

2. Cormier, Robert. **The Rag and Bone Shop.** New York: Delacorte Press, 2001. 154p. $15.95. ISBN 0 385 72962 6. [fiction] MJS, CG with high interest for boys. (*Teen Genre Connections,* 2005, pages 129 to 131.) An interrogator drives an innocent boy to crime.

3. Dostoevsky, Fyodor. Constance Garnett (trans.). **Crime and Punishment.** New York: Random House Publishing Group, 1996. 505p. $6.99pa. ISBN 0 553 211757. [classic] S/A, CG A young man commits murder to test his theory about exceptional men being above the law and achieves redemption through suffering. The story was written in 1865.

4. Myers, Walter Dean. **Monster.** New York: Harper Collins Publishers, 1999. 281p. $15.95. ISBN 0 06 028077 8. [fiction] JS, CG with high interest for boys. (*Booktalks and More,* 2003, pages 13 to 15.) Sixteen-year-old Steve Harmon structures his murder trial and related experiences into a movie script. The reader builds a verdict with the jury.

5. Zusak, Markus. **I Am the Messenger.** New York: Alfred A. Knopf, 2002. 357p. $20.50. ISBN 0 375 93099 X. [fiction] S, CG with high interest for boys. (*Booktalks and Beyond,* 2007, pages 143 to 146.) Nineteen-year-old Ed Kennedy witnesses a bank robbery, pursues the robber, becomes a hero, and receives aces that direct him to help people.

Swanson, James. Chasing Lincoln's Killer.

New York: Scholastic Press, 2009. 208p. $16.99.
ISBN-13: 978 0 439 90354 7. [nonfiction] JS, CG with high interest for boys

Themes/Topics: Abraham Lincoln, John Wilkes
Booth, spies

Summary/Description

After a brief explanation of the Civil War and its effect on post-war
Washington, D.C., Swanson begins with a description of the inaugural address that inspires Booth to shoot Lincoln and order the failed
assassinations of Vice-President Andrew Johnson, and Secretary of State
William H. Seward. Lincoln's visit to Ford's Theatre delivers a perfectly
timed, successful assassination. The shooting of Lincoln and the failed
attempts of his co-conspirators appear to be a Confederate plot. Slow
communications, Booth's cunning, missed opportunities, and Southern
sympathizers stymie government response. The assassin's portrait,
twelve-day flight, and conspirators' stories illuminate the time period
and crime. Pictures and documents highlight the text. "A List of Major
Participants" appears at the front of the book. An epilogue explains what
happens to each of the participants and why Booth ultimately fails in
history.

Values: Vanity drives Booth's conscience. He is a counterexample for
integrity and courage.

Read Aloud/Reader Response

1. Chapter 1, pages 13 and 14, beginning "Abraham Lincoln ate . . ."
   and ending ". . . to tell her." On the morning of the assassination,
   Lincoln tells his recurring dream.
2. Chapter 2, pages 33 to 45. The chapter describes Lincoln's assassination.
3. Chapter 3, pages 46 to 59. This chapter describes the attempted
   assassination of Seward.
4. Chapter 6, pages 105 to 107, beginning "It was time . . ." and ending
   ". . . the simplicity." The passage describes Lincoln's ride home.
5. Chapter 11, pages 165 to 177, beginning "It was day twelve . . ." and
   ending with the chapter. The passage describes Booth's death.

Booktalk

Hold up a picture of Lincoln. Ask the group what they know about him.

He gave his life for the Union. John Wilkes Booth killed him to
destroy that Union. Booth's plan was almost spontaneous. It hung on
Lincoln's decision to attend a play at Ford's Theatre. Booth, an actor,
knew the theater's floor plan and the play. He would use the setting
and the characters' lines to construct a different play. Conspirators

supported him. He believed that the world, in time, would praise him. In his drama, he would be the hero. But in history, Booth took on the villain's role. He envisioned a successful escape to spark Confederate victory and personal triumph. Instead, he was hunted like a dog. He died painfully and alone. Here is the story. Even though you know the ending, you won't be able to stop reading the details of *Chasing Lincoln's Killer.*

Curriculum Connections

1. (Research, American history) Using your library resources, learn more about John Wilkes Booth. Act as a resource person during the discussion.
2. (Compare and React, American history) Read *Manhunt,* the adult version of *Chasing Lincoln's Killer.* Comment on the differences between the two works.
3. (React, American history) What impressed you the most in the story of the assassination?

Related Works

1. Blackwood, Gary. **Second Sight.** New York: Dutton's Children's Books, 2005. 279p. $16.99. ISBN 0 525 47481 1. [fiction] MJS, CG In this fiction version, one of Booth's associates loses his courage, and Lincoln lives.
2. Giblin, James Cross. **Good Brother, Bad Brother: The Story of Edwin Booth and John Wilkes Booth.** New York: Clarion Books, 2005. 244p. $22.00. ISBN 0 618 09642 6. [nonfiction] MJS, CG with high interest for boys. Giblin explains the personal and historical contexts that produce brothers who leave very different marks on American history and culture.
3. Rinaldi, Ann. **An Acquaintance with Darkness**. New York: Harcourt Brace and Co., 1997. 294p. $16.00. ISBN 0 15 201294 X. [fiction] MJS, G Emily Bransby Pigbush discovers that her best friends are the center of President Lincoln's assassination.
4. St. George, Judith. **In the Line of Fire: Presidents' Lives at Stake.** New York: Holiday House, 1999. 144p. $18.95. ISBN 0 8234 1428 0. [nonfiction] MJS, CG St. George explains the assassinations of Abraham Lincoln, James Abram Garfield, William McKinley, and John Fitzgerald Kennedy; and the attempted assassinations of Theodore Roosevelt, Franklin Delano Roosevelt, Harry S Truman, Gerald Ford, and Ronald Reagan.

5. Swanson, James L. **Manhunt: The 12-Day Chase for Lincoln's Killer.** New York: HarperCollins, 2006. 464p. $15.95. ISBN-13: 978 0 06 051849 3. [nonfiction] S/A, CG with high interest for boys. *Manhunt* is the adult bestseller that inspired the young adult version, *Chasing Lincoln's Killer.* It includes documentation and a bibliography.

Dependability

 C§?D

Bauer, Joan. Peeled.

New York: G. P. Putnam's Sons, 2008. 248p. $16.99.
ISBN-13: 978 0 399 23475 0. [fiction] MJS, CG with high interest for girls

Themes/Topics: journalism, farm life, haunted houses, New York, conservation

Summary/Description

Hildy Biddle, high school reporter, lives with her extended family in the heart of New York apple country where a haunted house threatens the town's stability. Ominous warnings posted on the house, a psychic, a dead body, a corrupt mayor, and sensational news stories in the local newspaper push orchard owners to sell their land to a Boston developer planning to build a haunted theme park. With the help of a principled and disillusioned newspaper man and a local woman who is a survivor of the Polish Solidarity movement, Hildy and her fellow staff members uncover and foil the scheme.

Values: Hildy triumphs because she values family, truth, and hard work.

Read Aloud/Reader Response

1. Chapter 2, pages 18 to 19, "Want to Get Scared?" This article introduces the sensational series carried by the local paper about the haunted house.
2. Chapter 4, page 38, beginning "I snapped an apple . . ." and ending ". . . in one piece." Hildy recalls her father's lesson about peeling an apple.

3. Chapter 5, pages 50 to 51, beginning "Minska was at . . ." and ending with the chapter. Minska realizes the danger of poor information and simple solutions.
4. Chapter 13, pages 119 to 121, beginning "'How,' Baker Polton . . ." and ending "'that's what I know about.'" Baker Polton discusses reliable sources and how to get them.
5. Chapter 17, pages 153 to 155, beginning "I was at . . ." and ending ". . . 'bring the gate down.'" Hildy and Minska discuss propaganda and revolution.

Booktalk

High school reporter Hildy Biddle lives in rural New York where apples are the core of existence. And when Hildy thinks about proving herself as an ace reporter, she remembers her father's advice about peeling an apple. (*While you are talking, it might be appropriate to peel an apple as described in Read Aloud/Reader Response 2.*) Start at the top, and don't stop until you get to the bottom. That's advice that Hildy's father gave her before he died, and Hildy applies it to every job she does. So when a haunted house, a psychic, a dead body, and a theme park start making scary headlines in her hard luck, hardworking apple town, Hildy digs for the who, what, when, where, and why of all of them. She sharpens her pencil, gathers her friends, and together, they get those stories *Peeled.*

Curriculum Connections

1. (Research, journalism) Bauer cites three journalism books as research sources. Using library resources, find one of the books. Read and review it for the group, or investigate other books on journalism and share them with the group.
2. (Research, social studies) The Solidarity movement inspires Hildy and her journalism crew. Learn more about the movement. Act as a resource person during the discussion.
3. (Discussion, language arts) What makes Hildy Biddle appealing and believable?

Related Works

1. Bauer, Joan. **Backwater.** New York: G. P. Putnam's Sons, 1999. 185p. $16.99. ISBN 0 399 23141 2. (*Booktalks Plus*, 2001, pages 28 to 30.) Sixteen-year-old Ivy Breedlow shows her historian grit when she braves the wilderness to interview her hermit aunt.
2. Bauer, Joan. **Hope Was Here.** New York: G. P. Putnam's Sons, 2000. 186p. $16.99. ISBN 0 399 23142 0. [fiction] MJS, CG with

high interest for girls. (*Booktalks and More,* 2003, pages 258 to 260.) Hope, an excellent waitress for the Welcome Stairways Diner in Mulhoney, Wisconsin, uncovers a voter fraud scheme.

3. Bauer, Joan. **Rules of the Road.** New York: G. P. Putnam's Sons, 1998. 201p. $15.99. ISBN 0 399 23140 4. [fiction] MJS, CG with high interest for girls. (*Booktalks Plus,* 2001 pages 114 to 116.) Sixteen-year-old Jenna Boller acquires poise and an eye for quality when she is hired to drive for the owner of Gladstone Shoes.

4. Hiaasen, Carl. **Flush.** New York: Alfred A. Knopf, 2005. 263p. $16.95. ISBN 0 375 82182 1. [fiction] MJ, CG with high interest for boys. (*Booktalks and Beyond,* 2007, pages 121 to 123.) To clear his father's name, Noah Underwood exposes a gambling boat owner for dumping raw sewage into the water.

5. Hiaasen, Carl. **Hoot.** New York: Alfred A. Knopf, 2002. 292p. $15.95. ISBN 0 375 82181 3. [fiction] MJ, CG with high interest for boys. (*Teen Genre Connections,* 2005, pages 37 to 39.) Like Bauer, Hiaasen uses a cast of quirky characters to win an environmental fight with a would-be-developer.

Herrick, Steven. **Cold Skin.**
Honesdale, PA: Front Street, 2007. 279p. $18.95.
ISBN-13: 978 1 59078 572 0. [fiction in verse] S, CG

Themes/Topics: murder, fathers and sons, post World War II, Australia, coming of age

Summary/Description

In this post–World War II mystery set in an Australian mining town, nine voices react to the murder of a beautiful, talented teenage daughter of a war hero. Eddie, her friend and a member of one of the poorest families, suspects the school's abusive and perverted teacher. His investigation leads him to his own father who witnessed the murder. Thinking that the town will not believe him because of his reputation as a coward, the father pursues vigilante justice. He ties the murderer, the town mayor, to the train track on the bridge. The train will kill both the mayor and the father. Eddie's unsuccessful attempt to save the mayor's life foils his father's suicide plan and makes Eddie a town hero. The father goes to jail. Eddie leaves his hated schoolwork to work in the mines and pursues the girl he loves in spite of the town's social class labels.

Value: Eddie learns that personal integrity is more important than labels.

Read Aloud/Reader Response

1. Chapter 1, "Eddie," pages 11 to 12. Eddie introduces himself.
2. Chapter 4, "Mr. Carter," page 143. Mr. Carter is taken to the crime scene and realizes the impact on the town.
3. Chapter 5, "Mr. Carter," pages 185 to 186. Mr. Carter eliminates Eddie as a suspect.
4. Chapter 6, "Sergeant Grainger," pages 197 to 200. In the first passage, Mr. Carter tells the sergeant that the murderer is a man. In the second, Eddie's father tells him the murderer is a coward.
5. Chapter 8, "Eddie," pages 278 to 279. In this last passage, Eddie is in his new life.

Booktalk

In a small town, everybody knows everybody else. Burruga, Australia, isn't any different. According to Burruga, Eddie Holding is a loser from a loser family. Eddie agrees. He is strong and funny. But smart? Forget it. Eddie wants to leave school and work in the mines. Eddie loves one of the smartest and most beautiful girls in town, but Eddie's future will probably be like his dad's—menial farm work, a wife he doesn't want to go home to, and Friday nights in the local bar. Then the town has a murder. A beautiful girl, a standout, a friend of Eddie's is found by the river. Every man is a suspect, even Eddie. But Eddie has some suspects of his own. He does his own investigation. Who is guilty? More people than Eddie could imagine. Others are after that murderer too. Who will claim justice? Or who will exact revenge? Such a smart town should know who the murderer is. But sometimes guilt is hard to recognize, something to bury and turn away from, like a dead body with *Cold Skin*.

Curriculum Connections

1. (Research, social studies) Using library resources, learn more about how soldiers were chosen for military duty during World War II. Act as a resource person for the group.
2. (Create, language arts) Plan a dramatic reading for the nine voices of the novel.
3. (Create, language arts) Write the article that Mr. Carter might write about Eddie in five or ten years. Share it with the group.

Related Works

1. Brooks, Kevin. **Martyn Pig.** New York: The Chicken House, 2002. 240p. $10.95. ISBN 0 439 29595 5. [fiction] JS, CG with high

interest for boys. (*Booktalks and Beyond,* 2007, pages 114 to 116.) Hiding his father's accidental death from the police, Martyn Pig trusts an older, manipulative neighbor girl who betrays him.

2. Haddon, Mark. **The Curious Incident of the Dog in the Night-Time.** New York: Vintage Contemporaries, 2003. 226p. $12.00. ISBN 1 4000 3271 7. [fiction] S/A, CG with high interest for boys. (*Booktalks and Beyond,* 2007, pages 119 to 121.) When a brilliant, autistic teenager investigates the murder of his neighbor's dead dog, he uncovers the murderer and family secrets.

3. Harrison, Michael. **Facing the Dark.** New York: Holiday House, 2000. 128p. $15.95. ISBN 0 8234 1491 4. [fiction] MJS, CG (*Teen Genre Connections,* 2005, pages 135 to 137.) An accused murderer's son, Simon, and the victim's daughter, Charley, give their perceptions of the crime and its solution in alternating chapters.

4. Hesse, Karen. **Witness.** New York: Scholastic Press, 2001. 176p. $16.95. ISBN 0 439 27199 1. [fiction in verse] MJS, CG (*Booktalks and More,* 2003, pages 180 to 183.) This historical mystery, set in 1924 and told in verse by multiple voices, illustrates how small acts of kindness defeat the Ku Klux Klan invasion of a small Vermont town.

5. Lisle, Janet Taylor. **Black Duck.** New York: Philomel/Sleuth, 2006. 252p. $15.99. ISBN 0 399 23963 4. [fiction] MJS, CG with high interest for boys. (*Genre Talks for Teens,* 2009, pages 149 to 152.) When fourteen-year-old Ruben Hart and Jeddy McKenzie find a man's body on the beach, the boys become embroiled in a conflict between rival prohibition bootleggers.

❦❧

Marchetta, Melina. Jellicoe Road.

New York: HarperCollins/Harper Teen, 2006. 419p. $17.99.
ISBN-13: 978 0 06 143183 8. [fiction] S, CG with high interest for girls

Themes/Topics: abandoned children, family history, boarding schools, identity, Australia

Summary/Description

Taylor Markham, abandoned by her drug-addicted mother on Jellicoe Road at eleven, is seventeen and facing her past. She also leads her boarding school dormitory, which wages a traditional territory war with the Cadets and Townies. She struggles with this responsibility as she confronts the hostile cadet leader with whom she once ran away.

Hannah, the adult who has been like her family, disappears. Taylor also is discovering the roots of her confusing memories in the story of a tragic automobile accident that produced three orphans: her father, mother, and aunt. The town boy who saved them and the cadet who bonded with the four formed a family who created the town/ school/cadet wars as a game. The other leaders of the "warring" factions help her unravel her past, find her mother and Hannah, and open herself to friendship and love.

Values: Taylor discovers the danger of labels and the strength of love.

Read Aloud/Reader Response

1. "Prologue," pages 1 to 2. Hannah recalls the accident that began the friendship of Hannah, Web, Tate, and Fritz.
2. Chapter 2, pages 31 to 32, beginning "As his Cadet troop . . ." and ending ". . . planted the poppies." Jude Scanlon meets Hannah, Web, Tate, and Fritz.
3. Chapter 4, pages 56 to 59, beginning "'Do you know . . .'" and ending ". . . from my mother." Taylor remembers her first encounter with Jonah Griggs. The passage also alludes to the importance of personal history.
4. Chapter 11, pages 134 to 135, beginning "At night . . ." and ending ". . . state of fear." Taylor reflects on the Prayer Tree.
5. Chapter 27, pages 416 to 418, beginning "My mother took . . ." and ending with the chapter. This final chapter brings the journey from the beginning of the novel full circle.

Booktalk

Seventeen-year-old Taylor Markham is at war. She heads her Australian boarding school dorm, and the school wages an endless territory battle with the Townies and the Cadets. Each territory has its history. As the battle rages, those histories rage: drug addiction, prostitution, suicide, murder, and even a mysterious serial killer. Personal ghosts haunt Taylor's life: the mother who deserted her; the father she never knew; the stranger who stares at her; a hermit who puts a gun to his head; Hannah, her loyal adult friend who disappears; and the boy in the tree who invades her dreams. The war heats up. Taylor, confused and angry, starts a new and dangerous journey where her mother left her six years ago—on the beautiful and treacherous *Jellicoe Road*.

Curriculum Connections

1. (Research, language arts) The poppy is a central image in the novel. Read the passage cited in Read Aloud/Reader Response 2. Using library resources, learn more about symbolism of the poppy. Act as a resource person for the group.
2. (Discuss, language arts) Matthew 10:26 is the central quotation on the Prayer Tree. Discuss the significance of it and the Prayer Tree.
3. (Discuss, language arts) What is the difference between a trip and a journey?

Related Works

1. Brooks, Kevin. **Dawn**. New York: Scholastic Inc./Chicken House, 2009. 250p. $17.99. ISBN-13: 978 0 545 06090 5. [fiction] S, G Fifteen-year-old Dawn Bundy lives in a mental cave as she keeps secrets about her addicted mother and the father who deserted them.
2. Brooks, Kevin. **The Road of the Dead.** New York: Scholastic/ The Chicken House, 2006. 352p. $16.99. ISBN 0 439 78623 1. [fiction] JS, CG with high appeal for boys. (*Genre Talks for Teens,* 2009, pages 157 to 159.) Fourteen-year-old Ruben Ford and his sixteen-year-old brother Cole retrieve the body of his murdered sister whose death was the accidental result of a land-grabbing scheme.
3. Brooks, Martha. **Mistik Lake.** New York: Farrar, Straus and Giroux/Melanie Kroupa Books, 2007. 207p. $16.00. ISBN-13: 978 0 374 34985 1. [fiction] S, G (*Genre Talks for Teens,* 2009, pages 4 to 6.) In Mistik Lake, the family's summer retreat, seventeen-year-old Odella unravels the secrets that grip her family and discovers her own love.
4. Green, John. **Looking for Alaska.** New York: Dutton Books, 2005. 224p. $15.99. ISBN 0 525 47506 0. [fiction] S, CG (*Booktalks and Beyond,* 2007, pages 37 to 40.) A tragic car accident that kills his friend teaches Miles Halter to care for others.
5. Lee, Harper. **To Kill a Mockingbird.** New York: HarperCollins/ Harper Perennial, 2002. 336p. $12.95. ISBN-13: 978 0 06 093546 7. [classic fiction] JS/A, CG. First published in 1960 and awarded the Pulitzer Prize in 1961, this classic depicts a young girl learning that prejudice can be defeated. It is a major allusion in *Jellicoe Road.*

(ℭ ℭ)

Parker, Robert B. The Boxer and the Spy.

New York: Philomel Books, 2008. 210p. $17.99.
ISBN-13: 978 0 399 24775 0. [fiction] MJS, CG with high interest for boys

Themes/Topics: boxing, murder, corruption, friendship, diversity, love, conduct of life

Summary/Description

Fifteen-year-old Terry Novak, a boxer in training, and his best friend Abby pursue the mystery of a quiet boy's suicide. They discover that the school principal and a candidate for governor, who are having an affair, build houses using school students and district supplies and then keep the money. A senior school football star is the principal's enforcer, but Terry fights and beats him. After the football star threatens Abby, the detective duo and their supporters plot to expose the principal and the candidate. The football player fights Terry again. Terry wins. Humiliated and threatened with losing his scholarship, the player testifies about the murder, the disposal of the body, and the team's steroid use. Terry's trainer, a positive male mentor, gives a philosophical view of fighting. Eight Skycam passages supplement the narrative.

Value: Terry and Abby demonstrate their integrity as they fight for truth.

Read Aloud/Reader Response

1. Chapter 13, pages 59 to 63. Terry and Abby talk about being an adult.
2. Chapter 21, pages 97 to 100. George talks about fighting and taking a stand.
3. Chapter 26, pages 117 to 118, beginning "You ever just wanted to run?" and ending with the chapter. George and Terry talk about fear.
4. Chapter 30, pages 131 to 132, beginning "Heart got something to do . . ." and ending with the chapter. George talks about the relationship of courage, heart, and cruelty.
5. Chapter 36, pages 151 to 154. This chapter considers how one chooses friends.

Booktalk

Fifteen-year-old Terry and his maybe girlfriend Abby are fighters. Terry is a boxer in training and knows that fighting means more than fists.

A good fighter uses heart and head too. When Jason Green's body appears on the beach with no explanation but steroid abuse, Terry has the heart to ask some questions. The answer is "Back off." Terry's head tells him that shy Jason Green was no steroid user. And his head also registers that the people leaning on Terry the hardest are poster boys for steroid abuse. He could walk away. But he wants the truth, a truth that leads to important people who will spend money to keep him quiet. He will need high-powered help to stay alive. That's where Abby comes in. She will be his eyes and ears and find some more as well. The murderers will have the biggest fight of their lives with two natural born winners, *The Boxer and the Spy.*

Curriculum Connections

1. (Research, science) Using library resources, learn more about steroids. Act as a resource person for your group.
2. (Discuss, language arts) What do the Skycam chapters add to the novel?
3. (Create, physical education) George and Terry discuss how boxing makes a person grow. Choose another sport. List all the good qualities that it can develop.

Related Works

1. Brooks, Kevin. **The Road of the Dead.** New York: Scholastic/The Chicken House, 2006. 352p. $16.99. ISBN 0 439 78623 1. [fiction] JS, CG with high interest for boys. (*Genre Talks for Teens,* 2009, pages 157 to 159.) Two brothers retrieve their sister's body and discover her death to be the accidental result of a land-grabbing scheme.
2. Coy, John. **Crackback.** New York: Scholastic Press, 2005. 208p. $16.99. ISBN 0 439 69733 6. [fiction] JS, CG with high interest for boys. Pressured by his coach, teammates, and father to perform well in football, junior Miles Manning considers taking steroids.
3. Deuker, Carl. **Runner.** New York: Houghton Mifflin Co., 2005. 216p. $16.00. ISBN 0 618 54298 1. [fiction] JS, CG with high interest for boys. (*Booktalks and Beyond,* 2007, pages 70 to 73.) Chance Taylor's running ability pulls him into a terrorist plot.
4. Lisle, Janet Taylor. **Black Duck.** New York: Philomel/Sleuth, 2006. 252p. $15.99. ISBN 0 399 23963 4. [fiction] MJS, CG with high interest for boys. (*Genre Talks for Teens,* 2009, pages 149 to 152.) An unknown man's body on the beach puts Ruben Hart and Jeddy McKenzie in conflict with bootleggers and a town that prospers from the business.

5. Schmidt, Gary. **First Boy.** New York: Henry Holt and Co., 2005. 197p. $16.95. ISBN 0 8050 7859 2. [fiction] MJS, CG with high interest for boys. (*Genre Talks for Teens*, 2009, pages 138 to 141.). Fifteen-year-old Cooper Jewett learns that he was abandoned by his real parents whose identity endangers his life.

ぴ℀

Peacock, Shane. **Eye of the Crow.**
Toronto, ON, Canada: Tundra Books, 2007. 251p.
(The Boy Sherlock Holmes) $21.99.
ISBN-13: 978 0 88776 850 7. [fiction] MJ, CG with high interest for boys

Themes/Topics: Sherlock Holmes, nineteenth-century London, prejudice, theater

Summary/Description

Thirteen-year-old Sherlock Holmes prefers London's crimes and street life to school. His Jewish, well-educated parents cannot earn a living wage, and Sherlock is jeered as "Jew-boy" by the Irregulars, Malfactor's street gang. Holmes investigates a murder whose victim resembles his mother. An accused Arab boy claims his innocence. With his father's knowledge of birds, Malfactor's street smarts, and the investigative work of both a young girl and his mother, Holmes clears the Arab and secures the arrest of a prominent war veteran. He receives no credit for his solution, the young girl is seriously injured, and his mother is poisoned. The grieving young Holmes vows to investigate for justice, receive recognition, and distance himself from personal relationships. A London map introduces the novel.

Values: Holmes learns the importance of justice and fairness.

Read Aloud/Reader Response

1. "Preface," page ix. This short passage sets the story's tone and explains Holmes's position in the city.
2. Chapter 1, pages 6 and 7, beginning "When five o'clock comes . . ." and ending with the chapter. The passage describes Holmes's life on the streets.
3. Chapter 2, pages 13 to 15, beginning "Her name was . . ." and ending ". . . flew to him." The passage describes the mother and father's romantic but ill-fated love.
4. Chapter 8, page 71, beginning "Observation . . ." and ending ". . . made you weak." Holmes recalls his father's advice.

5. Chapter 22, pages 249 to 250, beginning "The tall thin boy's . . ." and ending with the novel. Holmes learns that Inspector Lestrade claimed the solution to the murder.

Booktalk

Ask the group to share what they know about Sherlock Holmes.

We know about the horrible and knotted crimes that he solves through deduction, but nothing about how he came to his career or fame. Even Dr. Watson once said, (*Read the quotation that appears on the page opposite "Contents"*). Now we have answers. The young Mr. Holmes was a school drop-out, a street wanderer. He suffered names like "Jew-boy." He loved to read about the latest crimes in the daily papers, and his best friends were the lowly of nineteenth-century London streets. What caused him to emerge as perhaps the most famous detective of all times? A murder of course. (*Read the "Preface" on page ix.*) When Holmes sees a young Arab accused of knifing that beautiful woman in Whitechapel, he is sure that the boy is innocent. He knows about prejudice. He will solve the mystery and free the boy. Easy? No. Clues lead him to the homes of the rich and powerful. He faces their weapons of prison, death, and treachery and ultimately sees the solution through the *Eye of the Crow*.

Curriculum Connections

1. (Research, social studies) Choose one of the important people that Holmes sees on London's streets. Learn about their contributions. Share your information with the group.
2. (Discuss, language arts) What do you think happens to Malfactor and Irene?
3. (Follow-Up, language arts) Read or view an Arthur Conan Doyle mystery. Discuss how Peacock made the young character consistent with Doyle's adult character.

Related Works

1. Abrahams, Peter. **Down the Rabbit Hole: An Echo Falls Mystery.** New York: Harper Collins Publishers/Laura Geringer Books, 2005. 375p. $16.89. ISBN 0 06 073702 6. [fiction] MJ, CG (*Booktalks and Beyond*, 2007, pages 111 to 114.) With Sherlock Holmes's technique, eighth-grader Ingrid Levin-Hill discovers a murderer and an imposter.
2. Altman, Steven-Elliot, and Michael Reaves (text) and Bong Dazo (illus.). **The Irregulars . . . in the service of Sherlock Holmes.** Milwaukie, OR: Dark Horse Books, 2005. 126p. $12.95. ISBN 1

59307 303 8. [graphic] MJS A band of street children penetrates an underground other world and helps clear Mr. Watson.

3.   Avi. **The Traitor's Gate.** New York: Atheneum Books for Young Readers/A Richard Jackson Book, 2007. 351p. $17.99. ISBN-13: 978 0 689 85335 7. [fiction] MJ, CG with high interest for boys. (*Genre Talks for Teens*, 2009, pages 141 to 144.) When his father is sent to debtor's prison, fourteen-year-old John Huffam contacts a hostile relative for help, secures his sister's marriage, and investigates the reasons for his father's lies and the spies who hound the family. An "Author's Note" connects the story to Charles Dickens.

4.   Lawrence, Iain. **The Convicts.** New York: Delacorte Press, 2005. 198p. $17.99. ISBN 0 385 90109 7. [fiction] MJ CG with high interest for boys. (*Booktalks and Beyond*, 2007, pages 128 to 131.). Tom leaves his near-insane mother when his father is sent to debtor's prison and journeys through the criminal system until he is reunited with his father.

5.   Mack, Tracy, and Michael Citrin (text) and Greg Ruth (illus.). **Sherlock Holmes and the Baker Street Irregulars: The Fall of the Amazing Zalindas, Casebook No. 1.** New York: Orchard Books, 2006. 259p. $16.99. ISBN 0 439 82836 8. [fiction] M, CG with high interest for boys. Sherlock Holmes and a band of street urchins investigate deaths that seem tied to the theft of a royal treasure.

Loyalty

ॲॐ

Bradbury, Jennifer. **Shift.**
New York: Simon & Shuster/Atheneum Books for
Young Readers, 2008. 256p. $16.99.
ISBN-13: 978 1 4169 4732 5. [fiction] JS

Themes/Topics: coming of age, friendship, father/son relationships, biking, senior trip

Summary/Description

High school senior Christopher Collins is investigated by the FBI when his best friend Win Coggans and the $19,000 he was carrying disappears on their graduation celebration bike trip out west. Win, dominated by his wealthy, controlling father and ignored by his socialite mother, has a history of spoiler behavior in the boys' friendship. He cleans out his bank account before the trip and decides to look for a home. He breaks away from Chris and backtracks to live with an elderly couple on a small Montana farm. Chris finishes the trip alone expecting Win to show up. Win's cryptic postcards and the FBI push Chris to find him. The angry reunion confirms that they must pursue independent lives. Both Chris and the FBI agent tell the father that Win cannot be found.

Values: The story shows the value of friendship, independence, family, and trust.

Read Aloud/Reader Response

1. Chapter 2, pages 16 and 17, beginning "My dad's a man . . ." and ending ". . . to go on this trip." Chris realizes that the trip will fulfill his and his father's dream.
2. Chapter 4, pages 26 to 28, beginning "Win's father's office . . ." and ending ". . . why he'd done it." Win's father attempts to control the trip with a check.
3. Chapter 8, pages 72 to 76, beginning "Three more cars . . ." and ending with the chapter. A church invites the boys to eat and hear the minister's message.
4. Chapter 17, pages 140 to 149. Chris is fixated on the postcard from Win. His new girlfriend, the FBI agent, and his father all ask him what he will do.
5. Chapter 20, pages 169 to 173, beginning "He was standing . . ." and ending with the chapter. In the wrestling match, Chris realizes his new power and Win's desire to let go. The passage parallels Read Aloud/Reader Response 3, which includes Jacob wrestling with the angel.

Booktalk

When Christopher Collins plans an after-graduation-cross-country-bike-trip with his best friend Win, all systems are go. Chris's dad offers encouragement, and Win's dad offers him a brand-new state-of-the-art bike. What could go wrong? Plenty. Win has always been a joker. When he suddenly disappears out west, Chris keeps riding. He is sure that Win will show up. Chris covers some miles, sees some scenery, and enjoys the peace and quiet. Then he reaches his destination and returns to life at home and school. Win doesn't. Win's high-powered father is on the case. The FBI knocks on Chris's door. The money from Win's bank account, $19,000, is missing. Chris can't explain. Then he gets some weird messages. Chris thinks Win is alive. Should he tell? Should he try to find him? Suddenly, a vacation and two pretty normal lives take one big *Shift*.

Curriculum Connections

1. (Research, life skills) Using library resources, research the money and supplies a cross-country biking trip requires. Act as a resource person during the discussion.
2. (Discuss, language arts) Compare the two fathers and the two sons. Read Aloud/Reader Responses 1 and 2 might be a good start for this discussion.
3. (React and Discuss, language arts) Rate the title on a scale of one to ten. Defend your opinion with references from the text.

Related Works

1. Cross, Gillian. **Phoning a Dead Man.** New York: Holiday House, 2002. 252p. $16.95. ISBN 0 8234 1685 2. [fiction] MJS, CG (*Teen Genre Connections*, 2005, pages 131 to 133.). When an American worker disappears in Russia, his sister and girlfriend try to find him and confront the Russian Mafia.
2. Hyde, Catherine Ryan. **Becoming Chloe.** New York: Alfred A. Knopf, 2006. 215p. $17.99. ISBN 0 375 93258 5. [fiction] S, CG with high interest for girls. (*Genre Talks for Teens*, 2009, pages 32 to 34.) Seventeen-year-old gay Jordon rescues a fragile street girl from rape, and together they seek beauty.
3. Kasischke, Laura. **Feathered.** New York: HarperTeen, 2008. 261p. $17.89. ISBN-13: 978 0 06 081318 5. [fiction] S, G (*Genre Talks for Teens*, 2009, pages 144 to 146.) Three high school seniors travel to Cancún for spring break and find their lives torn by drugs, drinking, and rape.
4. Plum-Ucci, Carol. **The Body of Christopher Creed.** New York: Harcourt, 2000. 248p. $17.00. ISBN 0 15 202388 7. [fiction] MJS, CG with high interest for boys. Torey Adams attends boarding school to avoid the rumors about the missing Christopher Creed, who ran away from his dominating mother.
5. Shoup, Barbara. **Everything You Want.** Woodbury, MN: Flux/Llewellyn, 2008. 312p. $16.95. ISBN-13: 978 0 7387 1100 3. [fiction] S, G A financial windfall teaches an awkward college freshman that money complicates relationships.

ᘓᘔ

Brittney, L. Nathan Fox: Dangerous Times.

New York: Feiwel and Friends/Macmillan, 2007. 283p. $16.95.
ISBN-13: 978 0 312 36962 0. [fiction] MJ, CG with high interest for boys

Themes/Topics: Elizabethan England, Othello,
spying, acting

Summary/Description

In this first book of the series, Sir Francis Walsingham, Queen Elizabeth's spymaster general, recruits thirteen-year-old actor and gypsy Nathan Fox as a spy. After training in military arts and cryptography, Nathan accompanies his mentor and his older sister, also a spy, to Venice where they try to build an alliance for the queen, via the renowned general Othello and are drawn into the violence, jealousy, and deceit of the Shakespearean plot. When he returns to Venice, he dictates his adventures to his friend William Shakespeare.

Values: Nathan learns the importance of skill, trust, and loyalty.

Read Aloud/Reader Response

1. "Introduction," pages iii to iv. This short passage describes the political situation in Elizabeth's England and Walsingham's place in it.
2. Chapter 1, pages 10 to 12, beginning "Nathan trotted beside . . ." and ending "'. . . the story is the thing.'" Shakespeare explains what he expects in a story.
3. Chapter 5, pages 66 to 81. In this chapter, Nathan learns about guns and their controversial place in warfare.
4. Chapter 6, pages 92 to 95, beginning "Walsingham and Pearce . . ." and ending ". . . could barely keep up." Nathan meets the queen.
5. Chapter 16, pages 207 to 208, beginning "That night . . ." and ending with the chapter. Nathan reflects on the battle.

Booktalk

Fourteen-year-old Nathan Fox lives for acting. One of his friends and favorite playwrights is William Shakespeare. Nathan can be male, female, or monster. He can jump, climb ropes, or juggle, and he knows that success lies in tiny details. But Nathan will soon be acting in a much different theater. This theater has an international stage. There is no applause. In fact, silence means success. And he must learn to kill. He will spy for Elizabeth, his queen. King Philip of Spain wants to make England a Catholic country again. Mary Queen of Scotts recently plotted to assassinate Elizabeth. The queen needs friends. Nathan is sent to Venice as her eyes and ears. Are her allies true? Will the queen and England be safe? Nathan must find the answers, through the clouds of love, fear, and jealousy that often mask the truth. And so begins the story of a Shakespearean James Bond in training, the story of *Nathan Fox: Dangerous Times.*

Curriculum Connections

1. (Research, language arts) Using library resources, learn more about *Othello*. Act as a resource person for the group during discussion.
2. (Discuss, language arts) In Read Aloud/Reader Response 2, Nathan and Shakespeare discuss what is required for a good play. Did *Nathan Fox* meet that standard?
3. (Discuss, language arts) Would you have hired Nathan Fox for the job? Be sure to support your opinion with specifics from the text.

Related Works

1. Gaiman, Neil (text), and Andy Kubert (illus.). **Marvel 1602: # 1–8.** New York: Marvel Comics, 2005. 248p. $19.99pa. ISBN 0 7851 1073 9. JS/A [graphic, fiction] (*Booktalks and Beyond,* 2007, pages 171 to 173.) A collection of Marvel characters interacts with historical characters (Queen Elizabeth I, James I of Scotland, and Virginia Dare and the Roanoke colony) to produce a fantastical conflict of good vs. evil.
2. Gratz, Alan. **Something Rotten.** New York: Penguin Group/Dial Books, 2007. 207p. (A Horatio Wilkes Mystery) $16.99. ISBN-13: 978 0 8037 3216 2. [fiction] JS, CG with high interest for boys. (*Genre Talks for Teens,* 2007, pages 130 to 132.) Horatio Wilkes visits his school friend Hamilton Prince in Denmark, Tennessee, to investigate the recent death of Rex Prince, Hamilton's father.
3. Janeczko, Paul B. (text), and Jenna LaReau (illus.). **Top Secret: A Handbook of Codes, Ciphers, and Secret Writing.** Cambridge, MA: Candlewick Press, 2004. 144p. $16.99. ISBN 0 7636 0971 4. [nonfiction] MJ, CG with high interest for boys. The author explains the how to of code breaking plus some related historical impact.
4. Rinaldi, Ann. **Nine Days a Queen: The Short Life and Reign of Lady Jane Grey.** New York: HarperCollins Publishers, 2005. 184p. $16.89. ISBN 0 06 054924 6. [fiction] MJ, G Born in 1537, Jane Grey, the great-granddaughter of Henry VII, is summoned to the court of Henry VIII to be with Mary, Elizabeth, and Edward—the

other three heirs to the throne—and learns about court intrigue and the dangers of being a queen.

5. Thomas, Resh Jane. **The Counterfeit Princess.** New York: Clarion Books, 2005. 197p. $15.00. ISBN 0 395 93870 8. [fiction] MJ, G Fourteen-year-old Iris loses her family and estate when the Duke of Northumberland arrests her father and mother, supporters of Princess Elizabeth. She acts as Elizabeth's double and is embroiled in royal intrigue.

ઈ૪ૢ

Bunce, Elizabeth C. A Curse Dark as Gold.

New York: Scholastic/Arthur A. Levine Books, 2008. 422p. $17.99.
ISBN-13: 978 0 439 89576 7. [fiction] JS, G

Themes/Topics: Rumpelstiltskin, love, coming of age, curses, ghosts, late eighteenth century, woolen mills

Summary/Description

Charlotte and Rosie Miller inherit their father's haunted, some say cursed, woolen mill and its debt. Their uncle arrives to take care of them and insists that they sell the mill to a rival and marry. Randall Woodstone, a banker, comes to foreclose. Jack Spinner appears and offers to spin gold out of straw for a price. Charlotte deals with Spinner to save the mill, sells the gold thread, and pays most of the debt. Woodstone and Charlotte marry and have a baby boy. The uncle sabotages Charlotte's efforts in the mill and runs up debt in her name. She returns to Jack Spinner, promises whatever he wants, but does not tell her husband. Her secrecy drives him away. Spinner claims the baby. Their confrontation reveals witch hunts, lies, treachery, theft, illegitimate children, and the death of the ghost's son. With the help of the community and her husband, she promises to bury Spinner next to his son. He returns her baby. The uncle, who was also under Spinner's control, leaves, and a document written by the father reveals that the owners of the rival mill stole his technology and have to pay the sisters.

Values: The story illustrates the importance of honesty, trust, responsibility, community, and family.

Read Aloud/Reader Response

1. Chapter 3, pages 36 to 41, beginning with the chapter and ending ". . . up the lane." Charlotte faces the idea of a curse or bad luck.

2. Chapter 7, pages 106 to 107, beginning "After he'd gone . . ." and ending with the chapter. Charlotte explains why she seeks help from Spinner.
3. Chapter 10, pages 130 to 136, beginning "Uncle Wheeler . . ." and ending ". . . further conversation." Charlotte and her uncle visit the House of Parmenter.
4. Chapter 18, pages 238 to 241, beginning "Building the new wheel . . ." and ending ". . . hands into my family." Charlotte's isolation grows as she researches the curse.
5. Chapter 27, pages 366 to 372, beginning "It must have been . . ." and ending with the chapter. Uncle Wheeler tells his story.

Booktalk

Ask one of the members of the group to tell the story of Rumpelstiltskin.

In Bunce's version, Charlotte Miller and her sister inherit a cursed and debt-ridden mill. Charlotte's sister conjures a solution. His name is Jack Spinner, and he will spin gold from straw, for a price. Jack Spinner isn't the misshapen man from the fairy tale. He can look as good or as rough as he wishes. He can read minds and hearts better than he can spin. Jack has dealt with Millers for generations. Charlotte strikes a bargain and learns its terrible price. She can save the mill and the town, but lose her love, family, and future. Can Charlotte unravel the sins of generations, or like her ancestors, will she be trapped in *A Curse Dark as Gold*?

Curriculum Connections

1. (Research, language arts) Using library resources, learn more about the Rumpelstiltskin tale and its "Name of the Helper" classification. Act as a resource person for the group.
2. (Discuss, language arts) Is the gold in the story evil?
3. (Discuss, language arts) After using your library resources to investigate other versions of the Rumpelstiltskin tale, discuss how Bunce's changes affect the story.

Related Works

1. Hettinga, Donald R. **The Brothers Grimm: Two Lives, One Legacy.** New York: Clarion Books, 2001. 180p. $22.00. ISBN 0 618 05599 1. [nonfiction] JS, CG Within the story of the two brothers, Hettinga lists all their publications and the tales they gathered.
2. Napoli, Donna Jo, and Richard Tchen. **Spinners.** New York: Puffin Books, 1999. 197p. $5.99pa. ISBN 0 14 131110 X. [fiction] JS, G

Rumpelstiltskin's daughter, a gifted spinner, grows up thinking her father is the drunken miller.

3. November, Sharyn, ed. **Firebirds: An Anthology of Original Fantasy and Science Fiction.** New York: Firebird/Penguin, 2003. 420p. $19.99. ISBN 0 14 250142 5. [fiction] MJS, CG This anthology includes variations on familiar stories and themes. "The Baby in the Night Deposit Box," pages 42 to 67, explores the importance of finding a safe and nurturing environment for children to learn wisdom and compassion.

4. Schmidt, Gary D. **Straw into Gold.** New York: Clarion Books, 2001. 172p. $15.00. ISBN 0 618 05601 7. [fiction] MJS, CG (*Teen Genre Connections*, pages 175 to 177.) Tousel, Rumpelstiltskin's foster son, solves the king's riddle to save rebels, discovers an heir to the throne, and finds his own gift of giving.

5. Vande Velde, Vivian. **The Rumpelstiltskin Problem.** New York: Houghton Mifflin Co., 2000. 116p. $15.00. ISBN 0 618 05523 1. [fiction] JS, CG (*Booktalks and More*, 2003, pages 213 to 215.) Vande Velde analyzes the story and retells it six different ways.

ॐॐ

Green, John. Paper Towns.

New York: Dutton Books, 2008. 305p. $17.99.
ISBN-13: 978 0 525 47818 8. [fiction] S, CG

Themes/Topics: missing persons, coming of age, friendship, Florida

Summary/Description

High school senior Quentin joins the senior next door, Margo Roth Spiegelman, whom he idolizes, for an evening of revenge. Afterward, she disappears, and he fears she is dead. As he and his friends track down the clues she leaves, they acquire new social status and self-knowledge. Quentin discovers the definitive clue to her whereabouts on graduation day. He and friends take a madcap trip to Agloe, an originally paper or fictitious New York town. They find an ungrateful Margo who has decided to break from her past and travel the world. The friends leave Quentin and Margo to say good-bye to their romantic visions and each other.

Values: Trying to find Margo, Quentin discovers that self-respect is more important than popularity, and that real friends help.

Read Aloud/Reader Response

1. "Prologue," pages 3 to 8. Quentin reveals his magical relationship with Margo.
2. Chapter 1, pages 14 to 15, beginning "I elbowed him . . ." and ending ". . . proved true." Quentin describes Margo's reputation.
3. Chapter 3, pages 104 to 105, beginning "'Listen, kid'" and ending ". . . always had." The detective compares Margo's relationship to other runaways.
4. "Agloe," page 282, beginning "I watch . . ." and ending ". . . than a person." Quentin and friends find Margo, and Quentin realizes his mistake.
5. "Agloe," pages 292 to 298, beginning "'And then you . . .'" and ending ". . . can be is me." Quentin and Margo clarify their identities.

Booktalk

(Read the opening paragraph of the "Prologue.")

Margo is the most fascinating girl in the senior class. Quentin is a nerd. She appears at his bedroom window just before midnight. She asks him to join her on a wild spree of revenge. Of course he says yes. The next day, she disappears. Is she a runaway? Overdramatic? Dead? Or all three? Quentin sniffs out the truth, where Margo really lives, in all her *Paper Towns*.

Curriculum Connections

1. (Research, social studies, language arts) Using library resources, learn more about map making and semantic mapping. Act as a resource person for the group.
2. (Research, language arts) Examine each of the allusions, especially Walt Whitman's *Leaves of Grass*. Act as a resource person for the group.
3. (React, language arts) Is finding Margo worth the trip? Be sure to use specifics from the text to support your answer.

Related Works

1. Dickinson, Emily. "Forever is composed of nows." Available: http://www.poetry foundation.org/archive/poem.html?id=182912 (Accessed January 24, 2010). This is the complete poem that Margo quotes to justify her behavior.
2. Eliot, T. S. "Choruses from the Rock." Available: http://ww.arak29. am/PDF-PPT/6-Literature/Eliot/Chtherock_eng.htm (Accessed January 24, 2010). This is the poem from which the line "Light, the

visible reminder of Invisible Light," which is central to the novel, comes.

3. Green, John. **An Abundance of Katherines.** New York: Dutton Dooks, 2006. 215p. $16.99. ISBN 0 525 47688 1. [fiction] JS, G (*Genre Talks for Teens,* 2009, pages 44 to 46.) Dumped by the nineteenth Katherine he has dated, Colin Singleton embarks on a road trip so that he might have the time and space to develop a mathematical formula predicting the length of romantic relationships.

4. Green, John. **Looking for Alaska.** New York: Dutton Books, 2005. 224p. $15.99. ISBN 0 525 47506 0. [fiction] S, CG (*Booktalks and Beyond,* 2007, pages 37 to 40.) Sixteen-year-old Miles Halter bonds with three students who help him explore the meaning of life and death.

5. Sandell, Lisa Ann. **A Map of the Known World.** (Self-Respect/Friendship, pages 20 to 22.) Cora, a talented cartographer, enters her freshman year and explores mental, emotional, and physical maps.

6. Whitman, Walt. **Leaves of Grass: The Original 1855 Edition.** New York: Dover Publications, 2007. 128p. $3.00pa. (Dover Thrift Editions Series) ISBN-13: 978 0 486 45676 8. [poetry] S/A, CG Quentin recommends the Penguin Classics version of the first edition. This edition also follows the arrangement of the 1891–1892 edition.

❧❧

Juby, Susan. **Getting *the* Girl: A Guide to Private Investigation, Surveillance, and Cookery.**

New York: HarperTeen, 2008. 341p. $16.99.
ISBN-13: 978 0 06 076525 5. [fiction] JS, CG

Themes/Topics: peer pressure, high school, popularity, mystery, humor, British Columbia

Summary/Description

Freshman Sherman Mack believes that a girl on whom he has a crush is about to be "defiled" or shunned by the school. He begins to investigate. A grade school friend is defiled instead. Because he escalates his investigation, another girl whom he realizes is his real girlfriend is targeted. Sherman and the girlfriend crack the case during a meal he prepares for his cooking class and to which he invites both the targets and targeters.

Values: Sherman demonstrates his acceptance and learns true friendship.

Read Aloud/Reader Response

1. Chapter 1, pages 4 to 5, beginning "See, at Harewood . . ." and ending ". . . about high school." Sherman explains the defiled.
2. Chapter 4, pages 26 to 28, beginning with the chapter and ending ". . . do anything to her." Sherman explains his devotion to girls.
3. Chapter 19, pages 158 to 159, beginning "You'd think . . ." and ending ". . . when kids are bad." Sherman contrasts his neighborhood and the more affluent one.
4. Chapter 33, pages 255 to 258. This chapter describes a defiled girl's return to school.
5. Chapter 41, pages 327 to 331, beginning "My head pounded" and ending with the chapter. Ed explains how, as the defiler, he just directed anger that was already there.

Booktalk

Freshman Sherman Mack loves two things in life, cooking and girls. Both are under attack. His single mother is more interested in buying burlesque costumes than food, so Sherman satisfies his cooking passion and appetite in his cooking class. But Sherman's passion for girls is messing up the meals. His ideal lady, an artistic loner named Dini Trioli, dates a junior who could throw Sherman into next week. Sherman can accept that. What he can't accept is the guy hurting Dini. Not hitting, but something even more serious, *defiling*. (See "Read Aloud/Reader Response" 1.) Sherman thinks that Dini is next on the defiled list, and Sherman decides, "No way." Maybe Sherman is a hero, but maybe Sherman is just looking out for Sherman. Dini will realize who really loves her. Then Sherman will have a surefire recipe for *Getting the Girl*.

Curriculum Connections

1. (Research, mental health) Using library resources, find out more about bullying aimed at girls. Act as a resource person for the group.
2. (React, language arts) Who was guilty in the defiling? You might consider re-reading Read Aloud/Reader Response 5.
3. (Discuss, language arts) Using the novel as a reference, distinguish between friendship and popularity. Is it possible to have both?

Related Works

1. Dessen, Sarah. **Just Listen.** New York: Penguin Group/Speak, 2006. 371p. $8.99pa. ISBN-13: 978 0 14 241097 4. [fiction] JS, G (*Genre Talks for Teens,* 2009, pages 24 to 27.) High school model Annabel Greene keeps silent about an attempted rape by her best friend's boyfriend, is slandered by the friend, and finds a true friend and justice with the "Angriest Boy in School."

2. Garfinkle, D. L. **Storky: How I Lost My Nickname and Won the Girl.** New York: G. P. Putnam's Sons, 2005. 184p. $16.99. ISBN 0 399 24284 8. [fiction] MJ, CG (*Booktalks and Beyond,* 2007, pages 63 to 65.) High school freshman Michael "Storky" Pomerantz seeks popularity in school, approval from his father, and a date with Gina. Instead he finds one good friend, academic success, a supportive step-father, and a loyal girlfriend.

3. Goobie, Beth. **The Lottery.** Victoria, BC: Orca, 2002. 272p. $16.95. ISBN 1 55143 161 0. [fiction] MJS, G (*Teen Genre Connections,* 2005, pages 33 to 35.) Fifteen-year-old Sally Hanson is "the victim" who, isolated from the rest of the student body, carries out harassment against students or faculty who offend, deny, or ignore the Shadow Council.

4. Juby, Susan. **Alice I Think.** New York: Harper Tempest, 2003. 290p. $16.89. ISBN 0 06 051544 9. [fiction] JS, G Sheltered and home-schooled by eccentric parents, a teenager humorously chronicles the difficulties of making the transition into regular high school.

5. Lubar, David. **Sleeping Freshmen Never Lie.** New York: Penguin Group/Speak, 2005. 279p. $6.99pa. ISBN-13: 978 0 14 240780 6. [fiction] MJ, CG with high interest for boys. (*Genre Talks for Teens,* 2009, pages 49 to 51.) Freshman Scott Hudson pursues a popular girl but finds better friends in the out-group.

Imagination: Fantasy, Science Fiction, and Paranormal Novels

Fantasy, science fiction, and paranormal deal with worlds that the Spinellis in *Today I Will* describe as "what if," but these worlds are grounded in reality. No matter how fantastic they become, they seem to focus on natural elements. What happens when we don't respect nature's forces, our own talents, or the abilities of others? Is the battle between good and evil waged by those who support natural forces and those who selfishly wish to destroy or control them?

Natural Talents

❧❧

Booraem, Ellen. The Unnameables.
New York: Harcourt, 2008. 316p. $16.00.
ISBN-13: 978 0 15 206368 9. [fiction] MJS, CG

Themes/Topics: utopias, satyrs, friendship, change, conduct of life

Summary/Description

Thirteen-year-old foundling Medford Runyuin lives in an island community centered on usefulness. Making an unnameable or frivolous product means punishment or banishment from the island. Medford, trained in carving and never truly accepted in the community, hides his beautiful, impractical carvings under his bed. Medford is refused a useful last name such as carver or carpenter at his Transition ceremony.

His foster father suggests that he live by himself in the woods. Here, he encounters a Goatman and a dog. The Goatman, like Medford, is journeying to adulthood but for a very different community. He is learning to control wind and encourages Medford's art. Medford's community discovers and imprisons them. Medford's friends rescue them. They discover that many citizens produce unnameables and that the community scholar distorts history to preserve simple usefulness. Finally, the community's artistic talent and even the Goatman's wild and dangerous relationship with wind prove useful.

Values: Medford demonstrates the importance of art and individual expression.

Read Aloud/Reader Response

1. Chapter 4, pages 36 to 46. The chapter illustrates the difference between Prudy and Medford.
2. Chapter 8, pages 80 to 91. In this chapter, the Goatman reveals a greater world with different ideas.
3. Chapter 14, pages 143 to 155. In this chapter, the authorities arrest Medford and the Goatman.
4. Chapter 18, pages 195 to 196, beginning "Medford imagined himself . . ." and ending ". . . couldn't decide." Medford weighs being embraced or banished by the community.
5. Chapter 25, pages 286 to 288, beginning "The crowd erupted . . ." and ending with the chapter. The trial is upended by the Goatman's talent and statement.

Booktalk

Baby Medford Runyuin washed up on the shore of the island on which he now lives. His Mainland parents drowned. The islanders gave him a foster family. Soon he will learn his adult name. Will it be Cobbler, Cook, or Carpenter? Like everyone on the island, he will be useful according to his name. The book says (*Read the italicized print on page 41*). And Medford truly wants to be useful, and accepted. He knows that the neat and orderly islanders don't know what to do with him, and that under his bed, they will find his terrible secrets. Then another foreigner appears. A Goatman. The Goatman hides nothing. He doesn't worry about neatness, names, or categories. He is learning to direct the wind, and he will practice even if the island and the people on it blow away. He doesn't worry about beds at all. He curls up under the house with his dog Stinky. What do the Goatman and

Medford have in common? The danger and the excitement of *The Unnameables*.

Curriculum Connections

1. (Research, language arts) The Goatman is a figure from Greek mythology known as a satyr. Using library resources, learn about the satyr's place in Greek mythology. Act as a resource person for the group.
2. (Research, language arts) Using library resources, learn more about utopias. Act as a resource person for the group.
3. (Discuss, language arts) Define the word *useful*. Be sure to use positive and negative examples from the novel and everyday life.

Related Works

1. Armstrong, Jennifer, and Nancy Butcher. **Fire Us Trilogy.** New York: HarperCollins. [fiction] MJS, CG (*Teen Genre Connections*, 2005, pages 204 to 210.)

   The Kindling: Book One. 2002. 224p. $15.89. ISBN 0 06 029411 6. After an adult-killing virus (fire us) sweeps the United States, seven orphans in Lazarus, Florida, band together as a family.

   The Keepers of the Flame: Book Two. 2002. 231p. $17.89. ISBN 0 06 029412 4. The ten travelers from *The Kindling*, discover a cult-like community in an abandoned mall. Each person in the group takes a Bible verse as a name.

   The Kiln: Book Three. 2003. 193p. $15.99. ISBN 0 06 008050 7. The group discovers that Angerman's father started the virus to purify the country. They kill him and move away from adults to form their own community.

2. Huxley, Aldous. **Brave New World.** New York: Perennial Classics, 1998. $11.95pa. ISBN 0 06 092987 1. [fiction] JS/A, CG Originally published in 1932, this novel projects a society of the future built on pleasure and instant gratification.

3. Rand, Ayn. **Anthem.** New York: Signet, 1995. 253p. $7.99pa. ISBN 0 451 19113 7. [fiction] S/A, CG In a post-apocalyptic world where all live for the community, one man chooses individuality. Inspired by Rand's view of Communism, the novel was first published in 1938. This edition includes an original text with revision markings and a reader's guide.

ℭℑℭℑ

Funke, Cornelia. Anthea Bell (trans.). Inkdeath.

New York: Scholastic/The Chicken House, 2008. 704p. $24.99.
ISBN-13: 978 0 439 86628 6. [fiction] MJS, CG

Themes/Topics: real life vs. fiction, loyalty, family,
relationships, heroism, trust, identity

Summary/Description

In this final volume of the *Inkheart* trilogy, Mo embraces the Bluejay persona and, with the Black Prince, fights the decaying Adderhead. The sinister Orpheus now writes the story and tries to substitute Mo for Dustfinger in death. The White Women, instead, send both Dustfinger and Mo to take back Adderhead's immortality. If Mo fails, he, Resa, and Meggie will die. Mo allies himself with the Black Prince, Dustfinger, Fenoglio, and Adderhead's daughter. Eventually, he succeeds by returning to his bookbinder identity. Adderhead dies, Orpheus flees to the North, and Mo, with his family, remains in the fictional world where Meggie finds a new love and the new son of Mo and Resa dreams of going to the real world.

Values: The characters are saved through their loyalty to and love for their families.

Read Aloud/Reader Response

1. Chapter 11, page 114, beginning "A longing for . . ." and ending ". . . poor Elinor." Elinor discovers that she loves her family more than her books.
2. Chapter 16, pages 161 to 164, beginning "Fenoglio!" and ending with the chapter. Fenoglio confronts Resa.
3. Chapter 25, pages 223 to 229. In this chapter, Mo meets Death and begins his task.
4. Chapter 45, page 413, beginning "All good stories . . ." and ending ". . . talkative thing." Fenoglio describes the relationship between questions and stories.
5. Chapter 76, pages 638 to 639. In this chapter, the Adderhead dies.

Booktalk

Hold up Inkheart *and* Inkspell. *Ask how many have read the books.*

The world is dark. Dustfinger died two months ago. Mo has embraced the identity of the Bluejay. With the Black Prince, he fights and must destroy Adderhead, the villain he made immortal. Fenoglio can't think of anymore to write, and the evil Orpheus has decided to take over the story to write himself to favor and riches. In the middle of all this danger and intrigue, Meggie is falling in love, and her mother and father are bringing a new life into the world. The world of books seems more complicated than the real world. In fact, it is becoming difficult to tell which world is real. And if Mo, Meggie, Resa, and Fenoglio cannot figure out where they fit, soon they will have worlds of neither fantasy nor reality. Soon they will have only *Inkdeath.*

Curriculum Connections

1. (Research, language arts) Using library resources, prepare a bibliography of works that deal with the blend of fiction and real life. Share your work with the group.
2. (Discuss, language arts) Who or what controls the book?
3. (Discuss, language arts) In Read Aloud/Reader Response 4, Fenoglio describes the relationship between questions and stories. What questions do you have at the end of this story that might lead to another story? Compare your questions with others in the group.

Related Works

1. Funke, Cornelia. Anthea Bell (trans.). **Inkheart.** New York: Scholastic Press/The Chicken House, 2003. 544p. $19.95. ISBN 0 439 53164 0. [fiction] MJS, CG (*Booktalks and Beyond,* 2007, pages 162 to 163.) Mo and Meggie become entangled with the dangerous fictional characters, which Mo, as Silvertongue, has read into existence.
2. Funke, Cornelia. Anthea Bell (trans.). **Inkspell.** New York: Scholastic Press/The Chicken House, 2005. 672p. $19.99. ISBN 0 439 55400 4. [fiction] MJS, CG (*Booktalks and Beyond,* 2007, pages 164 to 166.) Dustfinger returns to the fictional world through Orpheus and ultimately sacrifices his life to save Farid. Fenoglio loses control of his characters, and Mo becomes the Bluejay
3. McNamee, Eoin. **The Navigator: Chosen to Save the World.** New York: Random House/Wendy Lamb Books, 2006. 342p. $15.99. ISBN-13: 978 0 375 83910 8. [fiction] MJS, CG with high interest for boys. (*Genre Talks for Teens,* 2009, pages 180 to 182.) Young Owen, in a time shift, moves from his depressing life to his inherited role as the Navigator who will save the world.

4. Wooding, Chris. **Poison.** New York: Orchard Books, 2003. 273p. $16.99. ISBN 0 439 75570 0. [fiction] JS, G (*Booktalks and Beyond,* 2007, pages 176 to 178.) When the phaeries steal her baby sister, sixteen-year-old Poison decides to rescue her and discovers a fantasy/literary world in which she is the master author.
5. Zusak, Markus. **The Book Thief.** New York: Alfred A. Knopf, 2006. 552p. $21.90. ISBN 0 375 93100 7. [fiction] JS, CG with high interest for girls. (*Genre Talks for Teens,* 2009, pages 241 to 243.). Death tells the story of Liesel Meminger who uses books to shelter herself from the horrors of Hitler's Germany.

ॸॗॎॖ

Halam, Ann. **Snakehead.**
New York: Wendy Lamb Books, 2008. 287p. $16.99.
ISBN-13: 978 0 375 84108 8. [fiction] JS, CG

Themes/Topics: Perseus, Andromeda, Greek gods,
fate, conduct of life, coming of age

Summary/Description

Perseus lives with his mother and the rightful king of Serifos, now a tavern owner. Andromeda, a Phoenician princess fated to die for her country, arrives on the island. Perseus falls in love with her. Polydectes, the king, wants Perseus's mother for his wife. The marriage would make Perseus a direct rival for the throne. Polydectes tries to eliminate him and challenges him to bring back Medusa's head. Andromeda accompanies Perseus. Aided by the gods, Perseus retrieves the head, destroys Polydectes, and saves Andromeda from her fate. Perseus and Andromeda are allowed to marry. A "Cast of Characters" distinguishes between mythical and fictional characters in Serifos, the famous ship *Argo,* and Haifa. A map of significant places introduces the novel. A sketch of Pegasus, Cassiopeia, and Perseus and their constellations as well as an explanation of "Notable Places in the Story, Real and Mythical" concludes the novel.

Values: Through courage and responsibility, Perseus and Andromeda control their fates.

Read Aloud/Reader Response

1. Chapter 1, pages 15 to 17, beginning "My mother . . ." and ending with the chapter. Perseus observes the rich Taki's reaction to danger and disaster.

2. Chapter 2, pages 27 to 30, beginning "I must have been . . ." and ending ". . . onrush of darkness." Dicty explains why he did not fight for his place as king.
3. Chapter 3, pages 47 to 49, beginning "I was a princess . . ." and ending ". . . always hope." Danae tells her story.
4. Chapter 6, pages 126 to 130, beginning "I noticed . . ." to the end of the chapter. Andromeda and Perseus discuss gods, fate, and death.
5. Chapter 10, pages 220 to 223, beginning "They were monsters" and ending with the chapter. Perseus kills the Medusa and realizes the many layers to his deed.

Booktalk

Ask how many in the group know about the Medusa. Ask them to share what they know.

Medusa is a lady with a lifetime of bad hair days. Perseus is a big, god-touched teenager that no one in his town wants to fight. Andromeda is a newly arrived, beautiful Phoenician princess. What can a *Snakehead,* an oversized boy from a small island, and an elegant Phoenician royal have in common? Trouble from the gods. The gods set up Perseus to kill Medusa and perform several other off-the-wall tasks to prove that he is a hero and to satisfy their whims. They decide that Andromeda can prevent Phoenicia's biggest earthquake. All she has to do is give her life to a monster. As fate would have it, the tasks connect in Perseus. Will it be kill one and save one or kill two with one hero? Perseus isn't sure. He isn't even sure that the orders are coming from gods or just human wanna-be-gods. Perseus finds the answers when he accepts the face-to-face battle with Ms. *Snakehead.*

Curriculum Connections

1. (Research, language arts) Using your library resources, find the original story of Perseus. Act as a resource person during discussion.
2. (Research, language arts) Using your library resources, find out more about one of the other gods mentioned in the story. Act as a resource person during discussion.
3. (Discuss, language arts) What is the relationship between fate and free will in the story?

Related Works

1. Cadnum, Michael. **Starfall: Phaeton and the Chariot of the Sun**. New York: Scholastic, 2004. 128p. $16.95. ISBN 0 439 545331.

[fiction] MJS, CG In this revised Greek myth, the main character allows bullies to direct critical life decisions.

2. Galloway, Priscilla. **Snake Dreamer.** New York: Delacorte Press, 1998. 231p. $14.95. ISBN 0 385 32264 X. [fiction] MJ, G (*Booktalks and More*, 2003, pages 95 to 97.) Sixteen-year-old Dusa Thrashman's snake dreams draw her into Medusa's world where she learns to direct her own frightening powers.

3. Napoli, Donna Jo. **Beast.** New York: Atheneum Books for Young Readers, 2000. 260p. $17.00. ISBN 0 689 83589 2. [fiction] JS, CG (*Teen Genre Connections*, 2005, pages 171 to 173.) Orasmyn, a young Persian prince, selects an imperfect camel for sacrifice. The spirits change him into a lion so that he can learn about love and suffering.

4. Napoli, Donna Jo. **Sirena.** New York: Scholastic, 1998. 210p. $15.95. ISBN 0 590 383 38388 4. [fiction] JS, G (*Booktalks Plus*, 2001, pages 91 to 93.) The main character questions the model of heroism and learns that within fate, each person can build personal character.

5. Spinner, Stephanie. **Quiver.** New York: Alfred A. Knopf, 2002. 176p. $15.95. ISBN 0 375 81489 2. [fiction] JS, G (*Teen Genre Connections*, pages 177 to 179.) Combining the boar hunt, the race with the golden apples, and the transformation of Atlanta and her husband Hippomanes into lions, Spinner explains Atlanta's cruel marriage conditions and her capitulation to the Aphrodite-aided suitor.

ധ

Murdock, Catherine Gilbert. **Princess Ben.**

Boston, MA: Houghton Mifflin Co., 2008. 344p. $16.00.
ISBN-13: 978 0 618 95971 6. [fiction] JS, G

Themes/Topics: fairy tales, royalty, magic, coming of age, inferences

Summary/Description

Fifteen-year-old Princess Ben transforms from a difficult, over-weight, and slothful little girl to a worthy regent who saves her country from war and finds personal happiness. When Ben's parents are killed supposedly by a dragon, Ben is the ward of her childless, tyranni-cal aunt who tries to prepare her for the throne and a political marriage by teaching her courtly manners and slimming her down. Rebellious

Ben is sent to a stark tower room where she secretly taps into her inherited magical powers. Still fat and obnoxious, she flees the queen's ball and her intended prince whose kingdom she believes assassinated her mother and the king. Her underdeveloped magic lands her in the prince's war camp where, disguised as a boy, she learns about invasion plans, develops her personal strengths, and gets to know the prince. A much slimmer Ben escapes, returns to the kingdom, embraces her royal role, deters the prince's army with magic, successfully navigates the test of her royal abilities, and with the help of the prince, kills the dragon just before they discover their mutual love. The prince dies in battle, but Ben awakens him with a kiss.

Values: In her journey, Ben learns responsibility, self-control, industry, and true love.

Read Aloud/Reader Response

1. Chapter 3, pages 39 to 42, beginning "Lord Frederick . . ." and ending with the chapter. Princess Ben speaks with Lord Frederick after her mother's death.
2. Chapter 5, pages 71 to 78, beginning with "In the weeks that followed . . ." and ending with ". . .of being Satan himself." Princess Ben confronts the queen.
3. Chapter 6, pages 94 to 95, beginning "I spent the . . ." and ending ". . . not need another." Princess Ben discovers self-control to be the basis of spellwork.
4. Chapter 16, pages 257 to 258, beginning "I could . . ." and ending ". . . own treatment." Ben discovers that her own improved attitude improves the queen's attitude.
5. Chapter 20, pages 336 to 337, beginning "Even now, . . ." and ending ". . . returned to life." Ben describes her life-giving kiss to Florian.

Booktalk

Princess Ben isn't the fair damsel of most fairy tales. She is fat, obnoxious, and too dim-witted to carry on a conversation. So how will she protect the kingdom from hostile forces when her mother and the king die, and her father disappears? Her aunt Sophia, the reigning queen, answers that question. She will shape Ben up and marry her off to gain a strong, political alliance. Ben resists. The queen locks her up, gives her tedious lessons, and starves her. Ben rebels big time. In her tower, she has a secret—magic. Each day she learns more and eats more. Each day she thwarts the queen and wins. But victory brings her face-to-face with the enemy her aunt fears, the assassins who killed her family and want her country. Can she fight alone and win? Will magic help? Is her broom strong enough to lift her? Will the challenge crush her like a common Ben, or will trial by fire, dragon fire, forge a *Princess Ben*?

Curriculum Connections

1. (Research, language arts and mythology) Using your library resources, learn more about dragons. Act as a resource person during discussion.
2. (Research, language arts) Using your library resources, define and give examples of inferences. Apply your definition to the characters in the novel.
3. (Discuss, language arts) How do the terms *delusion* and *illusion* apply to the story?

Related Works

1. Ferris, Jean. **Once Upon a Marigold.** New York: Harcourt Brace and Co., 2002. 275p. $5.95pa. ISBN 0 15 205084 1. [fiction] MJS, G (*Booktalks and Beyond,* 2007, pages 173 to 176.) A dominated princess and an unwilling prince become a trend-setting royal couple after foiling the plot of an evil queen.
2. Haddix, Margaret Peterson. **Just Ella.** New York: Simon & Shuster Books for Young Children, 1999. 185p. $17.00. ISBN 0 689 82186 7. [fiction] MJS, G In this feminist Cinderella story, fifteen-year-old Ella discovers that the court centers on appearances and decides to control her own life.
3. Hale, Shannon. **Book of a Thousand Days.** New York: Bloomsbury, 2007. 306p. $17.95. ISBN-13: 978 1 599990 051 3. [fiction] JS, G (*Genre Talks for Teens,* 2009, pages 194 to 197.) Fifteen-year-old Dashti and her sixteen-year-old mistress are walled into a tower for seven years because the mistress wants to choose her own suitor. Dashti proves more competent and loyal.
4. Pierce, Tamora. **The Will of the Empress.** New York: Scholastic Press, 2005. 320p. $17.99. ISBN 0 439 44171 4. [fiction] MJS, G (*Genre Talks for Teens, 2009,* pages 207 to 210.) In this sequel to the *Circle Opens* quartet, the royal Sandry uses magic and maturity to resist a forced marriage and place her kingdom in good hands.
5. Wooding, Chris. **Poison.** New York: Orchard Books, 2003. 273p. $16.99. ISBN 0 439 75570 0. [fiction] JS, G (*Booktalks and Beyond,* 2007, pages 176 to 178.) In trying to rescue her sister, a difficult teen overcomes conflict and intrigue that prepares her for her role of the kingdom's master writer.

ɔʃʅɔ

Myers, Edward. Storyteller.

New York: Clarion Books, 2008. 283p. $16.00.
ISBN-13: 978 0 618 69541 6. [fiction] JS, CG

Themes/Topics: storytelling, royalty, conduct of life

Summary/Description

Seventeen-year-old Jack leaves home to pursue his storytelling talent. Accompanied by a talking midnight mynah, he travels to the Royal City where he tells stories to the king and his court and falls in love with the oldest princess, a talented poet and singer. When the king dies, the cruel prince and a power-hungry illusionist grab the throne and use the artists and storytellers as propaganda tools. The princess and Jack try to undercut the king with seemingly positive presentations. Eventually, the princess joins a Robin Hood–type highwayman who openly opposes the king. Jack trusts the illusionist's false promise that he will eventually be free to tell his own stories, discovers his mistake, and runs away. Trying to make reparation, Jack is captured and imprisoned. At Jack's execution, the mynah turns the crowd's sentiment to Jack. The prince is ousted, but the princess gives her throne to a former queen whose throne was also usurped. Jack and the princess marry and are content with a small home in the woods. Jack tells the story to his grandson.

Values: Jack and the princess learn the importance of honesty, courage, and love.

Read Aloud/Reader Response

1. Section 1, chapter 1, pages 5 and 6, beginning with the chapter and ending ". . . where I'll start." Jack explains the life of the storyteller.
2. Section 1, chapter 6, pages 24 to 27, beginning with the chapter and ending ". . . Jack Storyteller." Real and fictional worlds blend as Jack grows as a storyteller.
3. Section 2, chapter 15, page 56, beginning with the chapter, and ending ". . . of his art." Jack discovers the power of the story.
4. Section 4, chapter 53, pages 175 to 179. In this chapter, Jack and the princess make their first appearance as the king's public relations team.
5. Section 6, pages 282 to 283, beginning "Listen. For each of us . . ." and ending with the novel. Jack explains that each life is a story.

Booktalk

Seventeen-year-old Jack doesn't want to spend his life like his family, scratching an existence out of a farm and giving most of his crop to a king. He wants more and knows how to get it. With words. His village calls him Jack Storyteller. His new life will begin with "Once upon a time . . ." But "Once upon a time . . ." doesn't always end ". . . happily ever after." Telling stories can be dangerous. The world is full of bad guys: robbers, cruel kings, and some evil storytellers—liars. Jack meets them all. He finds good guys too: a wise deposed queen who rules over forest animals, a talking midnight mynah in love with a talking fish, a beautiful princess who can sing only sad songs, and even a Robin Hood with a golden coin eye. But the bad guys have the money and power. Money and power make a comfortable life. Which group will Jack choose? Hear the answer directly from the *Storyteller.*

Curriculum Connections

1. (Research, language arts) Using library resources, learn more about telling a story. Share what you find with the group.
2. (React, language arts) Cite one incident or statement in the story that made you think about language and stories differently. Share your choice with the group.
3. (Discuss, language arts) How does this story apply to the use of language today?

Related Works

1. Alexander, Lloyd. **The Golden Dream of Carlo Chuchio.** New York: Henry Holt and Co., 2007. 320p. $16.95. ISBN-13: 978 0 8050 8333 0. [fiction] JS, CG with high interest for boys. (*Genre Talks for Teens,* 2009, pages 123 to 126.) In this Arabian Nights–type tale, romantic orphan Carlo Chuchio discovers his personal fulfillment.
2. Anderson John David. **Standard Hero Behavior.** New York: Clarion Books, 2007. 273p. $16.00. ISBN-13: 978 0 618 75920 0. [fiction] JS, CG with high interest for boys. Fifteen-year-old Mason aspires to be a bard but discovers that the boss he seeks is a coward and that real heroes are needed to save the town.
3. Funke, Cornelia. **Inkheart.** New York: The Chicken House, 2003. 544p. $19.95. ISBN 0 439 53164 0. [fiction] MJS, CG (*Booktalks and Beyond,* 2007, pages 162 to 166.) In this first volume of the trilogy, Meg discovers the power that her father, a talented storyteller called Silvertongue, holds and that she shares.
4. Salinger, Michael (text), and Sam Henderson (illus.). **Well Defined: Vocabulary in Rhyme.** Honesdale, PA: Wordsong/Boyd Mills Press, 2009. [poetry] MJS, CG Poems define sixty-four words in free verse that describe real-life situations.

5. Wooding, Chris. **Poison.** New York: Orchard Books, 2003. 273p. $16.99. ISBN 0 439 75570 0. [fiction] JS, CG with high interest for girls. (*Booktalks and Beyond,* 2007, pages 176 to 178.) When phaeries steal her sister, sixteen-year-old Poison sets out to rescue her and discovers that the kidnapping was a catalyst for her to discover that she is the master writer, a human who controls all.

CSƏ

O'Brian, Caragh M. **Birthmarked.**
New York: Roaring Brook Press, 2010. 360p. $16.99.
ISBN-13: 978 1 59643 569 8. [fiction] JS, CG with high interest for girls

Themes/Topics: social class, environmental crisis, DNA, in-group/out-group, families

Summary/Description

Scarred as a baby, sixteen-year-old midwife Gaia Stone lives outside the city wall. Like her midwife mother, she marks each baby with a tattoo and gives the first three children that she delivers each month to the Enclave where they receive preferential treatment in a world dealing with the results of pollution and water shortage. When her parents are arrested, she enters the city illegally to find them and witnesses the Enclave's brutality. The leadership wishes to arrest a hemophilia gene that is killing their population. They need the birth records kept by Gaia's parents, but the parents will not cooperate. The father dies. Gaia finds her mother who dies giving birth to Gaia's baby sister. Gaia takes the baby and the Enclave's records and escapes the city with the help of the adopted son of the Enclave's leader whose capture suggests a sequel.

Values: Gaia values life and family over status and wealth.

Read Aloud/Reader Response

1. Chapter 6, page 66, beginning "Then, as noon . . ." and ending ". . . a vendor." Gaia notices how clothes identify social status.
2. Chapter 8, page 90, beginning "Capt. Grey . . ." and ending "'. . . genetic freaks.'" Captain Grey explains the Enclave's problem.
3. Chapter 10, pages 106 to 112, beginning "Back when . . ." and ending ". . . always say no." Gaia's father explains the history of advancing.
4. Chapter 15, page 174, beginning "When Winston . . ." and ending ". . . worlds collided." Gaia compares the house of the Protectorate with society as a whole.
5. Chapter 26, page 325, beginning "'Come on . . .'" and ending ". . . didn't like it." Gaia questions Leon's true character.

Booktalk

Sixteen-year-old Gaia is a midwife, like her mother. She lives outside the shining city called the Enclave. Each month, like her mother, she gives the first three babies that she births to the Enclave. Those babies will receive enough food, water, and shelter in a world that is baking to death. They are the lucky ones. But then her parents are taken away to the prison within the Enclave—no explanation. Gaia will follow them and maybe rescue them. Her journey will be hard and dangerous. She has to make it through the wall. Then she has to think of a disguise to hide the hideous scarred face that makes her stand out in the Enclave's perfect world. She prepares for it all. But she isn't prepared for the ugliness under that perfect façade. Filled with corruption, confusion, and disease, the Enclave is looking for answers to survive. What will it do when it finds them in a simple girl from the outside, an ugly girl who is *Birthmarked*?

Curriculum Connections

1. (Research, language arts) Using library resources, prepare a bibliography of futuristic books based on environmental disasters.
2. (Discuss, language arts) Why does the Enclave's population cooperate with the government?
3. (Discuss, language arts) What is the dividing line between good and evil in the story?

Related Works

1. Adlington, L. J. **The Diary of Pelly D.** New York: Harper Collins/ Greenwillow Books, 2005. 282p. $16.99. ISBN 0 06 076616 6. [fiction] JS, CG (*Booktalks and Beyond*, 2010, pages 178 to 181.) In a futuristic society on a non-Earth planet, fourteen-year-old Toni V finds the diary of Pelly D who was judged less worthy through gene testing.
2. Aronson, Marc. **Race: A History beyond Black and White.** New York: Atheneum Books for Young Readers/Ginee Seo Books, 2007. 322p. $18.99. ISBN-13: 978 0 689 86554 1. [nonfiction] S, CG Explaining race through the ancient "us" versus "strangers" thinking, Aronson traces persecution from the survival instincts of primitive tribes to a modern-day world in which them/us is experienced through possessions.
3. Collins, Suzanne. **The Hunger Games.** (Courage/ Perseverance, pages 78 to 80.) A teenage girl is selected for a country's survival games and becomes the symbol for a revolution against the privileged government.
4. Patterson, James. **Maximum Ride: The Angel Experiment.** New York: Warner Vision Books, 2005. 440p. $6.99pa. ISBN 0 446

61779 2. [fiction] JS, CG with high interest for boys. (*Booktalks and Beyond,* 2007, pages 181 to 183.) Fourteen-year-old Maximum Ride (Max) leads a six-member family made up of children who have been injected with bird DNA in a secret government experiment and raised in cages.

5.   Pfeffer, Susan Beth. **The Dead & the Gone.** New York: Harcourt, 2008. 321p. $17.00. ISBN-13: 978 0 15 206311 5. [fiction] JS, CG with high interest for boys. After a meteor hits the moon, seventeen-year-old Alex Morales fights to keep his sisters and himself alive as the city and world deteriorate.

Ƈ｝ʅɔ

Reeve, Philip. **Here Lies Arthur.**
New York: Scholastic Press, 2008. 339p. $16.99.
ISBN-13: 978 0 545 09334 7. [fiction] JS, CG

Themes/Topics: legends, loyalty, King Arthur, coming of age, conduct of life

Summary/Description

Gwyna the Mouse, the daughter of a dead slave woman, is saved from death by a bard, Myriddin. She masquerades as the Lady of the Lake, delivers the magic sword to Arthur, and is disguised as a boy to become Myriddin's ward and servant. She learns about warfare, manipulation, unknightly attitudes, and an abusive, power hungry, and superstitious Arthur whom Myriddin's stories build into a hero. When she is no longer able to pose as a boy, she becomes Gwenhwyfar's servant until Myriddin betrays her confidence and tips off Arthur concerning Gwenhwyfar's affair with his maimed nephew whom Arthur brutally kills. Gwyna sees the truth about the treacherous Arthur and the misguided and now dying Myriddin. She returns, buries Myriddin, and comes upon the battle between Arthur and the brother of the nephew Arthur killed. The dying Arthur is crawling through the mud. Gwyna agrees to throw Arthur's sword back into the water, returns to see Arthur die, and plunders his corpse.

Values: Gwyna learns to value truth and authenticity over the power and glory produced by false words.

Read Aloud/Reader Response

1.   Chapter 1, pages 3 to 7. In this chapter, Gwyna introduces herself.
2.   Chapter 8, page 42, beginning "It was the first time . . ." and ending

". . . bear of a man." Gwyna describes seeing Arthur for the first time without his helmet and armor.

3.   Chapter 9, pages 52 to 57, beginning "We rode through a land . . ." and ending "'. . . than most of them.'" Gwyna describes Arthur's pattern of war and the view of the gods.

4.   Chapter 19, pages 122 to 123, beginning with the chapter and ending ". . . happier that way." Gwyna describes how her experience with Myriddin is changing her life and mind.

5.   Chapter 46, pages 307 to 313. In this chapter, Gwyna explains how her life and Myriddin's life became entwined.

Booktalk

Ask the group to share what they know about King Arthur.

Gwyna, the daughter of a dead slave woman, knows a different Arthur. When Arthur attacks her master's home, she runs but is caught. Her captor or savior is not a soldier but a bard, the man who tells the world about wonderful Arthur. When she agrees to travel with him, he transforms her just as he transforms Arthur. She becomes the mysterious Lady of the Lake, a boy soldier, and a deadly spy. Soon she isn't sure who she is or who Arthur is or who Myriddin, her master bard, is. She must transform *herself* now, into a thinker. But how can a person think in the blood, guts, and screams of war? Does she sort it all out? Does she get to tell her own story, the true Arthur story? Not the pretty one about the ladies and the knights? You be the judge when you read Gwyna's version of the legendary king—*Here Lies Arthur.*

Curriculum Connections

1.   (Research and Compare, language arts) Using library resources, research the Arthurian legend. Compare the image to Arthur in *Here Lies Arthur.*

2.   (Discuss, language arts) How would you interpret the title in relation to the novel? Be sure to read the introductory quotation from Sir Thomas Malory's *Le Morte d' Arthur.*

3.   (Discuss) After reading this novel, do you think that the Arthurian legend is still relevant today? Support your answer with specifics from the novel.

Related Works

1.   Gardner, John. **Grendel.** New York: Vintage Books, 1989, reissue ed. 192p. $10.95pa. ISBN 0 679 72311 0. [fiction] S/A The monster from *Beowulf,* whose life has been characterized by the "Shaper," tells his own story.

2. Kerven Rosalind. **King Arthur.** New York: DK Publishing, 1998. 63p. (Eyewitness Classics) $14.95. ISBN 0 7894 2887 3. [nonfiction] MJS, CG (*Booktalks Plus*, 2001, pages 131 to 133.) Kerven explains the Arthurian legend and the themes of good and evil surrounding it.

3. Mathews, John. **King Arthur: Dark Age Warrior and Mythic Hero.** New York: Rosen Publishing, 2008. 127p. (Prime Time History) $39.95. ISBN-13: 978 1 4042 1364 7. [reference] JS, CG Mathews presents a scholarly history of the Arthurian legends as well as its influence on modern culture and extensive research sources. Chapter 5, "Ladies of the Lake," explains the stories of the women surrounding the legend.

4. Sandell, Lisa Ann. **Song of the Sparrow.** New York: Scholastic Press, 2007. 416p. $16.99. ISBN-13: 978 0 439 91848 0. [fiction, poetry] JS, G (*Genre Talks for Teens*, 2009, pages 197 to 199.) Seventeen-year-old Elaine lives in Arthur's war camp with her father and brothers, overcomes her jealousy of Gwynivere, finds her true love, and earns a place at the Round Table.

5. Vande Velde, Vivian. **The Book of Mordred.** Boston, MA: Houghton Mifflin Co., 2005, 342p. $18.00. ISBN 0 618 50754 X. [fiction] JS, CG (*Genre Talks for Teens*, 2009, pages 199 to 202.) Three connected stories portray Mordred as a questioning rebel in the disintegrating and rigid Arthurian court.

Nature's Power

Gaiman, Neil. **Dave McKean (illus).** The Graveyard Book.

New York: Harper Collins, 2008. 312p. $17.99.
ISBN-13: 978 0 06 05 3092 1. [fiction] MJS, CG with high interest for boys

Themes/Topics: dead, supernatural, cemeteries, acceptance

Summary/Description

Bod is raised by cemetery ghosts after a secret society hit man kills his family. His guardian, neither living nor dead, protects him from danger and helps him transition to the real world. Bod's own encounters with ghouls, an ancient tomb, school-yard bullies, and a human friend teach him the world's dangers and boundaries and prepare him for a final confrontation with the secret society and the departure from his home.

Values: Growing up with death, Bod values the potential of life for love and accomplishment.

Read Aloud/ Reader Response

The entire book is suitable for a read aloud. The following are possible selections.

1. Chapter 1, pages 6 to 9, beginning with the chapter and ending ". . . no child." Jack murders Bod's family.
2. Chapter 4, pages 100 to 104, beginning "Bod went back . . ." and ending "'. . . what I mean.'" Bod discovers the cemetery's unconsecrated ground.
3. Chapter 6, pages 178 to 181, beginning "'I think . . .'" and ending ". . . find you a school." Bod learns his history and resolves to prepare for the outside world.
4. Chapter 7, page 289, beginning "How could . . ." and ending ". . . world safer." Silas explains erasing Scarlett's memory.
5. Chapter 8, page 306, beginning "Do you know what . . ." and ending ". . . *path untaken.*" Bod leaves the graveyard.

Booktalk

Read aloud pages 2 to 9, beginning with the chapter and ending "There was no child." You may wish to show the illustrations as you read.

That child was Nobody Owens. He took a walk that night, and that is why this live boy lives in a graveyard. His mother made the ghost of Mrs. Owens promise to take care of him. There are plenty of retired teachers there as well as loving families, so he can easily learn about our world and have a normal life. Well, a normal life if you don't count the ghosts, ghouls, and ancient curses. Plus, the man who killed Bod's family is still looking for Bod, and the secret society that sent him is giving him some deadlines or else. Oh sure, Bod has the Hounds of God on his side, but monsters and killers are waiting for their chance, and when they see an opening, well, Bod's encounters are all right here in *The Graveyard Book.*

Curriculum Connections

1. (Research, social studies) Tour a local graveyard. Note the inscriptions on the gravestones and share them with the group.
2. (Research, language arts) Using library resources, learn more about theories of ghosts, ghouls, and spirits of the night. Share your information with the group.

3. (Discuss, language arts) What life lessons does Bod learn by living with the dead?

Related Works

1. Farmer, Nancy. **The Sea of Trolls.** Atheneum Books for Young Readers/A Richard Jackson Book, 2004. 459p. $17.95. ISBN 0 689 86744 1. [fiction] MJ, CG with high interest for boys. (*Booktalks and Beyond*, 2007, pages 160 to 162.) Eleven-year-old Jack, overworked and underappreciated by his father, is captured by Berserkers and discovers his powers within the life force.
2. Heneghan, James. **The Grave.** New York: Farrar, Straus and Giroux/Frances Foster Books, 2000. 245p. $17.00. ISBN 0 374 32765 3. [fiction] MJS, CG with high interest for boys. (*Booktalks and More*, 2003, pages 65 to 67.) Foster child Tom Mullen falls into a grave, time travels to Ireland of 1847, and finds his life.
3. McCaughrean, Geraldine. **The Stones Are Hatching.** New York: Harper Collins, 1999. 230p. $15.95. ISBN 0 06 028765 9. [fiction] MJ, CG with high interest for boys. Eleven-year-old Phelim discovers his connections with his father and the creatures from the Old Magic who tell him to save Britain.
4. McNamee, Eoin. **The Navigator: Chosen to Save the World.** New York: Random House/Wendy Lamb Books, 2006. 342p. $15.99. ISBN-13: 978 0 375 83910 8. [fiction] MJS, CG with high interest for boys. (*Genre Talks for Teens*, 2009, pages 180 to 182.) Owen overcomes his fears and discovers that he, like his father, is a key player in a battle between the Resisters and the Harsh, two ancient communities that emerge from extended sleeps and battle for the survival of the world.
5. Rowling, J. K. **Harry Potter and the Sorcerer's Stone.** New York: 1997. 509p. $17.95. ISBN 0 590 35340 3. MJS, CG with high interest for boys. (*Booktalks Plus*, 2001, pages 181 to 182.) Harry discovers his wizard blood and confronts Voldemort who killed his parents.

☙❧

Klass, David. Timelock: Book III.

New York: Farrar, Straus and Giroux/Frances Foster Books, 2009. 246p.

(The Caretaker Trilogy) $17.99. ISBN-13: 978 0 374 32309 7.

[fiction] JS, CG with high interest for boys

Themes/Topics: global warming, ecology, interpersonal relations, destiny, time travel

Summary/Description

In this final volume, Jack Danielson who has decided to remain a present-day human and stay with his high school love, is spirited away to the deserts of the future where he battles cyborgs, zombie warlocks, ninjas, and scorpions. He reunites with his mother who is preparing to rescue his father from public execution and the earth from destruction. Eko transports P. J. to the Amazon to retrieve the Star of Dann, which Jack and his mother use to rescue Jack's father. Jack, his father, P. J., Eko, Gisco, and Kidah travel to the Arctic to confront the Death Lord and the destructive Omega Box. Jack's father saves Jack, kills the Death Lord, and dies. Gisco destroys the Omega Box. After the battle, Kidah decides to lock time to secure the future. Jack fulfills his destiny and takes Eko for his wife. They time travel to a nature-filled world where Jack is the honored leader. Kidah dies locking time, and P. J. continues with her life on Earth.

Values: Jack shows courage, resolve, and ultimately the responsibility of a leader.

Read Aloud/Reader Response

1. Part 1, chapter 20, pages 76 to 80. This chapter centers on the Star of Dann and Jack's responsibility in world salvation.
2. Part 2, chapter 27, pages 100 to 104. In this chapter, Eko and P. J. enter each other's minds.
3. Part 2, chapter 28, pages 104 to 106. This chapter reviews Jack's bid for independence and shows Eko's determination to retrieve the star.
4. Part 3, chapter 41, pages 149 to 151, beginning "Usually when I panic . . ." and ending ". . . healing may begin." Jack has a vision of a man who understands the folly of modern man and the hope for the future.
5. Part 4, chapter 54, pages 198 to 202. P. J. and Eko arrive to help Jack and present the arguments for choice vs. duty.

Booktalk

We followed Jack Danielson through *Firestorm* and *Whirlwind*. (*Hold up both books.*) Now the end is here. In the most thrilling book of the *Caretaker* trilogy, Jack fights the final battle to save the earth. (*Hold up the book.*) He has to survive the scorching deserts of the future, cyborgs, zombie warlocks, suicidal ninjas, and super-sized scorpions. He has to navigate acid pools and fatal detection systems to meet Mom and Dad, the people who threw him away. If he makes it, he gets to battle for the world. But what about another battle? There is a battle in his heart over whether to live the ordinary, relatively worry-free life of a human with his high school love P. J. or embrace his duty to the future with the new Eve, Eko. That battle could make the confrontation with the Dark Lord look like a walk in the park, that is, if Jack survives. And will any fighting mean a thing if Jack and the world are trapped in a *Timelock*?

Curriculum Connections

1. (Research, language arts) Using your library resources, prepare a bibliography of fiction and nonfiction dealing with ecology issues.
2. (Discuss, language arts) Do you agree with Jack's choice at the end of the novel? Use details from the novel to support your opinion.
3. (Discuss, language arts) Read "The Road Not Taken" by Robert Frost. Discuss it in relation to Jack's situation.

Related Works

1. Card, Orson Scott. **Ender's Game.** New York: TOR, 1991. 234p. $6.99pa. (Ender) ISBN 0 812 55070 6. [fiction] JS/A In this first book of the series, six-year-old Ender trains as a battle commander of brilliant children who will save their world from ant-like aliens.
2. Evans, Kate. **Weird Weather: Everything You Didn't Want to Know about Climate Change but Probably Should Find Out.** Toronto, ON, Canada: Groundwood Books, 2007. 96p. $15.95. ISBN-13: 978 0 88899 838 5. [graphic, nonfiction] JS, CG Evans makes the case that we must act now against global warming. It includes Web sites, "Interactive Online Games," and "Recommended Further Reading."
3. Frost, Robert. "The Road Not Taken." Poets.org. Available: http://www.poets.org/viewmedia.php/prmMID/15717. (Accessed May 10, 2010). Frost's poem addresses the power of choice and the doubt that each difficult choice brings.
4. Klass, David. **The Caretaker Trilogy.** New York: Farrar, Straus and Giroux/Frances Foster Books. [fiction] JS, CG with high interest for boys. (*Genre Talks for Teens,* 2009, pages 119 to 123.)

> **Firestorm: Book I**. 2006. 287p $17.00. ISBN 0 374 32307 0. Jack Danielson, a brilliant, athletic, and handsome high school senior discovers that his mission, as a visitor from the future, is to save the earth.
>
> **Whirlwind: Book II.** 2008. 295p. $17.00. ISBN-13: 9780374323080. Jack and Gisco race to the Amazon to rescue P. J. from the Dark

Lord and enlist the help of Kidah, the powerful time-traveling shaman.

꒜꒘

Lloyd, Saci. The Carbon Diaries, 2015.
New York: Holiday House, 2008. 330p. $17.95.
ISBN-13: 978 0 8234 2190 9. [fiction] JS, CG with high interest for girls

Themes/Topics: family life, rationing, energy conservation, climate change, England

Summary/Description

After the Great Storm crisis, the United Kingdom sets a carbon ration of 200 points per month. Laura watches her family and community deal with blackouts, fuel shortages, and looting. The freezing winter is followed by a searing summer that requires water rationing and riot police. Laura bonds with her savvy elderly neighbor; fantasizes about the boy next door; stays connected with her band, the Dirty Angels; and reluctantly meets her school requirements. When a killer storm hits, the family discovers that their love transcends lost jobs, school failures, black market activity, and a women's rights movement. Laura realizes her ability to help others, her love for a bandmate, and a stronger relationship with her family. She commits to success in school and a new world. The book contains graphic illustrations and articles, a glossary, and a list of EcoLinks. Some language and situations could be considered controversial.

Values: Laura learns the importance of self-reliance, love, and cooperation.

Read Aloud/Reader Response

1. "January" diary entries Wed., Jan. 28, and Thurs., Jan. 29, pages 23 to 25. The entries describe people adjusting to outages and shortages.
2. "February" diary entry Thurs., Feb. 19, pages 43 to 45. Laura chooses Arthur for her needy person.
3. "February" diary entry Sat., Feb. 21, pages 46 to 49, beginning with the entry and ending ". . . like each other anymore." The Smart Meter brings out family secrets.
4. "Autumn. September," diary entry Wed., Sept. 9, pages 224 to 225, beginning with the entry and ending "Maybe I will." Adi explains how the crisis is adjusting his future.

5. "November," diary entry Thurs. Nov. 5, pages 265 to 267. Arthur talks about dealing with a national crisis.

Booktalk

Laura is in a crazy family and a hot band, the Dirty Angels. All face a big crisis—the weather. The government decides on carbon rationing. (*Hold up a plastic gift card.*) It works just like a gift card. A person has a 200-point carbon allowance. When it's gone, the card stops. Sounds like a good, responsible idea—for somebody else. But most people, like Laura, don't have time to count points. There is the traveling band and the gorgeous boy next door who might want to be her boyfriend. Then there is passing all those stupid school courses so that she will have the piece of paper she needs to be part of any future that is left. After a freezing winter, and a searing drought, the worst storm in history is coming. Can a girl find love and happiness in that mess? Laura has the answer in *The Carbon Diaries, 2015*.

Curriculum Connections

1. (Research, social studies, language arts) At the end of the novel, Lloyd lists EcoLinks. Choose one of the sites, evaluate it, and share your information with the group.
2. (Create, environmental science, language arts) Keep a carbon-reduction diary of your own. Record how those conservation decisions affect your life.
3. (Discuss, language arts) *The Carbon Diaries, 2015* deals with recycling humans as well as ecology. Agree or disagree and support your opinion with specifics from the novel.

Related Works

1. Anderson, M. T. **Feed.** Cambridge, MA: Candlewick Press, 2003. 235p. $16.99. ISBN 0 7636 1726 1. [fiction] JS, CG with high interest for boys. (*Teen Genre Connections*, 2005, pages 201 to 203.) As the environment deteriorates, a population focuses on consumerism via chips installed in their brains.
2. Lloyd, Saci. **The Carbon Diaries, 2017.** New York: Holiday House, 2010. 336p. $17.95. ISBN-13: 978 0 8234 2260 9. [fiction] JS, CG with high interest for girls. In this sequel, Laura faces responsibilities to her family, university studies, and band while trying to survive in a world suffering food and water shortages, disease, and political conflict.

3. Pfeffer, Susan Beth. **The Dead & the Gone.** New York: Harcourt, 2008. 321p. $17.00. ISBN-13: 978 0 15 206311 5. [fiction] JS, CG with high interest for boys. After a meteor hits the moon, seventeen-year-old Alex Morales fights to keep his sisters and himself alive as the city and world deteriorate.

4. Rosoff, Meg. **How I Live Now.** New York: Random House/Wendy Lamb Books, 2004. 194p. $18.95. ISBN 0 385 90908 X. [fiction] S, CG (*Booktalks and Beyond,* 2007, pages 184 to 186.) The world faces destruction through terrorism and self-destructive choices.

5. Tanaka, Shelley. **Climate Change.** Toronto, CA: House of Anansi Press/Groundwood Books, 2006.144p. $15.95. ISBN-13: 978 0 88899 783 8. [nonfiction] JS, CG Tanaka explains climate change and the tough questions and solutions it brings.

ॐ

Pierce, Tamora. **Melting Stones.**
New York: Scholastic Press, 2008. 320p. $17.99.
ISBN-13: 978 0 545 05264 1. [fiction] JS, G

Themes/Topics: magic, nature, coming of age

Summary/Description

Fourteen-year-old Evvy, a stone mage in training, accompanies Rosethorn and Myrrhtide to an island community to investigate a mysterious disruption in the island's plant and water supply. Evvy and her wise rock companion Luvo discover that the source of the problem is the birth of a volcano. Evvy uses her magic to reach the spirits trying to burst from the earth, redirects them, and saves the island.

Values: Evvy discovers her generosity and learns to value people as well as rocks.

Read Aloud/Reader Response

This novel was first released as an audiobook in 2007. You may wish to listen and read. Below are some passages suggested for response.

1. Chapter 2, page 25, beginning "'I am a *green* . . .'" and ending ". . . like a dog." Evvy compares Rosethorn's attitude toward status to Myrrhtide's.

2. Chapter 5, pages 58 to 59, beginning "I remember slow . . ." and ending ". . . think of pain." Luvo recalls his birth and his decision to connect with the rest of nature.

3. Chapter 8, pages 100 to 114. In this chapter, Evvy meets Flare and Carnelian.
4. Chapter 13, page 190, beginning "'Ifs just . . .'" and ending with the chapter. Evvy recalls Briar's advice on how to cope with problems.
5. Chapter 22, pages 310 to 311, beginning "I'd lived . . ." and ending ". . . wake up in time." Evvy knows who she is and how she will direct her life.

Booktalk

Hold up the books of the Circle Opens *quartet. Ask how many people are familiar with them.*

The Winding Circle has a new chapter. Fourteen-year-old Evvy likes rocks (*Hold up some*) more than people. Her best friend is a talking rock. Rocks give her magic or help her discover her magic. She isn't sure which. Now she is on a boat with the powerful mage Rosethorn. The trip isn't pleasant. Rock people don't enjoy water trips, but an island's plants and water are dying, and the Winding Circle has promised to help. The mages discover that the problems aren't in the plants or water. Those are just the symptoms. The problems are deeper, in the rocks. Who is the expert? Right. Evvy, the mage in training. Evvy is in charge, the one to blame for mistakes, the one to save the people or destroy them. These rocks are like her, violent, unpredictable, and sometimes selfish. Can she control them and save the island, or should she join them? It would be so nice to blend into the world she loves, a world that lets her belong without questions, a world of *Melting Stones.*

Curriculum Connections

1. (Research, science) Using your library resources, learn more about volcanoes and their origins. Act as a resource person during the discussion.
2. (Create, language arts, art) Present each of the characters in graphic format or choose a small portion of the story to tell in graphic format.
3. (React, language arts) Evvy changes a great deal by the end of the story. Is she maturing or selling out? Be sure to use specifics from the text to support your response.

Related Works

1. Pierce, Tamora. **The Circle Opens Quartet**. New York: Scholastic Press. [fiction] MJ

Magic Steps. 2000. 272p. $16.95. ISBN 0 590 39588 2. G Fourteen-year-old Sandry realizes her magical responsibilities when she moves with her uncle, mentors a dancer, and confronts two assassins and a decadent mage.

Street Magic. 2001. 304p. $16.95. ISBN 0 590 39628 5. CG Fourteen-year-old Brian Moss mentors the stubborn Evvy and defeats the evil woman who wishes to control her magic.

Cold Fire. 2002. 368p. $16.95. ISBN 0 590 39655 2. G Daja and Frostpine teach meditation to magically gifted twins and uncover a pyromaniac.

Shatterglass. 2003. 368p. $16.95. ISBN 0 590 39683 8. G Trisana Chandler helps a glassmaker gifted with lightning magic to focus his powers and clear himself of murder accusations. Like the other three lead characters in the *Circle Opens* quartet, she helps a young orphan discover her magic.

2.   Pierce, Tamora. **The Will of the Empress.** New York: Scholastic Press, 2005. 320p. $17.99. ISBN 0 439 44171 4. [fiction] MJS, G (*Genre Talks for Teens,* 2009, pages 207 to 210.) Sandry's Discipline Cottage friends help her escape a forced marriage.

ᘓᘔ

Shusterman, Neal. The Skinjacker Trilogy.
[fiction] MJS, CG

Concluding volume forthcoming.

Themes/Topics: after-life, interpersonal relationships,
families, monsters, control

Everlost.

New York: Simon Pulse, 2006. 377p. $6.99pa.
ISBN-13: 978 0 689 87238 9.

Summary/Description

When their cars collide, fourteen-year-old Nick and Allie are trapped in Everlost, an area between Earth and their final destinations. Lief, who died when he was eleven, greets them and warns them about the McGill, the most formidable monster in Everlost. Allie tries to return home, and the three encounter fifteen-year-old Mary Hightower who lives in the Twin Towers, writes about Everlost life, and cares for Afterlight kids. Against Mary's advice, Allie affects the real world and seeks more knowledge from the Haunter who traps Lief and Nick in barrels, which the McGill steals. Allie finds the McGill and promises to teach him how to use the real world. Her plan helps Nick escape and seek help from Mary. Facing his sister, the McGill turns back into his fourteen-year-old body and flees from his victims but later saves Allie from plunging to the earth's center. Nick teams with Mary who has actually been holding children back from their destinations. When he frees them, she characterizes him as a monster. Mary's former assistant assumes the McGill role.

Values: Allie and Nick demonstrate loyalty and courage as they defeat bullies.

Read Aloud/Reader Response

1. Chapter 5, Page 51. The excerpt from Mary Hightower's book explains self-image in Everlost.
2. Chapter 7, pages 75 and 76, beginning with the chapter and ending ". . . September day." The story explains the place of the Twin Towers in Everlost.
3. Chapter 8, Page 106. The excerpt from Mary Hightower's book explains the place of routine for Afterlights.
4. Chapter 15, pages 195 to 196, beginning "Although not even . . ." and ending ". . . strong and fearless." Lief and Nick adjust differently to the pickle barrels.
5. Chapter 30, page 373, beginning "Perhaps Mary was . . ." and ending ". . . passing through." Nick reflects on Mary's concept of Everlost.

Booktalk

Fourteen-year-old Allie and Nick never met in life. Their cars crashed head on. They went to sleep and woke up dead with a guide who will be eleven forever. They have all the time in this new world to get to know each other. What is the point? To get back to life. But the trip from point A to point B isn't so simple. They will face gangs, monsters, and advice that can pound them to the center of the earth's magma or numb them with repetition. The live world was dangerous enough. It got them killed. But this world's dangers have eternal consequences, and before they "get where they are going," they have to survive *Everlost*.

Everwild.

New York: Simon and Shuster/BFYR, 2009. 424p. $16.99.
ISBN-13: 978 1 4169 5863 5.

Summary/Description

Three new characters complicate the relationships among Mary, Nick, Allie, and Mikey. Milos, a skinjacker, expands Allie's skinjacker skills. He searches for his former girlfriend, skinjacker Jackin' Jill who causes accidents to bring more children into the afterlife. Allie leaves him to look for her family, but not before he causes Mikey to become jealous, leave, and expand his monster transformation powers. Milos finds Jackin' Jill with Mary who wants to use Jill's secret to expand her power. Nick finds Zin, a female Confederate soldier who can take items from the real world. He helps her learn to cram things back into the world. Allie finds her family and discovers that she is not dead, but in a coma. Milos frees her from the boy she has used to get that information, but Allie runs away when Milos wants to make her part of Mary's plan. Mary sets her confrontation with Nick in Graceland, a vortex that intensifies dominant traits. Nick, the Chocolate Ogre, melts. Zin and Allie cram Mary into the real world, but Mary's forces defeat Nick's, and Milos captures Allie. Mikey learns that Allie is a prisoner and rebuilds Nick, and they set out to release her. Milos rescues Mary from the real world.

Values: Allie and Nick courageously fight for what they believe but learn from new experiences.

Read Aloud/Reader Response

1. Chapter 3, pages 20 to 21, beginning "In spite of everything . . ." to ". . . *could* be." Nick reveals his vision of his love for Mary.
2. Chapter 4, page 27, beginning "It was . . ." and ending ". . . the name 'Everlost.'" Allie ponders the power Mary has through language.
3. Chapter 10, page 130, beginning "There was a house . . ." and ending with the chapter. Mikey's reaction to an abandoned house reveals his identity.
4. Chapter 23, pages 259 to 265. In this chapter, Zin crams a corsage into the living world.
5. Chapter 35, page 375, beginning "There was a good reason . . ." and ending ". . . beautiful." Allie reacts to Mikey, the monster.

Booktalk

Hold up Everlost. *Ask how many people have read it.*

We know that in *Everlost*, Allie and Nick wake up dead to a new world of mystery and monsters. They become part of that mystery, and in this second book of the *Skinjacker* trilogy, they become major players. Allie is still determined to return home even if Mary and the sinister, seductive skinjacker Milos try to keep her in Everlost forever. Mary names Nick, who challenges her plans, the Chocolate Ogre. Nick can't stop thinking about his name and is turning into a mound of chocolate. And Allie's love makes Mikey, the McGill monster, more human everyday, maybe. Mary plans to expand Everlost with Milos and friends even if they destroy the living world. Can Allie and friends stop her? Two different views of good and evil mean war, and Everlost becomes *Everwild*.

Curriculum Connections

1. (Research, language arts) Using your library resources, prepare a bibliography of works that deal with the after-life.
2. (Discuss, language arts) Using specifics from these stories, what makes a monster?
3. (Discuss, language arts, art) Portray the characters or a scene from these stories in graphic format.

Related Works

1. Carey, Janet Lee. **The Beast of Noor.** New York: Atheneum Books for Young Readers, 2006. 497p. $16.95. ISBN-13: 978 0 689 87644 8. [fiction] MJ, CG with high interest for boys. (*Genre Talks for Teens*, 2009, pages 167 to 169.) Fifteen-year-old Miles and his thirteen-year-old sister discover their own strengths when they enter the supernatural world to confront a huge and raging beast of the dark woods.
2. Jenkins, A. M. **Repossessed.** New York: HarperCollins/HarperTeen, 2007. 218p. $15.99. ISBN-13: 978 0 06 083568 2. [fiction] JS, CG (*Genre Talks for Teens*, 2010, pages 35 to 37.) Kiriel, a fallen angel, enters the body of a teenager and experiences God's creation.
3. Sleator, William. **Hell Phone.** New York: Amulet Books, 2006. 237p. $16.95. ISBN 0 8109 5479 6. [fiction] MJ, CG with high interest for boys. (*Genre Talks for Teens*, 2010, pages 164 to 166.) A cheap cell phone pulls seventeen-year-old Nick Gordon into a murder plot and death.
4. Soto, Gary. **The Afterlife.** New York: Harcourt, 2003. 161p. $16.00. ISBN 0 15 204774 3. [fiction] JS, CG (*Teen Genre Connections*,

2005, pages 294 to 296.) Stabbed to death in a restroom, eighteen-year-old Jesús changes the real world and himself after death.

5.　Zevin, Gabrielle. **Elsewhere.** New York: Farrar, Straus and Giroux, 2005. 277p. $19.95. ISBN 0 374 32091 8. [fiction] MJS, G (*Booktalks and Beyond*, 2007, pages 188 to 190.) Liz dies in a traffic accident shortly before her sixteenth birthday and prepares for her return to Earth in *Elsewhere*.

ভ৩ ৩ভ

Tan, Shaun. Tales from Outer Suburbia.

New York: Scholastic/Arthur A. Levine Books, 2009. 96p. $19.99.
ISBN-13: 978 0 545 05587 1. [illustrated stories and poems]
MJS/A, CG with high interest for boys

Themes/Topics: differences, gifts, new experiences

Summary/Description

Fifteen very short off-the-wall tales explore the mystery and magic of cryptic advice, multiple cultures, creativity, nature, love, bullies, government, pets, and exploration. The author's signature illustrations accompany each story. They sometimes support and sometimes tell the story.

Values: The stories highlight creativity, tolerance, awareness, gratitude, and fairness.

Read Aloud/Reader Response

Each story is suitable for a read aloud, and the read aloud should include the pictures. Displaying them on a large screen while the stories are read will increase the impact.

Booktalk

Ask how many in the group have read The Arrival *by Shaun Tan. Hold up the book.*

The Arrival tells a beautiful story with only pictures. (*Leaf through the book and direct the pictures toward the audience as you speak.*) In it, Shaun Tan explores the magic of coming to a new country (any country), finding hospitality, settling in, and then passing that hospitality on to others. In *The Arrival*, Tan proved that he could be a master storyteller with just pictures. Now he has a new story, with a new message, and his delivery is a little different. (*Hold up* Tales from Outer Suburbia *and leaf through the pages as you speak, but be sure to open and com-*

ment on the table of contents, which is made up of stamps that accent "delivery.") This time, he uses words and pictures. He talks about taking advice, small gifts, the challenges of love, strangers, nature, and just seeing or listening. And maybe, after reading the stories and looking at the pictures again and again, you will find your home in *Tales from Outer Suburbia.*

Curriculum Connections

1. (Research, language arts and art) Using your library resources, learn about illustrators who have used art rather than action plots to communicate ideas. Act as a resource person for the group during the discussion. Bring examples of their work.
2. (Research and Discuss, language arts) Using library resources, define *tale.* Find and define other narrative forms. Is *tale* an appropriate word for the title of Tan's book?
3. (React, language arts, art) Choose your favorite picture and story. Explain your choice.

Related Works

1. Muth, Joh. **Zen Shorts.** New York: Scholastic Press, 2005. 36p. $17.99. ISBN-13: 978 0 439 33911 7. [fiction, picture book] CMJS/A, CG Stillwater the panda tells three stories that reflect Zen philosophy.
2. Ryan, Pam Muñoz (text), and Peter Sís (illus.). **The Dreamer.** New York: Scholastic Press, 2010. 384p. $17.99. ISBN-13: 978 0 439 26970 4. [fiction] MJS, CG Combining biography, fiction, personal fantasy, and sensory illustrations, Muñoz and Sís tell the story of Neftalí Reyes who grows into one of the most famous poets of Chile by following the calls of nature's beauty, his gift of words, and the demands of social responsibility.
3. Selznick, Brian. **The Invention of Hugo Cabret.** New York: Scholastic Press, 2007. 544p. $22.99. ISBN-13: 978 0 439 81378 5. [fiction] M, CG (*Genre Talks for Teens,* 2009, pages 152 to 154.) A combination of pictures and words tells the story of the orphan who maintains the train station clocks and becomes friends with George Méliès, a pioneer French filmmaker.
4. Sís, Peter. **The Wall: Growing Up behind the Iron Curtain.** New York: Farrar, Straus and Giroux/Frances Foster Books, 2007. 56p. $18.00. ISBN-13: 978 0 374 34701 7. [graphic, nonfiction] MJS, CG (*Genre Talks for Teens,* 2009, pages 255 to 257.) In this illustrated memoir, Sís describes childhood in Soviet-controlled

Czechoslovakia and the brief glimpses of Western life that changed his thinking and his life.

5.   Tan, Shaun. **The Arrival.** New York: Scholastic/Arthur A. Levine Books, 2007. 128p. $19.99. ISBN-13: 978 0 439 89529 3. [wordless graphic] The story, told completely in pictures, communicates the joy of arrival to a new country and how that joy is passed to others.

Waters, Daniel. Generation Dead.

New York: Hyperion Books, 2008. 392p. $8.99pa.
ISBN-13: 978 142 310 922 8. [fiction] JS, CG with high interest for girls

Themes/Topics: zombies, friendship, prejudice, love

Summary/Description

Oakvale High establishes a program for these "differently biotic" students, teenagers who die but come back to life. Phoebe, still living, draws her two friends into the support group, and they interact with differently biotic students. Adam, one of those friends, deals with a differently biotic student, Tommy, who wants to play on the football team. Adam becomes more sympathetic as the coach encourages the team to harass Tommy. When Tommy dates Phoebe, Adam realizes that he loves her. Tommy invites her to a dance. Afterward they go to a party at an abandoned house where the undead gather. Adam joins them, rescues Phoebe from an attack by members of the football team, and is killed. Because of Phoebe's love, he returns to life.

Value: Within the romantic story is a strong theme of tolerance and acceptance.

Read Aloud/Reader Response

1.   Chapter 1, pages 6 to 7, beginning "She looked . . ." and ending ". . . shooter games." Phoebe wonders about the undead life.
2.   Chapter 2, page 22, beginning "Gino Manetti . . ." and ending ". . . had changed." The passage shows the difference between Pete and Adam.
3.   Chapter 5, page 48, beginning "The Pain . . ." and ending ". . . in life." Adam rethinks his reputation and football friendships.
4.   Chapter 14, pages 171 to 172, beginning "'It is an . . .'" and ending ". . . Phoebe's head." Karen compares being undead to being Goth.

5. Chapter 17, pages 207 to 208, beginning *"Week three . . ."* and ending *". . . change happened."* Tommy's blog discusses using consumerism to help an idealistic cause.

Booktalk

Live. Dead. Now a third category, undead. Dead American teens are coming alive again, maybe half alive. Oakvale High School decides to make a place for them and call them "living impaired" instead of zombies. When that name becomes negative, the label is "differently biotic." Phoebe is a Goth, open to the mysteries of death and life. She notices one differently biotic boy. He notices her. They join a support group. She invites her friends. It's a positive start for blending life and death, except not everyone is with the program. Some people don't want these half alive people in their school. It isn't murder if the person is already dead, is it? But murderers don't always kill the person they aim for. Sometimes they get the people standing next to the target. And the escalating violence may mean an entire *Generation Dead*.

Curriculum Connections

1. (Research, language arts) Using library resources, learn more about the principles of Goth and the concept of zombies. Share your information with the group.
2. (Research, social studies) Using library resources, learn more about the roots of prejudices. Share your information with the group.
3. (Discuss, language arts) List the negative and positive forces in the novel. Use specific support from the novel to support your choices. Compare your list with the lists of others in the group.

Related Works

1. Aronson, Marc. **Race: A History Beyond Black and White.** New York: Atheneum Books for Young Readers/Ginee Seo Books, 2007. 322p. $18.99. ISBN-13: 978 0 689 86554 1. [nonfiction] S, CG Explaining race through the "us" versus "strangers" thinking of the ancient world, Aronson traces the history of man persecuting man from the survival instincts of primitive tribes to a multi-cultural modern-day world.
2. Cabot, Meg. **Haunted: A Tale of the Mediator.** New York: HarperCollins Publishers, 2003. 246p. $15.99. ISBN 0 06 029471 X. [fiction] JS, G In her junior year, Susannah Simon finds herself in a supernatural struggle with seventeen-year-old Paul Slater whom she believes tried to kill her and eliminate the 150-year-old ghost she loves.

3.   Leavitt, Martine. **Keturah and Lord Death.** Asheville, NC: Front Street, 2006. 216p. $16.95. ISBN-13: 978 1 932425 29 1. [fiction] JS, G (*Genre Talks for Teens,* 2009, pages 178 to 180.) Sixteen-year-old Keturah Reeve builds a relationship with Lord Death, which allows her to help others and accept her own death.

4.   Walters, Daniel. **Generation Dead: Kiss of Life.** New York: Disney/Hyperion Books, 2009. 416p. (Generation Dead Series) $16.99. ISBN-13: 978 142310923 5. [fiction] JS, CG with high interest for girls. Adam, who died trying to save Phoebe, struggles as an undead person, and Phoebe sorts out her feelings for both Adam and Tommy, who is expanding his efforts for equal justice.

5.   Zevin, Gabrielle. **Elsewhere.** New York: Farrar, Straus and Giroux, 2005. 277p. $19.95. ISBN 0 374 32091 8. [fiction] MJS, G (*Booktalks and Beyond,* 2007, pages 188 to 190.) Fifteen-year-old Liz dies and is rejuvenated in *Elsewhere.*

Heritage: Historical Books

History and historical fiction show us how those who have gone before us struggled for and value what we guard today. Most peoples, past and present, want the freedom to express themselves and establish their own communities. Within those communities, they want some guarantee of equality and recognition. Accomplishing those strong communities requires leaders to give us hope and raise the bar.

Freedom

Anderson, Laurie Halse. Chains.

New York: Simon & Shuster Books for Young Readers, 2008. 316p. (Seeds of America) $16.99. ISBN-13: 978 1 4169 0585 1. [fiction] JS, CG with high interest for girls.

Themes/Topics: Revolutionary War, slavery, epilepsy, conduct of life

Summary/Description

In 1776, Isabel and her younger sister Ruth, an epileptic, are sold after their mother and owner die, even though her master freed them in her will. The new owners are loyalists. Curzon, a slave boy owned by a rebel, recruits Isabel as a spy. Her owner's wife becomes more abusive, and Isabel gives information to the rebels. The rebels take information but refuse to help when Ruth is sold. Because Isabel protests the sale and tries to escape, her owner's wife has Isabel's face branded with an "I" for "Insolence." Curzon helps Isabel heal. The British occupy New York, and Curzon fights for the rebels. He is captured and held in a British prison. Isabel smuggles him table

179

scraps, negotiates with his guards and fellow prisoners for his safety, and engineers his escape. An appendix explains the novel's historical base.

Values: Courage and loyalty keep Isabel and Curzon strong.

Read Aloud/Reader Response

1. Chapter 4, page 25, beginning "Momma said . . ." and ending ". . . cracked in the wind." Isabel reflects on her family being trapped in the Americas.
2. Chapter 13, page 79, the chapter's introductory quotation. The letter from Abigail Adams to her husband, John Adams, suggests that wives may also be slaves.
3. Chapter 23, pages 146 to 148. In this chapter, Isabel is branded.
4. Chapter 38, pages 246 to 247, beginning "After the carriage left . . ." and ending ". . . guide someone home." Isabel realizes that no one can enslave her soul unless she allows it.
5. Chapter 41, pages 267 to 269, beginning "The sun rose . . ." and ending with the chapter. Isabel reflects on paths to freedom.

Booktalk

Thirteen-year-old Isabel sees her mother and owner die of smallpox. She has one hope, freedom. Before she died, her owner freed Isabel and her sister Ruth, but the owner's nephew sells them from Rhode Island to New York. The year is 1776. A revolution for freedom is blooming, and her new owners are determined to stop it. They will crush the rebels as well as Isabel and Ruth. The rebels in New York would like Isabel to spy for them. As an ignored nobody in an influential home, she has access to crucial information about the British plans for invasions and assassinations. But what will that information mean for Isabel? Freedom? Slavery? Or Death? Isabel, the slave, decides to be a free agent. She will work for Isabel, for Ruth, and for anyone or any country willing to break their *Chains*.

Curriculum Connections

1. (Research, history) Using library resources, learn more about slavery in the Northern states during the American Revolution. Act as a resource person for your group.
2. (Research, history) Using library resources, learn more about *Common Sense* by Thomas Paine. Act as a resource person for the group.
3. (Discuss, language arts) Who are the villains and heroes in this novel? Explain your choices with specifics from the story.

Related Works

1. Allen, Thomas B. **George Washington, Spymaster: How the Americans Outspied the British and Won the Revolutionary War.** Washington, DC: National Geographic, 2004. 184p. $16.95. ISBN 0 7922 5126 1. [nonfiction] MJS, CG with high interest for boys. (*Booktalks and Beyond,* 2007, pages 215 to 218.) Allen portrays Washington as a spymaster who eventually defeats the British with wit rather than might.

2. Anderson, M. T. **The Astonishing Life of Octavian Nothing: Traitor to the Nation; Volume I: The Pox Party.** Boston, MA: Candlewick Press, 2006. 351p. (The Astonishing Life of Octavian Nothing: Traitor to the Nation) $17.99. ISBN 0 7636 2402 0. [fiction] JS, CG (*Genre Talks for Teens,* 2009, pages 217 to 220.) During the American Revolution, Octavian and his mother live in a scholarly Boston house, where Octavian learns he is a slave being assessed for his African intelligence.

3. Aronson, Marc. **The Real Revolution: The Global Story of American Independence.** New York: Clarion Books, 2005. 238p. $21.00. ISBN 0 618 18179 2 [nonfiction] JS, CG (*Booktalks and Beyond,* 2007, pages 218 to 221.) Aronson frames the American Revolution in world events.

4. Cox, Clinton. **Come All You Brave Soldiers.** New York: Scholastic Press, 1999. 189p. $15.95. ISBN 0 590 47576 2. [nonfiction] JS, CG (*Booktalks Plus,* 2001, pages 155 to 157.) Cox explains how slaves and indentured servants tried to choose the side that would give them liberty and then, after the war, had freedom denied.

5. Nelson, Marilyn. Pamela Espeland (notes and annotations). **Fortune's Bones: The Manumission Requiem.** Asheville, NC: Front Street, 2004. 32p. $16.95. ISBN 1 932425 12 8. [nonfiction] JS, CG (*Booktalks and Beyond,* 2007, pages 247 to 249.) With notes and pictures accompanying six poems, the author tells the story of one of the last slaves in Connecticut.

 ☙❧

Anderson, M. T. The Astonishing Life of Octavian Nothing: Traitor to the Nation; Volume II: The Kingdom on the Waves.

Cambridge, MA: Candlewick Press, 2008. 561p. $22.99.
ISBN-13: 978 0 7636 2950 2. [fiction] JS, CG with high interest for boys

Themes/Topics: Revolutionary War, slavery, loyalty, freedom, conduct of life

Summary/Description

After escaping with Dr. Trefusis and saving his life, Octavian joins Lord Dunmore's Ethiopian Regiment in Norfolk and reunites with Pro Bono. Acting on inaccurate information, the British face an overwhelming rebel force and retreat to their ships. The regiment lives in near-slave-like conditions. Octavian hears the various hardships that slaves endure and learns about African folklore and mythology. He faces hostility from his fellow soldiers and scorn from the British. He learns about his mother's trip to the New World, which casts doubt on her royalty but reveals her intelligence and cunning. Dunmore's situation deteriorates, and the slaves become expendable. Dr. Trefusis is killed in a rebel assault. Octavian flees North where he realizes the gap between philosophical ideals and the real world and seeks a more civilized society. The Author's Note explains the story's factual base and the role of history in each person's life.

Values: Octavian realizes the value of heritage and personal freedom.

Read Aloud/Reader Response

1. Section 5, pages 102 to 103, beginning with the chapter and ending ". . . a soldier." Octavian describes how he became a British soldier.
2. Section 6, pages 128 to 132. In this section, Octavian becomes Octavian Nothing.
3. Section 6, pages 162 to 163. In this section, Pomp illustrates the futility of immortality.
4. Section 7, pages 346 to 349, beginning "The Tale of Oshun" and ending with the chapter. Octavian wonders about his mother's life in relation to "The Tale of Oshun."
5. Section 8, pages 559 to 561. In this passage, Octavian reflects on his experiences.

Booktalk

Hold up a copy of The Astonishing Life of Octavian Nothing: Traitor to the Nation; Volume I: The Pox Party. *Ask people who have read the book to share their reactions.*

After rebelling against men who claim their own freedom but enslave and torture him, Octavian is on the run with his savior, Dr. Trefusis, to find safety with the British. But can the British hold Boston? Octavian seeks work, but few people need a scholar. Fists and fire rule. Octavian joins fellow slaves in Lord Dunmore's Ethiopian Regiment. He will fight for men's rights, not just read about them. They go South where a slave rebellion can defeat the rebels once and for all. The ship is a school that teaches Octavian about his African roots, his regal mother, jealousy, loyalty, and betrayal. Most important, he learns that each man must guard his personal liberty even in *The Kingdom on the Waves.*

Curriculum Connections

1. (Research, social studies) Using library resources, learn more about Lord Dunmore. Act as a resource person for the group.
2. (Research, social studies) Using library resources, learn more about slavery in colonial America. Act as a resource person for the group.
3. (Discuss, language arts) List the other stories told within this story. Explain why these stories and stories in general are important.

Related Works

1. Anderson, M. T. **The Astonishing Life of Octavian Nothing: Traitor to the Nation; Volume I: The Pox Party.** Cambridge, MA: Candlewick Press, 2006. 351p.$17.99. ISBN 0 7636 2402 0. [fiction] JS, CG (*Genre Talks for Teens,* 2009, pages 217 to 220.) Octavian and his mother, Cassiopeia, live in a house of Boston scholars who pamper them but study them to assess African intelligence.
2. Aronson, Marc. **Race: A History Beyond Black and White.** New York: Atheneum Books for Young Readers/Ginee Seo Books, 2007. 322p. $18.99. ISBN-13: 978 0 689 86554 1. [nonfiction] S, CG Aronson traces the history of man persecuting man from the survival instincts of primitive tribes to a multi-cultural modern-day world.
3. Aronson, Marc. **The Real Revolution: The Global Story of American Independence.** New York: Clarion Books, 2005. 238p. $21.00. ISBN 0 618 18179 2. [nonfiction] JS, CG (*Booktalks and Beyond,* 2007, pages 218 to 221.) Aronson frames the American Revolution in world events and considers the dynamic of slavery.
4. Draper, Sharon. **Copper Sun.** New York: Atheneum Books for Young Readers, 2006. 302p. $16.95. ISBN-13: 978 0 689 82181 3. [fiction] JS, CG (*Genre Talks for Teens,* 2009, pages 87 to 90.) Stolen from her village by slavers, Amari survives to tell the stories of destruction and cruelty.
5. Murphy, Jim. **The Real Benedict Arnold.** New York: Clarion Books, 2007. 264p. $20.00. ISBN-13: 978 0 395 77609 4. [nonfiction] JS, CG with high interest for boys. (*Genre Talks for Teens,* 2009, pages 249 to 252.) Murphy examines the dynamics that shape Arnold and his final decision to side with the Loyalists.

ଔଓ

Engle, Margarita. **The Surrender Tree: Poems of Cuba's Struggle for Freedom.**

New York: Henry Holt & Co., 2008. 169p. $16.95.
ISBN-13: 978 0 8050 8674 4. [novel in verse] JS, CG

Themes/Topics: Cuba, war, healing, slavery, concentration camps, conduct of life

Summary/Description

Participants who fought for freedom in the Cuban wars from 1868 to 1899 tell their stories in poems. Rosa, the healer, tends the sick and wounded regardless of their loyalties. Lieutenant Death, the son of a slavehunter, hunts slaves and stalks Rosa, whom he considers a witch. The rebel José marries Rosa, protects her, and also heals. Lieutenant General Weyler explains his plans to crush the rebellion and invents concentration camps to starve the rebels. Silvia, a concentration camp victim, loses her family and, with the help of the death-cart driver, finds her way to Rosa who teaches her healing. The "Author's Note" explains the historical context. A "Chronology" explains the early efforts for independence. "Selected References" list the author's main sources.

Values: The rebels demonstrate loyalty, tolerance, and generosity.

Read Aloud/Reader Response

The entire novel is suitable for dramatic reading. Selections below are of particular interest.

1. Part 1, "Lieutenant Death," page 6, and "Rosa," page 8. Both selections show how the slavehunters use words and symbols to intimidate.
2. Part 1, "Rosa," page 22. Labeled a witch, Rosa treats friend and enemy.
3. Part 2, "Rosa," page 58. Rosa heals the enemy.
4. Part 3, "Rosa," page 69, and "José," page 70. Rosa and José define slavery.
5. Part 3, "Silvia," page 158. Silvia addresses the imperfect peace.

Booktalk

Read "Rosa," page 16.

This poem captures Rosa's life. She is a slave and a healer in nineteenth-century Cuba, a century that saw more than one war for independence. With a good heart and knowledge of plants and flowers, she heals both allies and enemies. What does she receive in return? Sometimes a smile, sometimes thanks, sometimes a chicken, and always more enemies. The slavehunters want to capture or kill her and crush the people that she helps. Even her ears, cut from her head in death, will bring them money and praise. But Rosa fights for her freedom and democracy for her country. Will her dream live or die at *The Surrender Tree*?

Curriculum Connections

1. (Research, language arts, social studies) Using library resources, learn more about José Martí. Share the information with the group.
2. (Discuss, language arts) Why did Margarita Engle choose simple characters to tell their stories rather than the more world-famous ones?
3. (Research, social studies) Using library resources, examine events in the United States over the time period of the Cuban rebellions? Prepare a timeline for the group.

Related Works

1. Bagdasarian, Adam. **Forgotten Fire.** New York: DK Publishing, 2000. 273p. $17.95. ISBN 0 7894 2627 7. [fiction] MJS, CG (*Booktalks and More,* 2003, pages 49 to 51.) Twelve-year-old Vahan Kenderian recounts his life between 1915 and 1918 as the youngest son in a prosperous Armenian family during the Armenian holocaust in Turkey.
2. Draper, Sharon. **Copper Sun.** New York: Atheneum Books for Young Readers, 2006. 302p. $16.95. ISBN-13: 978 0 689 82181 3. [fiction] JS, CG (*Genre Talks for Teens,* 2009, pages 87 to 90.) Fifteen-year-old Amari is stolen from her village by slavers and eventually escapes to the Spanish, slavery-free Fort Mose in Florida.
3. Giblin, James Cross. **The Life and Death of Adolf Hitler.** New York: Clarion Books, 2002. 246p. $21.00. ISBN 0 395 90371. [nonfiction] MJS, CG (*Teen Genre Connections,* 2005, pages 250 to 252.) Giblin portrays a disturbed and dedicated individual who appealed to the prejudices and fears of the German people after World War I. Like Lieutenant General Weyler, he used concentration camps.
4. Kraft, Betsy Harvey. **Theodore Roosevelt: Champion of the American Spirit.** New York: Clarion Books, 2003. 180p. $19.00. ISBN 0 618 14264 9. [nonfiction] JS, CG Kraft describes one of the most dynamic public figures of the time. Pages 51 to 66 describe

his involvement in the Spanish-American War and its effect on his career.

5.   Martí, José. **Versos sencillos/Simple Verses.** Houston, TX: Arte Público Press, 1997. 123p. (Recovering the U.S. Hispanic Literary Heritage) $12.95. ISBN 1 55885 204 2. [poetry] S, CG This is the first complete English translation of *Versos sencillos* written by Martí in the United States during his years of exile and revolution. The volume includes both the original Spanish and the English translation. The "Introduction" explains Martí's place in the political, literary, and intellectual history of the Americas.

ᘓᘔ

Warren, Andrea. **Under Siege! Three Children at the Civil War Battle for Vicksburg.**

New York: Farrar, Straus and Giroux/Melanie Kroupa Books, 2009. 166p. $21.95.
ISBN-13: 978 0 374 31255 8. [nonfiction] MJS, CG

Themes/Topics: Vicksburg siege, 1863; Civil War, 1861–1865; Mississippi history

Summary/Description

From December 1862 to July 4, 1863, Ulysses S. Grant holds Vicksburg, Mississippi, the key to controlling the Mississippi River. The three young people described in the siege are Lucy McRae, a daughter of a privileged family. Twelve-year-old Frederick Grant, General Grant's son, and eleven-year-old Willie Lord, the son of an Episcopal minister from New York. Lucy and Willie experience the shelling, looting, flight to the countryside, and life in the caves. Fred visits his father on the battleground and suffers a leg wound, infection, and disease. The adults within the narrative include the soldiers, officers, prominent townspeople who aid the resistance, and the slaves who choose their loyalties. The "Afterword" follows up on each person featured. "Facts about the War" include specifics about Vicksburg and the Civil War. "Children Orphaned by the War" explains the post-war rise of orphanages and orphan trains. "Women in the War" tells how women supported the fighting. "Reconstruction" addresses generally the period following the war. "For More about the Civil War," "Selected Bibliography," and "Endnotes" list sources for further reference including a film and Web sites.

Values: The account shows courage and loyalty on both sides of the fighting.

Read Aloud/Reader Response

1. Chapter 1, pages 9 to 19. The four sections of this chapter describe pre-battle Vicksburg.
2. Chapter 3, pages 27 to 29, beginning with the chapter and ending with ". . . all around him." The passage describes how Fred and family join Grant in war.
3. Chapter 4, pages 39 to 40, beginning with the chapter and ending ". . . hope for the best." The passage introduces Willie Lord and his family.
4. Chapter 9, pages 81 to 86, beginning with the chapter and ending ". . . William Siege Green." The passage describes life in the caves.
5. Chapter 13, pages 118 to 121, beginning "At ten . . ." and ending with the chapter. The passage describes the surrender.

Booktalk

Ask what the group knows about the Civil War. Show a map of the Vicksburg area.

If either side, North or South, were to win the war, it had to have Vicksburg because the Vicksburg position controlled the Mississippi River. Grant was sent to take the city. Pemberton defended it. Grant anticipated a swift victory. He was wrong. Vicksburg held out for forty-seven days. The citizens hunkered down in snake-filled, slimy caves. Constant shelling threatened instant death. The Union soldiers fatally charged impossible fortifications. And in the thick of the battle were three young people: Lucy McRae, the privileged daughter of a wealthy family; Willie Lord, the son of a minister transplanted from the North; and Fred Grant, General Grant's son. They hid, ran, fought, and lived to tell their stories *Under Siege!*

Curriculum Connections

1. (Research, social studies) Using library resources, learn more about General Grant. Share the information with the group.
2. (Research and Create, social studies) Using library resources, create a timeline of Civil War battles that features Vicksburg and Gettysburg.
3. (Research, social studies) The author suggests further sources. Choose one of those sources and share the information that you find with the group.

Related Works

1. Abnett, Dan (text), and Dheeraj Verma (illus.). **The Battle of Gettysburg: Spilled Blood on Sacred Ground.** New York: Rosen Central, 2007. 48p. (Graphic Battles of the Civil War) $29.25. ISBN-13: 978 1 4042 0777 6. [graphic] MJS, CG Gettysburg ended on the same day as the Battle for Vicksburg. The two victories secured a Northern victory.
2. Fraser, Mary Ann. **Vicksburg: The Battle That Won the Civil War.** New York: Henry Holt and Co., 1999. 100p. $16.95. ISBN 0 8050 6106 1. [nonfiction] JS, CG Fraser explains Vicksburg's geographic, economic, and emotional importance.
3. McKissack, Patricia C., and Frederick L. McKissack. **Days of Jubilee: The End of Slavery in the United States.** New York: Scholastic Press, 2003. 144p. $18.95. ISBN 0 590 10764 X. [nonfiction] MJS, JS Civil War diaries, letters, and slave narratives describe how slaves gained freedom through the Underground Railroad, rebellion, military service, the Emancipation Proclamation Act, and the Thirteenth Amendment.
4. McMullan, Margaret. **How I Found the Strong: A Novel of the Civil War.** Boston, MA: Houghton Mifflin Co., 2004. 136p. $15.00. ISBN 0 618 35008 X. [fiction] MJS, CG with high interest for boys. (*Booktalks and Beyond,* pages 210 to 213.) Ten-year-old Frank Russell stays on the Mississippi farm. His father and fourteen-year-old brother join the Confederate army. Eventually, he and his father help their slave flee North.
5. Rinaldi, Ann. **Girl in Blue.** New York: Scholastic, 2001. 320p. $15.95. ISBN 0 439 07336 7. [fiction] MJ, G (*Teen Genre Connections,* 2005, pages 149 to 151.) Fifteen-year-old Sarah Louisa leaves her abusive father to join the Union army. She becomes a respected soldier, a skilled nurse, and eventually a Pinkerton detective and spy.

Equality

ঙ্গ

Bruchac, Joseph. March toward the Thunder.
New York: Dial Books, 2008. 298p.
ISBN-13: 978 0 8037 3188 2. [fiction] MJS, CG with high interest for boys

Themes/Topics: Abenaki Indians, Civil War, Irish Brigade's Virginia Campaign, summer of 1864, conduct of life

Summary/Description

Motivated by the Union army's pledge to free the slaves and his desire for good wages, fifteen-year-old Abenaki Indian/Canadian Louis joins the Fighting 69th, an Irish Brigade known for bravery. He fights in the 1864 Virginia Campaign and encounters prejudice, friendship, and horrific war. When he is seriously wounded, his mother, a Native American healer, arrives at the Union hospital and cares for him. When healed, he contemplates rejoining the soldiers to whom he has grown close. Maps of Virginia and the Fighting 69th's progress introduce and conclude the novel. An "Author's Note" explains Bruchac's ties to the story. "The Irish Brigade" explains the Fighting 69th. The "Selected Bibliography" provides a list of the most useful sources.

Values: The story demonstrates loyalty, courage, and idealism.

Read Aloud/Reader Response

1. Chapter 5, pages 41, beginning "'Do not just look . . .'" and ending ". . . *listen to the corporal.*" Louis recalls the basic knowledge that guides him in service.
2. Chapter 10, pages 82 to 86, beginning *"Can I do this?"* and ending with the chapter. Louis meets the challenge of war, one step at a time.
3. Chapter 16, pages 122 to 126, beginning "The sergeant leaned . . ." and ending with the chapter. Sergeant Flynn explains his views on humanity.
4. Chapter 29, pages 232 to 238, beginning "Sure enough . . ." and ending with the chapter. A poor Rebel explains his views on the war.
5. Chapter 36, pages 283 to 286. In this final chapter, Louis shows that his motivation for fighting is his loyalty to his fellow soldiers.

Booktalk

Fifteen-year-old Louis isn't old enough to fight in the United State's Civil War, legally. As an Abenaki Indian from Canada, he doesn't have anything to fight about. But he can earn enough money for his mother to buy a piece of land and help one man come out from under the heel of another, so he signs up on the Union side. Louis is in the fierce Fighting 69th, the only Native American in the Irish Brigade. His nickname is Chief. He feels alone and isolated, until the fighting starts. Everyone's blood runs red. Differences of skin and background disappear. Louis fights in the Irish Brigade's bloody Virginia Campaign. The Union generals can't match Confederate skill. A Blue victory is up to the enlisted foot soldier and noncommissioned officers. Each battle makes Louis more committed. But someone's bullet has Louis's name on it in his *March toward the Thunder.*

Curriculum Connections

1. (Research, social studies) Using library sources, learn more about the Virginia Campaign of 1864. Act as a resource person for the group.
2. (Research, social studies) Louis meets significant historical figures. Learn more about one. Act as a resource person for the group.
3. (Reaction, language arts) Should Louis have served in the Fighting 69th? Be sure to use specifics from the story to support your answer.

Related Works

1. Bruchac, Joseph. **Code Talker: A Novel about the Navajo Marines of World War Two.** New York: Dial Books, 2005. 231p. ISBN 0 8037 2921 9. [fiction] MJS, CG Navajo Ned Begay tells his grandchildren about his life and service in the Navajo marine unit that led him to a military medal in World War II.
2. Haskins, Jim. **Black, Blue & Gray: African Americans in the Civil War.** New York: Simon & Shuster, 1998. 154p. $16.00. ISBN 0 689 80655 8. [nonfiction] MJS, CG Haskins details African American service in the Civil War and the higher risk black soldiers took in relation to white soldiers.
3. McMullan, Margaret. **How I Found the Strong: A Novel of the Civil War.** Boston, MA: Houghton Mifflin Co., 2004. 136p. $15.00. ISBN 0 618 35008 X. [fiction] MJS, CG with high interest for boys. (*Booktalks and Beyond,* 2007, pages 210 to 213.) Ten-year-old Frank Russell stays on the farm to safeguard family and property while his father goes to war. Eventually, they save the family slave and guide him North.
4. Paulsen, Gary. **Soldier's Heart: Being the Story of the Enlistment and Due Service of the Boy Charley Goddard in the First Minnesota Volunteers.** New York: Delacorte Press, 1998. 106p. $15.95. ISBN 0 385 32498 7. [fiction] JS, CG with high interest for boys. A young soldier enthusiastically enlists but returns home physically and emotionally wounded.
5. Severance, John B. **Braving the Fire: A Civil War Novel.** New York: Clarion, 2002. 149p. $15.00. ISBN 0 618 22999 X. [fiction] MJS, CG Fifteen-year-old Jem Bridwell from Maryland, a Civil War border state, joins the Barlow Boys to get some glory.

ௐ

Davis, Tanita S. Mare's War.

New York: Alfred A. Knopf, 2009. 343p. $16.99.
ISBN 978 0 375 85714 0. [fiction] JS, G

Themes/Topics: automobile travel; grandmothers; African Americans; U.S. Army; Women's Army Corps; World War II, 1939–1945; sisters; family life; Alabama

Summary/Description

Teenagers Octavia and Tali accompany their grandmother on a road trip where they learn about her growing up black in Alabama and serving in World War II. Threatened by her mother's boyfriend and rejected by her mother, the teenaged Marey Lee (grandmother) illegally signs up for the army. In her training and service, she develops skills, physical strength, and metal resolve that free her from her hometown and help her support and protect her younger sister. After the war, she marries, has a child, leaves her philandering husband, goes to school, builds a career, and lives with a lesbian friend she met in the army. On this road trip, she passes on her life lessons to her indulged granddaughters.

Values: Marey Lee teaches her granddaughters strength, independence, and courage.

Read Aloud/Reader Response

1. Chapter 2, pages 20 to 21, beginning "Two old women . . ." and ending ". . . *Marey Lee.*" The grandmother describes a confrontation on the bus.
2. Chapter 5, pages 37 to 41. This chapter describes confrontation with Toby.
3. Chapter 8, page 62, beginning "Live a little . . ." and ending ". . . till you try." Octavia reacts to the imperative "Live a little."
4. Chapter 12, pages 102 to 103, beginning "But I am . . ." and ending with the chapter. Marey Lee is determined to stay in the army.
5. Chapter 37, pages 327 to 332, beginning "Staff Sergeant Hill . . ." and ending with the chapter. Marey Lee confronts her mother.

Booktalk

When you see Marey Lee Boylen, you don't think grandmother. The woman drives a red sports car and wears high heels, wigs to the extreme, and push-up bras. And don't ever call her Grandma. To sisters Octavia and Tali, she is an embarrassment. They will be embarrassed big-time this summer. The girls' parents promised that just the sisters will take a road trip with grandma to a family reunion. Trapped in a car with this show-off dictator, Tali, the older, fights all the way. Octavia, the younger, tries to stay under the radar. But Grandma is ready for them both. She was practically born fighting. She held her head high in a segregated South with a mother who would have preferred not to have children. She took care of her younger sister. And then she fought in a war, World War II. She had to run away from home and lie about her age to do it, but she helped save the world and herself. She never turned back. The girls get a glimpse of that life and "Live a Little" themselves when they learn about *Mare's War.*

Curriculum Connections

1. (Research, history) Using library resources, learn more about women's service in World War II. Act as a resource person for the group.
2. (React, language arts) What was the most surprising part of Marey Lee's story? Compare your reaction with others in the group.
3. (Discuss, language arts) Using library resources, learn more about discrimination against African Americans during the 1930s and 1940s. Share the information with the group.

Related Works

1. Bradley, Kimberly Brubaker. **For Freedom: The Story of a French Spy.** New York: Delacorte Press, 2003. 181p. $17.99. ISBN 0 385 90087 2. [fiction] MJ, G (*Booktalks and Beyond,* 2007, pages 123 to 125.) In 1942, Suzanne Good becomes a spy for the French Resistance.
2. Connolly, John. **The Book of Lost Things.** New York: Atria Books, 2006. 339p. $23.00. ISBN-13: 978 7432 9885 8. [fiction] S/A, CG (*Genre Talks for Teens,* 2009, pages 220 to 222.) Knocked unconscious in a German air raid, a young British boy has a coming-of-age experience with fantasy characters.
3. Hostetter, Joyce Moyer. **Blue.** Honesdale, PA: Calkins Creek Books, 2006. 193p. $16.95. ISBN-13: 978 1 59078 389 4. [fiction] MJS, G (*Genre Talks for Teens,* 2009, pages 225 to 227.) Thirteen-year-old Ann Fay Honeycutt becomes the man of the house when her father serves in World War II but fights her own battles against polio and prejudice.

4. Mosher, Richard. **Zazoo.** New York: Clarion, 2001. 248p. $16.00. ISBN 0 618 13534 0. [fiction] MJS, CG (*Teen Genre Connections, 2005*, pages 262 to 264.) Zazoo, a Vietnamese orphan, learns about her adopted French grandfather's role in the French Resistance during World War II.
5. Whelan, Gloria. **Summer of the War.** New York: HarperCollins Children's Books, 2006. 176p. $15.99. ISBN-13: 978 0 06 008072 3. [fiction] MJ, G (*Genre Talks for Teens*, 2009, pages 238 to 240.) Fourteen-year-old Mirabelle conflicts with her sophisticated cousin when they spend the summer of 1942 with her grandparents in the upper Great Lakes.

ᘓᘔ

Frost, Helen. **Crossing Stones.**
New York: Farrar, Straus and Giroux, 2009. 184p. $16.99.
ISBN-13: 978 0 374 31653 2. [novel in verse] JS, CG with high interest for girls

Themes/Topics: World War I, women's rights, family, love, coming of age

Summary/Description

In a series of poems structured in the shapes of stones and water, four friends react to events from April 1917 to January 1918. Muriel, the main speaker, seeks a single, independent life. Frank, who loves her, fights in France and dies. Ollie, Muriel's brother, lies about his age, fights in France, and loses his arm. Emma, Frank's sister, wants a domestic life with Ollie. The four young people come from two families that are separated by a stream filled with crossing stones. Muriel is conflicted over her feelings for Frank and her resentment about the assumption that she will marry him and stay in the area. As they exchange letters while he is overseas, his thinking changes; she grows closer to him and then loses him. Ollie, wounded and suffering post-traumatic stress, finds love with Emily. Muriel joins her suffragette aunt in Washington, D.C., who works for women's rights and social justice.

Values: The four young people demonstrate commitment, self-respect, and independence.

Read Aloud/Reader Response

The entire book is an excellent read aloud. The suggestions below focus heavily on Muriel.

1. "Moral Compass," pages 9 to 10. Muriel is brought to task for challenging the war and questions why women should reserve their judgments.
2. "Socks," pages 14 to 15. Muriel claims the right to plan her own life.
3. "A Greater Good," pages 20 to 21. Muriel graduates.
4. "Rocking," pages 34 to 35. Muriel's mother assesses her.
5. "I Can See Myself," page 159. Emma compares herself to Muriel and concludes that staying home and building a family requires "pluck" also.

Booktalk

Muriel is about to graduate from high school, and World War I is exploding her peaceful life. The boy to whom she feels the closest is about to help fight it. That bothers Muriel, but it bothers her more that her family thinks that they will marry and settle down. Then Muriel will keep house the rest of her life. Can people plan another person's life? Her government and family seem to be saying yes. Muriel says no. Then cryptic messages come from her wild aunt, a single woman making big changes in Washington. Should Muriel join her, or will she have to save her? Yes, Muriel is about to graduate, but not just from high school. The lessons taught by war, grief, and social change are about to graduate Muriel and the three young people she has been closest to all her life from childhood into adulthood. Talking is one thing. Walking the walk is different, and to make it over a restless stream of life, all four will navigate slippery *Crossing Stones*.

Curriculum Connections

1. (Research, social studies) Using library resources, learn more about the women's suffrage movement of the early twentieth century. Act as a resource person for the group.
2. (Research, social studies) Using library resources, learn why World War I was a pivotal war for the United States. Act as a resource person for the group.
3. (Research and Discuss, language arts, social studies) "In the Doorway," page 151, uses two quotations from *Anne of Green Gables*. Why are these quotations significant to the story and to Muriel's life? Be sure that before the discussion you research the origin of "God's in his heaven, all's right with the world."

Related Works

1. Adams, Colleen. **Women's Suffrage: A Primary Source History of the Women's Rights Movement in America.** New York: Rosen Central/Primary Source, 2003. 64p. (Primary Sources in American History). $29.25. ISBN 0 8239 3685 6. [nonfiction] JS, CG Original documents, pictures, and explanatory narrative present the women's rights cause of primarily the late nineteenth and early twentieth centuries.

2. Morpurgo, Michael. **Private Peaceful.** New York: Scholastic Press, 2003. 202p. $16.95. ISBN 0 439 63648 5. [fiction] JS, CG with high interest for boys. Private Peaceful waits for his older brother to be executed and reviews how they came to this point.

3. Murphy, Jim. **Truce.** New York: Scholastic Press, 2009. 128p. $19.99. ISBN-13: 978 0 545 13049 3. [nonfiction] MJS, CG Murphy explains the lies and ambitions that launched World War I and how the truce declared at Christmas of 1914 illustrates the humanity of European troops. He refers to the mud that became part of Ollie's trauma.

4. Remarque, Erich Maria. **All Quiet on the Western Front.** New York: Fawcett Crest, 1975. 296p. $4.95pa. ISBN 0 449 21394 3. [fiction] S/A A young German soldier, pressured to go to war and disillusioned by what he sees, tells this anti-war story, set in World War I and first published in 1928.

5. Spillebeen, Geert (text), and Terese Edelstein (trans.). **Kipling's Choice.** Boston, MA: Houghton Mifflin Co., 2005. 160p. $16.00. ISBN 0 618 43124 1. [fiction] JS, CG (*Booktalks and Beyond,* 2007, pages 213 to 215.) As eighteen-year-old John Kipling dies, he and the reader review his privileged but demanding life as the son of Rudyard Kipling, England's poet laureate whose work extolled risk and patriotism.

❧❧

Gratz, Alan. The Brooklyn Nine: A Novel in Nine Innings.

New York: Dial Books, 2009. 299p. $16.99.
ISBN-13: 978 0 8037 3224 7. [fiction] JS, CG

Themes/Topics: baseball, immigration, New York, Civil War, vaudeville, discrimination, World War II, Cold War, perfectionism, U.S. history

Summary/Description

Nine short stories ranging from 1845 to 2002 chronicle the lives of the Schneider/Snider/Flint family. Ten-year-old German Felix Schneider comes to the United States as a stowaway. Helping a volunteer fire department baseball team put out the Manhattan fire, he burns his legs and loses his job as a delivery runner in the garment district. He becomes a tailor, sews a baseball, and passes it to his son. The son carries the ball to the Civil War and exchanges it for a homemade Confederate bat. In 1864, Arnold Schneider loses the bat to a drunken baseball hero. The Schneider name changes to Snider when the father of feisty Walter Snider faces anti-Semitism. Walter sees similar discrimination against black players and gives up on the Dodgers. Walter's math-wiz daughter, a numbers runner, manipulates baseball bets to help her exploited customers. Her daughter, Kat, stars in the All-American Girls Baseball League. Kat's son endures bullies, Sputnik, and the Dodgers leaving Brooklyn. His son, Michael, is suddenly pitching a perfect Little League game, and Michael's son Snider, working in his uncle's antique store, is drawn into the story of a handmade baseball. The "Author's Note" provides a brief historical sketch for each story.

Values: The family hands down a tradition of fairness, tolerance, and hard work.

Read Aloud/Reader Response

1. "First Inning: Play Ball," pages 10 to 11, beginning "Felix ran . . ." and ending ". . . young city." The paragraph describes Broadway, the *American* New York.

2. "Fourth Inning: The Way Things Are Now," pages 128 to 132, beginning "The reaction . . ." and ending with the chapter. Brooklyn players abuse a black player.

3. "Fifth Inning: The Numbers Game," pages 144 to 150, beginning with section 2, and ending ". . . *have* to add that!" Frankie meets John Kieran.

4. "Sixth Inning: Notes of a Star to Be," pages181 to 182, beginning "Um, hi . . ." and ending ". . . this forever." Kat talks about war changing women's roles.

5. "Ninth Inning: Provenance," pages 293 to 299, beginning "Mr. McNamara . . ." and ending with the chapter. In ignorance, Snider and Dave sell the family memorabilia, but Snider keeps the original ball.

Booktalk

Hold up a baseball. Ask what it is.

Everybody recognizes a baseball. People go to stadiums and root for players who make more in a year than most fans make in their lifetimes. Why? Maybe the game is in America's blood. Parents, grandparents, and great-grandparents talk about where they were when a home run won the game or a double play lost it. But baseball is a bigger than family fun, memories, or money. It wasn't always professional or such a spectator sport. It helped make foreigners Americans, and discriminated against American citizens. It advanced civil rights, and helped us face war and fears. In nine innings, Alan Gratz shows us what baseball taught us about playing fair. He tells a family's story, nine generations of baseball, in *The Brooklyn Nine*.

Curriculum Connections

1. (Research, social studies) Using library resources, learn more about the organization of professional baseball. Share the information with the group.
2. (Research, social studies) Using library resources, choose the time period setting of one story. Find out more about that period. Share the information with the group.
3. (React, language arts) Which story was your favorite? Explain why.

Related Works

1. Bartoletti, Susan. **No Man's Land: A Young Soldier's Story.** New York: The Blue Sky Press, 1999. $15.95. 169p. ISBN 0 0590 38371 X. [fiction] MJS, CG with high interest for boys. (*Booktalks Plus*, 2001, pages 37 to 39.) Fourteen-year-old Thrasher Magee joins the Confederate army and discovers that baseball and food can silence guns.
2. Giff, Patricia Reilly. **All the Way Home.** New York: Dell Yearling, 2001. 169p. $5.99pa. ISBN 0 440 41182 3. [fiction] MJ, G Eleven-year-old Mariel lives a few blocks from Ebbets Field with her "almost mother" Loretta and learns about faith and love.
3. Hopkinson, Deborah. **Shutting out the Sky: Life in the Tenements of New York 1880–1924.** New York: Scholastic, Orchard Books, 2003. 134p. $17.95. ISBN 0 439 37590 8. [nonfiction] MJS, CG This volume illustrates the living conditions in the tenements of New York. A picture of a tenement baseball game appears on page 75.

4. Lupica, Mike. **Heat.** New York: Puffin Books, 2006. 220p. $6.99pa.
    ISBN-13: 978 0 14 240757 8. [fiction] MJ, CG with high interest for
    boys. (*Genre Talks for Teens,* 2009, pages 79 to 81.) Twelve-year-old
    Michael Arroyo's unusual height and strong pitching skills threaten
    his Little League eligibility and U.S. residency.
5. Nelson, Kadir. **We Are the Ship: The Story of Negro League
    Baseball.** New York: Hyperion/Jump at the Sun, 2008. 96p. $18.99.
    ISBN-13: 978 0 7868 0832 8. [nonfiction] MJS/A, CG with high
    interest for boys. (*Genre Talks for Teens,* 2009, pages 252 to 255.)
    Nine innings (chapters) and spectacular pictures show the glamour
    and grit of the Negro League.

ტ̶ო̶

Hesse, Karen. **Brooklyn Bridge.**
New York: Feiwel and Friends, 2008. 229p. $17.95.
ISBN-13: 978 0 312 37886 8. [fiction] MJS, CG

Themes/Topics: coming of age, family life, Brooklyn, teddy
bears, social class, homeless persons, immigrants, Russian
American Jews, 1903

Summary/Description

Fourteen-year-old Joseph Michtom lives in Brooklyn, New York,
during the early 20th century. His father and mother, Russian immigrants, are consumed by their invention, the teddy bear, while Joseph
laments the lack of family time and fantasizes about a trip to Coney
Island. Interacting with siblings, aunts, uncles, and neighbors, he uncovers
family secrets and learns everyone has talents and limitations. Eventually,
the mother and father share their prosperity not only with the family but
also with the guests at the wedding of Joseph's uncle. They take everyone
to Coney Island. Here, Joseph discovers another uncle in hiding and the
truth behind his cousin's death, which he feared that he had caused. In
contrast to the prosperous Michtom family, a series of sketches outlines
the bleak lives of homeless children under the Brooklyn Bridge.

Values: Joseph learns the importance of family, generosity, forgive-
ness, and hard work.

Read Aloud/Reader Response

The sketches of life under the Brooklyn Bridge would be an effective
dramatic reading.

1. Chapter 2, page 19, beginning "What Mama didn't . . ." and ending ". . . the lucky break." Joe explains how prosperity separates him from his former life.
2. Chapter 5, pages 57 to 65. In this chapter, Joe's aunt, the Queen, dies.
3. Chapter 9, pages 100 to 101, beginning "Lizzie Kaplan spoke so softly . . ." and ending ". . . nothing about Coney Island." Lizzie Kaplan tells how the Queen saved her life.
4. Chapter 14, pages 129 to 132. In this chapter, Joe helps Jake realize the American dream.
5. Chapter 26, pages 224 to 225. In this final chapter, Joe reflects on luck.

Booktalk

Fourteen-year-old Joe Michtom lives in Brooklyn. The year is 1903. His mother and father, Russian Jewish immigrants, just invented the teddy bear. Now, Joe's life is all about cutting and sorting bear parts, or wrapping and mailing finished bears. The rest of the time, he complains and fights with his parents. Their American dream is his nightmare. Joe wants to leave the bears and see Coney Island's glitter. He misses his mother, father, and the way the family used to be. But if Joe is unhappy with his luck, he should look at the unlucky. He meets a few: his neighbor who had his head smashed in before coming to America and his aunt who will never understand love. Then there is the homeless world. Joe is part of that world too. Poor, swindled, and abused children live there at night. Their families are hunger, cold, fear, and death. They all live together— under the *Brooklyn Bridge.*

Curriculum Connections

1. (Research, social studies) Using library resources, learn more about New York at the turn of the century. Act as a resource person for the group.
2. (Research, social studies) Using library resources, learn more about the teddy bear and the man who inspired it. Act as a resource person for the group.
3. (Discuss, language arts) Why do you think that Hesse combined the Brooklyn Bridge stories with Joe's?

Related Works

1. Brown, Don. **The Notorious Izzy Fink.** New Milford, CN: Roaring Brook Press/A Deborah Brodie Book, 2006. 150p. $16.95.

ISBN 1 59643 139 3. [fiction] MJ, CG, with high interest for boys. Irish/Jewish Sam Glodsky stands up to the Russian Izzy Fink when both thirteen-year-olds hire on to work for a local gangster.

2. Hopkinson, Deborah. **Shutting out the Sky: Life in the Tenements of New York 1880–1924.** New York: Scholastic/ Orchard Books, 2003. 134p. $17.95. ISBN 0 439 37590 8. [nonfiction] MJS, CG Personal stories of courageous young residents illustrate living conditions in New York tenements.

3. Karr, Kathleen. **The Boxer.** New York: Farrar, Straus and Giroux, 2000. 169p. $16.00. ISBN 0 374 30921 3. [fiction] MJ, CG with high appeal for boys. (*Booktalks and More,* 2003, pages 128 to 130.) Fifteen-year-old John Aloysius Xavier Woods becomes a boxer in New York's Lower East Side during the late nineteenth century to help support his mother and five brothers and sisters.

4. Newton, Robert. **Runner.** New York: Alfred A. Knopf, 2007. 201p. $18.99. ISBN-13: 978 0 375 93744 6. [fiction] MJ, CG with high interest for boys. (*Genre Talks for Teens,* 2009, pages 230 to 233.) In 1919, fifteen-year-old Charlie Feehan works for a crime boss so that he can support his newly widowed mother and baby brother.

5. Peck, Richard. **The Teacher's Funeral: A Comedy in Three Parts.** New York: Dial Books, 2004. 190p. $16.99. ISBN 0 8037 2736 4. [fiction] JS, CG (*Booktalks and Beyond,* 2007, pages 202 to 204.) This early-twentieth-century story explores a young man's coming of age in a one-room country school.

Leadership

ෆ෨

Bruchac, Joseph. **Jim Thorpe: Original All-American.**

New York: Dial Books/Walden Media, 2006. 276p.
ISBN 0 8037 3118 3. [biographical novel] JS, B

Themes/Topics: sports hero, amateur status, education and sports, Native American life, racism, stereotyping

Summary/Description

After Jim Thorpe runs away from several Indian schools, his father sends him to the Carlisle Indian School in Pennsylvania, as far as possible from the Sac and Fox Reservation. Under the guidance of Pop Warner, the school coach, he becomes a privileged member of the Carlisle track and field, football, and baseball teams. In spite of prejudice, family problems, differences in culture, and exploitation, Thorpe represents the United States in the 1912 Olympics. He loses his awards and medals because, at one point, he was paid to play baseball for a non-school team. The public outcry does not restore Thorpe's Olympic status, but he signs with professional teams, marries his school sweetheart, and helps found the National Football League (NFL). An author's note explains Thorpe's post-Carlisle life and provides a bibliography.

Values: Jim Thorpe's life illustrates courage, determination, and fairness.

Read Aloud/Reader Response

1. Chapter 13, pages 67 to 72, beginning "There's one more . . ." and ending with the chapter. The Hopis surprise the coach and inspire Thorpe.
2. Chapter 16, pages 84 to 88, beginning "Joining the football . . ." and ending with the chapter. Thorpe joins the football team.
3. Chapter 30, pages 183 to 184, beginning "Some of the stories . . ." and ending with the chapter. Thorpe gives an example of the racist press.
4. Chapter 34, pages 210 to 212, beginning "Our names . . ." and ending with the chapter. Thorpe describes the ironies of his Olympic experience.
5. Chapter 37, pages 239 to 241, beginning "For Pop Warner . . ." and ending "'could do it better.'" Carlisle defeats Army, and Thorpe receives the credit from Army player Dwight Eisenhower.

Booktalk

Show the book's cover. Ask the group to share their knowledge of Jim Thorpe.

The Jim Thorpe Trophy for the NFL Most Valuable Player was instituted in 1954, a year after Jim Thorpe died. The Pennsylvania town where he was buried was named after him. He may be the greatest athlete in the first part of the twentieth century. To Native Americans, Thorpe is a warrior and leader as great as Black Hawk and Crazy Horse. Thorpe was born on a reservation. He played for Carlisle, a small Indian school where countless students were abused and died. He won Olympic medals before he was allowed to be a U.S. citizen. He overcame loneliness, grief, poverty, prejudice, and disgrace. But he always remembered what he learned in the Carlisle Indian School, "Keep a-goin'." He did. That made him a hero. That made him *Jim Thorpe: Original All-American.*

Curriculum Connections

1. (Research, social studies) Using library resources, learn more about the Carlisle School. Share the information with the group.
2. (Discuss, language arts, social studies) Does the Thorpe story change the meaning of *All-American* for you?
3. (Create, language arts, art) Rewrite one of the book's scenes in graphic format.

Related Works

1. Alexie, Sherman (text), and Ellen Forney (illus.). **The Absolutely True Diary of a Part-Time Indian.** New York: Little, Brown & Co., 2007. 228p. $16.99. ISBN-13: 978 0 316 01368 0. [fiction] JS, CG with high interest for boys. (*Genre Talks for Teens,* 2009, pages 269 to 272.) Intellectually gifted but physically challenged Arnold Spirit leaves the reservation school to attend the more prosperous white school.
2. Bruchac, Joseph. **Code Talker: A Novel about the Navajo Marines of World War Two.** New York: Dial Books, 2005. 231p. $16.99. ISBN 0 8037 2921 9. [fiction] MJS, CG with high interest for boys. In this novel about the heroic Navajos in World War II, Bruchac includes the prejudice encountered at the white man's school.
3. Bruchac, Joseph. **Geronimo.** New York: Scholastic Press, 2006. 384p. $16.99. ISBN 0 439 35360 2. [fiction] MJS, CG with high interest for boys. (*Genre Talks for Teens,* 2009, pages 243 to 246.) Willie, Geronimo's adopted grandson, tells the story of the eighty-year-old Geronimo.
4. Bruchac, Joseph. **Wabi: A Hero's Tale.** New York: Dial Books, 2006. 198p. $16.99. ISBN 0 8037 3098 5. [fiction] MJS, CG (*Genre Talks for Teens,* 2009, pages 189 to 191.) In this Abenaki story, a weak owl with unusual powers becomes human, an winning athlete, and an outstanding warrior.
5. Carvell, Marlene. **Sweetgrass Basket.** New York: Dutton Children's Books, 2005. 243p. $16.99. ISBN 0 525 47547 8. [novel, poetry] JS, G. (*Booktalks and Beyond,* 2007, pages 244 to 246.) Sent to the Carlisle Indian Industrial School in 1879 after their mother's death, Mattie and Sarah Tarbell encounter cruelty, prejudice, and ignorance.

CꙄꙄ

Heiligman, Deborah. **Charles and Emma: The Darwins' Leap of Faith.**

New York: Henry Holt and Co., 2009. 268p. $18.95.
ISBN-13: 978 0 8050 8721 5. [nonfiction] JS, CG

Themes/Topics: Charles Darwin, Emma Wedgwood, naturalists, family life, nineteenth century

Summary/Description

Starting with Darwin's debate over whether to marry, Heiligman traces Charles's intellectual journey, grounded in love and honesty, which allowed him to find a remarkable wife, nurture ten children, and challenge the spiritual, intellectual, and eventually economic status quo. Heiligman emphasizes the couples' great devotion in spite of the differences between their religious beliefs as they deal with a lively family, the death of three children, Charles's frail health, and the controversy concerning his work. A photo section provides a visual context for the family. A family tree shows the blending of the Darwin and Wedgwood families. Source notes accompany each chapter. An extensive "Selected Bibliography" includes the literary works alluded to as well as the primary and secondary sources consulted, including the two Web sites central to the research. An index allows easy access to the material.

Values: The Darwins' love, tolerance, diligence, and commitment allowed them to achieve a happy marriage and Darwin to realize an outstanding career.

Read Aloud/Reader Response

1. Chapter 1, pages 5 to 16. In this chapter, Darwin lists the pros and cons of marriage.
2. Chapter 10, pages 71 to 72, beginning "Emma knew . . ." and ending "'. . . are so guilty.'" Charles takes a stand on slavery.
3. Chapter 13, pages 90 to 93, beginning with the chapter and ending ". . . in real life." Charles and Emma settle into marriage.
4. Chapter 23, pages 162 to 165, beginning "Charles was a . . ." and ending with the chapter. The passage describes the Darwin household.
5. Chapter 26, pages 180 to 186. The chapter shows how Emma helped Darwin clarify and present his theory.

Booktalk

Ask what the group knows about Charles Darwin.

Often, we think of Darwin as a severe man bold enough to tell people that their ancestors were monkeys. Not so. The real Darwin was sensitive, thoughtful, and honest. And that monkey thing was kind of a negative spin. Darwin loved an ordered world. He wanted a traditional family and chose an intelligent wife who birthed their ten children and helped him to birth his books, especially the world-altering *On the Origin of Species*. Were they alike? Somewhat. Did they agree? On some things. But one of the best parts of their relationship was their agreement to disagree and respect their differences. Emma believed in a Bible-based, traditional religion. Darwin did not. Some said that difference would destroy their family and separate them for eternity. They took that chance. Here is their most unusual, or maybe usual, story, *Charles and Emma: The Darwins' Leap of Faith*.

Curriculum Connections

1. (Research, social studies, science) Using library resources, learn more about Darwin's work. Share your information with the class.
2. (Research and Analysis, social studies, language arts, science) Choose one source listed in Heiligman's "Selected Bibliography," read or examine it, and share it with the group.
3. (Discuss, language arts) What surprised you about the Darwins?

Related Works

1. Hoose, Phillip. **The Race to Save the Lord God Bird.** New York: Farrar, Straus and Giroux/Melanie Kroupa Books, 2004. 196p. $20.00. ISBN 0 374 36173 8. [nonfiction] JS, CG (*Booktalks and Beyond*, 2007, pages 100 to 102.) This narrative about the Lord God Bird begins in 1809 with specimen hunters shooting birds to study them.
2. Larson, Gary. **There's a Hair in My Dirt: A Worm's Story.** New York: HarperCollins Publishers, 1998. 59p. $15.95. ISBN 0-06-019104-X. [fiction, illustrated fable] MJS, CG Hearing the story of a fair young maiden's romantic tour through the forest, a young worm learns the importance of his life within survival of the fittest.
3. McClafferty, Carla Killough. **Something Out of Nothing: Marie Curie and Radium.** New York: Farar, Straus and Giroux, 2006. 134p. $18.00. ISBN 0 374 38036 6. [nonfiction] MJS, CG (*Booktalks and Beyond*, 2007, pages 223 to 225.) Working against the establish-

ment but with keen observation and her husband's support, Marie Curie makes a world-changing discovery.

4. Schanzer, Rosalyn. **What Darwin Saw: The Journey That Changed the World**. Washington, DC: National Geographic, 2009. 48p. $17.95. ISBN 978 1 4263 0396 8. [nonfiction] MJ, CG Combining whimsical illustration, original quotations, and engaging narrative, Schanzer chronicles the four-year-plus journey of the *Beagle*.

5. Stewart, Melissa. **Life without Light: A Journey to Earth's Dark Ecosystems.** New York: Franklin Watts, 1999. 128p. $22.00. ISBN 0 531 11529 1. [nonfiction] MJS, CG (*Booktalks and More,* 2003, pages 240 to 241.) Man's descended to the ocean floor and discovered creatures adapted to chemosynthesis.

☙❧

Hoose, Phillip. Claudette Colvin: Twice toward Justice.

New York: Farrar, Straus and Giroux/Melanie Kroupa Books, 2009. 133p. $19.95.
ISBN-13: 978 0 374 31322 7. [nonfiction] MJS, CG with high interest for girls

Themes/Topics: civil rights; African Americans; Montgomery, Alabama; segregation; bus boycotts; *Browder v. Gayle;* 1955–1956

Summary/Description

With narrative and personal interviews, Hoose describes Claudette Colvin's life in relation to the mid-1950s Montgomery civil rights movement. Colvin, a high school junior, refused to give up her bus seat to a white woman in Montgomery, Alabama, before the Rosa Parks incident. Colvin's action spurred the Montgomery bus boycott. Because of her family's poverty, Colvin's age, and rumors of instability, the NAACP chose Parks as the face of their resistance. In *Browder v. Gayle,* the "landmark busing case," Colvin agreed to testify but, after the trial, was ignored or vilified as an unstable, single, teenage mother. Hoose combines narrative, photographs, personal interviews, sidebars, and source notes. His bibliography includes books, articles, and Web sites. An index provides easy access to information.

Values: Colvin demonstrates courage, integrity, and humility.

Read Aloud/Reader Response

1. Chapter 3, pages 23 to 24, beginning "Jeremiah Reeves's arrest . . ." and ending ". . . for a long time." Claudette explains why the Reeves case was important.

2. Chapter 3, pages 25 to 27, beginning "Miss Geraldine Nesbitt . . ." and ending with the chapter. Claudette explains the importance of this teacher in her life.
3. Chapter 5, page 45, beginning "Now I was . . ." and ending with the chapter. Claudette explains the personal implications of her decision not to move on the bus.
4. Chapter 6, page 52, beginning "I only went . . ." and ending ". . . bored with it." Claudette explains her relationship with Rosa Parks.
5. Chapter 8, pages 74 to 75, beginning "We talked to all . . ." and ending with the chapter. Claudette talks about her baby and her resolve to testify in the trial.

Booktalk

Invite people in the group to share what they know about Martin Luther King or Rosa Parks. Ask how many have heard of Claudette Colvin.

Rosa Parks gets credit for ending segregation on busses in Montgomery, Alabama, in the 1950s, but Claudette Colvin, a junior in high school, made an earlier, louder protest. She risked beatings, jail, and death and was ignored by the nation and the people she helped. Why isn't her name in the history books? Being a poor teenager is just part of the reason. Phillip Hoose knew Claudette's story was worth telling. It is a story about personal trouble and strength in a time of national crisis. It is for everyone who has done the right thing and been wronged because of it. This teenager believed that she could make a difference and did: *Claudette Colvin: Twice toward Justice.*

Curriculum Connections

1. (Research, social studies, language arts) Read quotations introducing the parts and chapters. Choose one. Using library resources, learn about the speaker. Share your information with the group.
2. (Discuss, social studies) How does Colvin's story affect your view of the civil rights movement?
3. (Discuss, language arts and social studies) Describe Claudette Colvin's character.

Related Works

1. Fradin, Dennis Brindell, and Judith Bloom Fradin. **Fight On! Mary Church Terrell's Battle for Integration.** New York: Clarion Books, 2003. 181p. $17.00. ISBN 0 618 13349 6. [nonfiction] MJS, CG Born during the Civil War, Terrell experienced her

parents' divorce, excellent educational opportunities, and the stings of discrimination.

2. Fradin, Dennis Brindell, and Judith Bloom Fradin. **Ida B. Wells: Mother of the Civil Rights Movement.** New York: Clarion Books, 2000. 178p. $18.00. ISBN 0 395 89898 6. [nonfiction] MJS, CG (*Booktalks and More,* 2003, pages 249 to 252.) Born a slave in 1862, Ida B. Wells became one of the first African American investigative reporters. She was a lifelong civil rights activist.

3. Kidd, Sue Monk. **The Secret Life of Bees.** New York: Penguin Books, 2002. 302p. $14.00. ISBN 0 14 200174 0. [fiction] S/A, G (*Booktalks and Beyond,* 2007, pages 196 to 199.) In 1964, fourteen-year-old Lily Owens runs away with her African American nanny who is arrested and beaten for trying to vote and stands up to her abusive father.

4. Lee, Harper. **To Kill a Mockingbird.** New York: HarperCollins/ Perennial Classics, 2002. 323p. $11.95. ISBN 0 06 093546 4. [fiction] JS, CG A child of the Depression sees her father defend an African American accused of raping a white woman. The novel was written in 1960, received the Pulitzer Prize in 1961, and became a movie in 1962.

5. Shone, Rob (text), and Nick Spender (illus.). **Rosa Parks: The Life of a Civil Rights Heroine.** New York: The Rosen Publishing Group/Rosen Central, 2007. 47p. (Graphic Biographies) $29.95. ISBN-13: 978 1 4042 0864 3. [graphic] MJS, CG Shone depicts Rosa Parks in the context of the civil rights movement. Claudette Colvin appears on page 16. Fred Gray appears on page 17.

 C҉Ͽ

Sandler, Martin W. **Lincoln through the Lens: How Photography Revealed and Shaped an Extraordinary Life.**

New York: Walker & Co., 2008. 97p. $19.99.
ISBN-13: 978 0 8027 9666 0. [nonfiction] MJS, CG

Themes/Topics: Lincoln, photography, portraits, Civil War

Summary/Description

Sandler demonstrates how photography enhanced Lincoln's career and legacy. Every other page of the book presents a large photograph or illustration of a central image or person in Lincoln's life.

Supplementary images appear on the opposite pages. A Lincoln quotation introduces each two-page section up to the assassination. Then the focus shifts to his killers, the controversy about photographs of his dying and death, and the memorials erected for the protection of his remains and honor to his memory. "Places to Visit" lists museums, historic sites, and Web sites. "Further Reading and Surfing" cites additional young adult books about Lincoln and his times as well as Web sites. Sources for information and quotations and an index are included.

Values: Lincoln's life demonstrates diligence, integrity, humility, curiosity, tolerance, determination, honesty, commitment, sincerity, compassion, and sacrifice.

Read Aloud/Reader Response

1. "Introduction," page 2. The text is an overview of Lincoln's life.
2. The introductory quotation of each section, beginning with page 4 and ending on page 74, represents a significant character trait or value of Lincoln.
3. "Humble Beginnings," page 12. The text illustrates Lincoln's goal of self-education.
4. "A Turning Point," page 16. The text describes Lincoln's trip to New Orleans where he witnessed the slave markets.
5. "The Miracle of History," page 92. The text comments on how Lincoln's character and leadership, through his words and the words of those around him, lived after him.

Booktalk

President Obama won an election with new technology that communicated his story and vision to the public. When we look at this man (*Hold up the book and show the front and back covers*), a hero of President Obama's, we don't think high tech. Yet the high tech of his time, the camera, propelled him into the White House and into history. He was the most photographed person of the period. (*Show page 8.*) These are just a few of those pictures. (*Keep turning the pages as you speak.*) That same technology allowed the war that began and ended during his presidency, the Civil War, to be seen by the world. It glimpsed the evils of slavery and revealed the slaughter of battle. It even brought a swifter end to the men who killed Lincoln. Generations know the life, times, death, and legend of *Lincoln through the Lens*.

Curriculum Connections

1. (Research, photography) Using library resources, learn more about the works of Mathew B. Brady. Organize a presentation of Brady's work and his assistants' work.
2. (Research, photography) Using library resources, learn more about how an official presidential photographer enhanced a president's image. Organize a presentation.
3. (Research, social studies, language arts) Choose one of the selections from "Further Reading and Surfing." Review it, and present it to the group.

Related Works

1. Blackwood, Gary. **Second Sight.** New York: Dutton's Children's Books, 2005. 279p. $16.99. ISBN 0 525 47481 1. [fiction] MJS, CG In this alternative history, one of Booth's associates loses his courage, and Lincoln lives.
2. Burchard, Peter. **Lincoln and Slavery.** New York: Atheneum Books for Young Readers, 1999. 196p. $17.00. ISBN 0 689 81570 0. [nonfiction] MJS, CG (*Booktalks and More,* 2003, pages 252 to 254.) Burchard traces Lincoln's intellectual and political journeys to the Emancipation Proclamation.
3. Fradin, Dennis Brindell. **Bound for the North Star: True Stories of Fugitive Slaves.** New York: Clarion Books, 2000. 205p. $20.00. ISBN 0 395 97017 2. [nonfiction] MJS, CG (*Teen Genre Connections,* 2005, pages 30 to 33.) First-person accounts of Mary Prince, Eliza Harris, Henry "Box" Brown, and Harriet Tubman outline the horrors of slavery and the heroic efforts to escape it.
4. Stowe, Harriet Beecher. **Uncle Tom's Cabin or Life Among the Lowly.** Pleasantville, NY: The Reader's Digest Association, 1991. 416p. $20.00. ISBN 0 89577 367 8. [fiction] S/A Written in 1852 and published again in the 1960s during the civil rights movement, this novel describes why even the most positive slave/owner relationships are evil. The "Afterword" by Alfred Kazin points out that negative stereotypes about the book come from post–Civil War dramatizations rather than from the book itself.
5. Swanson, James. **Chasing Lincoln's Killer.** (Problem Solving/ Conscience, pages 118 to 121.) Beginning with a brief explanation of the Civil War and how it affected Washington, D.C., immediately after the war, Swanson begins his fast-moving narrative with a description of the inaugural address that inspires Booth to shoot Lincoln.

ᘓᘔ

Weatherford, Carole Boston. Floyd Cooper (art). **Becoming Billie Holiday.**

Honesdale, PA: Boyds Mills Press/Wordsong, 2008. 117p. $19.95.
ISBN-13: 978 1 59078 507 2. [fictional verse memoir] JS, CG

Themes/Topics: jazz, Harlem, 1920s and 1930s, prejudice

Summary/Description

Using Billie Holiday song titles for each poem, Weatherford creates a fictional memoir of Holiday's childhood and young adulthood. Born Eleanora Fagan, Holiday, the speaker, recalls her dysfunctional family life, delinquent behavior, battles with racial prejudice, and discovery of jazz through which she created the Billie Holiday identity. The novel's art work highlights her conflicts. Two pages of brief biographies describe famous persons mentioned in the poems. An "Afterword" explains the author's journey to the book. A list of references and suggestions for further reading and listening are springboards to more information.

Values: Holiday's life is a combination of creativity, persistence, and courage.

Read Aloud/Reader Response

The entire book would make a strong dramatic presentation with readers of various ages reading the parts. Some of the material requires a mature audience.

1. "Ghost of Yesterday," page 25. Eleanora tells about her grandmother.
2. "God Bless the Child," page 30. Eleanora recalls her second baptism.
3. "Ain't Nobody's Business if I Do," page 45. Eleanora talks about her attitude at eleven.
4. "I'm in a Low Down Groove," page 90. Billie tells about her relationship with the blues.
5. "I Don't Know if I'm Coming or Going," pages 102 to 103. Billie tells about her relationship with the Artie Shaw band and their confrontation with racism.

Booktalk

Has anyone here ever heard of Billie Holiday? (*Give time for answers. If there are no answers, play a few of her songs if possible.*) That is what

Billie Holiday sounded like. She was born Eleanora Fagan in 1915 to a single mother and became one of the great ladies of jazz like Ella Fitzgerald, Sarah Vaughan, and Dinah Washington. Billie Holiday did more than sing the blues, she lived them: desertion, poverty, racism, delinquency, and drug abuse. (*Read "Left Alone," page 19; "Gloomy Sunday", page 28; "Ain't Nobody's Business if I Do," page 45; or "Do You Know What It Means to Miss New Orleans?" page 100.*) The titles of these poems are the titles of the songs she sang. Suffering created her voice. If you have never heard of her, this book is a great introduction. If you love her music, you will want to know more about her life. Read the verses. Look at the pictures. (*Show some of the illustrations as you are speaking.*) Then you will know a little about *Becoming Billie Holiday.*

Curriculum Connections

1. (Research, social studies, language arts) Using library resources, learn more about at least one of the people cited in the biographies on pages 114 to 115. Share your information with the group.
2. (Research, language arts) Choose one reference or source from "Further Reading and Listening" on page 116. Read or review it. Share the information with the group.
3. (Research) Each poem title is a Billie Holiday song. Using those songs, make a sound track for a dramatic reading of the book.

Related Works

1. Fradin, Dennis Brindell, and Judith Bloom Fradin. **Ida B. Wells: Mother of the Civil Rights Movement.** New York: Clarion, 2000. 178p. $18.00. ISBN 0 395 89898 6. [nonficton] MJS, CG (*Booktalks and More,* 2003, pages 249 to 252.) Born a slave in 1862, Ida B. Wells became one of the first African American investigative reporters and maintained her civil rights activism throughout her life.
2. Myers, Walter Dean. **Harlem Summer.** New York: Scholastic Press, 2007. 176p. $16.99. ISBN-13: 978 0 439 36843 8. [fiction] MJ, CG with high interest for boys. (*Genre Talks for Teens,* 2009, pages 267 to 269.) Sixteen-year-old Mark Purvis learns about the shady and sunny sides of Harlem and life when he works for both Fats Waller and the newspaper *The Crisis* in his 1925 summer.
3. Nelson, Kadir. **We Are the Ship: The Story of Negro League Baseball.** New York: Hyperion/Jump at the Sun, 2008. 96p. $18.99. ISBN 978 0 7868 0832 8. [nonfiction] MJS/CG with high interest for boys. (*Genre Talks for Teens,* 2009, pages 252 to 255.) Nine innings (chapters), illustrated with Nelson's spectacular oil paintings

of league life, explain the beginnings, development, and end of the Negro League.

4. Nelson, Marilyn. **Carver: a Life in Poems.** Asheville, NC: Front Street, 2001. 103p. $16.95. ISBN 1 886910 53 7. [biography in poems] MJS, CG (*Teen Genre Connections*, 2005, pages 42 to 44.) In a series of poems, Nelson emphasizes Carver's dedication to nature and education, outstanding mental ability, artistic talent, religious faith, work ethic, love of nature, and humbling generosity.

5. Nolan, Han. **Born Blue.** New York: Harcourt, 2001. 177p. $17.00. ISBN 0 15 201916 2. [fiction] JS, CG (*Teen Genre Connections*, 2005, pages 13 to 15.) Placed in an abusive foster home, Janie bonds with seven-year-old, African American Harmon who introduces her to the music of lady blues singers around whom she focuses her life.

Openness and Tolerance: Multiple Cultures Books

In *Race: A History beyond Black and White,* Marc Aronson takes us back to a time when primitive people saw two groups, us and enemies. He explains how these instincts linger today and warns us about how they complicate blending cultures. As the world shrinks, it is even more important to respect our own culture and the culture of others, have empathy for those whose cultures are rapidly changing, and believe in something beyond ourselves.

Respect

Bruchac, Joseph. **The Way.**

Plain City, OH: Darby Creek Publishing, 2007. 164p. $16.95.
ISBN-13: 978 1 58196 062 4. [fiction] MJS, CG with high interest for boys

Themes/Topics: martial arts, self-confidence, Abenaki Indians, family, divorce, bullying

Summary/Description

Cody LeBeau, an Abenaki Indian, deals with bullying in his high school by imagining he is a skilled ninja but believes he is a loser. His father left, and his mother earns a meager salary at the prosperous Koacook Tribe's casino. Then his mother's half-brother John arrives. John, an accomplished martial arts fighter, prepares for a lucrative contest at the casino. He camps behind the LeBeau trailer and trains Cody in the Way, which allows one to breathe, walk (run), listen, and see more effectively. Cody builds self-confidence and strength. When his mother admits that she and Cody's father are divorcing, Cody avoids the inward focus of self-pity and self-blame. He focuses instead on an odd alliance of students he previously separated as bullies and victims. Sure that the group is planning a Columbine-type massacre, he overcomes injury and pain to foil the plot and briefly becomes a media hero. Uncle John wins the contest and will share his winnings with Cody and his mother.

Values: Cody learns determination, self-reliance, and true responsibility.

Read Aloud/Reader Response

1. Chapter 1, pages 5 to 8. In this chapter, Cody begins his day with his ninja fantasy.
2. Chapter 3, pages 22 to 24, beginning "My mind flashed back . . ." and ending "Weird." Cody describes Stump's strange reaction to being pantsed.
3. Chapter 6, pages 43 to 48. In this chapter, Cody meets his Uncle John.
4. Chapter 15, pages 117 to 118, beginning *"Dad's not . . ."* and ending ". . . in the world?" Cody realizes that he can control only his own attitude.
5. Chapter 19, pages 139 to 141, beginning with the chapter and ending "'. . . were going to kill.'" Cody relates the tradition of painting the face for battle to the would-be shooters.

Booktalk

Cody LeBeau thinks he is a target because he is a loser. The Koacook casino where his mother works funds his high school. Cody, an Abenaki, doesn't share in the wealth and lives with his mother in a beat-up trailer park. Cody gets batted around like the other losers. Sometimes he imagines that he is an unconquerable ninja. Sometimes, he daydreams about everyone crying over his grave. Mostly he hides. But the bullies have loser radar. Then Uncle John shows up. Cody never heard of him. But Uncle John has a lot to say, and most of it is about bullies. He doesn't talk about other guys though. He talks about Cody being his own bully. John spent part of his own life letting the bully in his head beat him down. Now he is on the rise as a martial arts fighter. Can Cody hitch on to his uncle's star? No. It's one star, one person, but Uncle John can show him *The Way.*

Curriculum Connections

1. (Research, physical education) Using library resources, examine at least three different self-defense or martial arts ways of thinking. Act as a resource person for the group.
2. (Discuss, language arts, mental health) Identify all the bullies in the novel. Describe each one, and explain why each is included. Use specifics from the novel.
3. (Research, mental health) Using library resources, learn more about bullying and self-confidence. Create a display or bibliography of the best sources that you find.

Related Works

1. Freedman, Russell. **Who Was First? Discovering the Americas.** New York: Clarion Books, 2007. $19.00. ISBN-13: 978 0 618 66391 0. [nonfiction] MJS CG Freedman discusses groups that may have first discovered the Americas and the cultures that formed the Native American populations and beliefs.
2. Koja, Kathe. **Buddha Boy.** New York: Farrar, Straus and Giroux/ Frances Foster Books, 2003. 117p. $16.00. ISBN 0 374 30998 1. [fiction] MJS, CG with high interest for boys. (*Booktalks and Beyond,* 2007, pages 40 to 43.) Jinsen, a new and talented art student, relies on Buddhist training and beliefs to deal with bullies.
3. Mikaelsen, Ben. **Touching Spirit Bear.** New York: HarperCollins Publishers, 2001. 241p. $15.95. ISBN 0 380 97744 3. [fiction] MJS, CG with high interest for boys. (*Booktalks and More,* 2003, pages 80 to 82.) From his Tlingit parole officer, fifteen-year-old bully Cole Mathews learns about himself and the ramifications of his crime.
4. Muth, Joh. **Zen Shorts.** New York: Scholastic Press, 2005. 36p. $17.99. ISBN-13: 978 0 439 33911 7. [fiction, picture book] CMJS/A, CG In this picture book, Stillwater the panda tells three stories that reflect the Zen philosophy.
5. Ramen, Fred. **Native American Mythology.** New York: Rosen Central, 2008. 64p. (Mythology Around the World) $29.95. ISBN-13: 978 1 4042 0738 7. [nonfiction, myths] MJS, CG Ramen explains the common elements of Native American mythology. The stories center on creation, animals, tricksters, and heroes. "The Bear's Wife," tells about a Tlingit girl marrying a grisly who transforms himself into a human. She then becomes a bear.

ርኇ፝፝ጜ

Calcines, Eduardo F. Leaving Glorytown: One Boy's Struggle under Castro.

New York: Farrar, Straus and Giroux, 2009. 221p. $17.95.
ISBN-13: 978 0 374 34394 1. [nonfiction] MJS, CG with high interest for boys

Themes/Topics: Cuban history, 1959 to 1990; refugees; family life; faith

Summary/Description

In 1959, Eduardo Calcines is three, and Castro comes to power. Calcines describes the slow starvation, destruction of cultural and religious customs, the nationalization of successful businesses, and the random violence visited on the citizens. Fearing that Eduardo will be drafted into the Cuban army at fifteen, the family applies for an exit visa when Eduardo is eleven. For three years the family is ostracized and persecuted. The father is sent to a work camp. Calcines is ignored or harassed in school. The mother sells on the black market to keep her family alive. The grandparents council Calcines and his little sister to react passively and remember Christ's suffering. Any violation could cancel the visa. When their names are drawn, the family endures the separation from their extended family and the final, harassment-filled exit process. The epilogue relates their success in America.

Values: The Calcines family demonstrates love, loyalty, courage, and industry.

Read Aloud/Reader Response

The short chapters are excellent read alouds. The following might have special interest.

1. "The Bay of Pigs," pages 19 to 25. Five-year-old Calcines sees his father and uncle arrested during the Bay of Pigs and learns about the Committee for the Defense of the Revolution, a "kind of a cross between the Gestapo and a Neighbor Watch program."
2. "Gusanos" pages 69 to 72, beginning "My teacher that year . . ." and ending "'. . . on the map?'" Calcines' teacher berates him because his family has applied for emigration.
3. "The Ashes of Spring," pages 114 to 115, beginning "That spring . . ." and ending ". . . came first." Calcines describes his Uncle Tío William after his release from prison.

4. "Señora Santana," pages 153 to 156, beginning "I'll kill him . . ." and ending ". . . among the birds." Calcines rages against Castro, and his grandfather counsels him about hatred.

5. "Planning to Escape," pages 195 to 199, beginning "At last . . ." and ending with the chapter. Calcines describes his family's departure from his grandparents

Booktalk

Invite the group to share what they know about Fidel Castro.

Castro's revolution took place in 1959. Eduardo F. Calcines was three. He stayed in Cuba until he was fourteen. Then his family came to America. It is a simple story, isn't it? They get on a plane and leave. No. Calcines tells his not-so-simple story here, a story of persecution, starvation, imprisonment, and death. Fidel Castro, the great savior of Cuba, tolerated no one being better, no one disagreeing. He wanted to grind everyone down to his will. *He* would decide who would be privileged and who would be deprived. The Calcines family disagreed. It meant ripping apart their family and risking their lives. Here is their story, *Leaving Glorytown.*

Curriculum Connections

1. (Research, social studies) Using your library resources, learn more about the Cuban Revolution and the modern Cuba that it produced. Act as a resource person for the group.

2. (Discuss, language arts) Choose the incident that has the most impact for you. Explain why you chose it.

3. (Follow-Up, language arts) Write to the editor and ask what you would like to know about the Calcines family.

Related Works

1. Aronson, Marc. **Race: A History Beyond Black and White.** New York: Atheneum Books for Young Readers/Ginee Seo Books, 2007. 322p. $18.99. ISBN-13: 978 0 689 86554 1. [nonfiction] S, CG Aronson traces the history of persecution from the primitive to modern-day worlds. The book illustrates the revolutionary mentality of Castro's Cuba.

2. Ellis, Deborah. **I Am a Taxi.** Toronto, ON, Canada: House of Anansi Press/Groundwood Books, 2006. 204p. (The Cocalero Novels) $16.95. ISBN-13: 978 0 88899 735 7. [fiction] MJ, CG with high interest for boys. (*Genre Talks for Teens*, 2009, pages 285 to 287.) Diego turns to drug production to support his family living in prison.

3. Link, Theodore. **Communism: A Primary Source Analysis.** New York: The Rosen Publishing Group/Primary Source/Rosen Central, 2005. 64p. (Primary Sources of Political Systems) $29.95. ISBN 0 8239 4517 0. [nonfiction] MJS, CG Historical documents and pictures trace Communism from the Greeks to the twentieth century.

4. Mikaelsen, Ben. **Tree Girl.** New York: HarperCollins Children's Books, 2004. 240p. $16.99. ISBN 0 06 009004 9. [fiction] JS, CG Gabriela Flores flees her Guatemalan village with her baby sister when U.S.-trained troops begin a systematic Indian massacre.

5. Osa, Nancy. **Cuba 15.** New York: Delacorte Press, 2003. 277p. $17.99. ISBN 0 385 90086 4. [fiction] JS, G Fifteen-year-old Violet Paz learns her Cuban heritage as she plans for her ". . . quinceañero (KEEN-say-ahn-YEH-ro), or quince . . ." a coming of age ceremony for womanhood.

᛭᛭

Ehrenberg, Pamela. **Ethan, Suspended.**

Grand Rapids, MI: Eerdmans Books for Young Readers, 2007. 266p. $16.00.
ISBN 978 0 8028 5324 0. [fiction] M, CG with high interest for boys

Themes/Topics: grandparents; friendship; race relations; middle schools; Washington, D.C.; personal responsibility

Summary/Description

Suspended from his school for throwing rocks at another student, thirteen-year-old Ethan is sent to live with grandparents in Washington, D.C. His parents are divorcing, and his sister is starting college. Ethan makes friends through his classes and a jazz band where he plays the oboe, the only instrument available. He tries to protect his neighbor who is involved in running drugs, and he raises money for instruments, lessons, and band camps for inner-city youth. He learns about his family's history as he studies Washington, D.C., within the civil rights movement. Realizing the difference personal decisions make, Ethan returns to his Pennsylvania home resolved to stay in touch with his Washington family and friends. The "Author's Note" suggests related books and Web sites.

Values: Ethan grows in tolerance, personal responsibility, and friendship.

Read Aloud/Reader Response

1. Chapter 6, pages 68, beginning "And it was beginning . . ." and ending with the chapter. Ethan wants adult answers from his family.
2. Chapter 14, pages 140 to 141, beginning "I picked up the . . ." and ending ". . . of the house for." Mr. Harper and Ethan discuss the relevance of music in the world.
3. Chapter 14, pages 142 to 146, beginning "I started to walk past . . ." and ending ". . . longer than necessary." Ethan and Sharita bond through their love of music.
4. Chapter 21, pages 215 to 223, beginning "As my mom . . ." and ending with the chapter. Ethan learns his grandfather's store was the center of civil rights rioting.
5. Chapter 22, pages 231 to 232, beginning "Then still coloring . . ." and ending with the chapter. Ethan's grandmother explains why they stayed in the neighborhood.

Booktalk

Thirteen-year-old Ethan is suspended from his suburban school. Mom doesn't want him. Dad isn't too excited about him either. They are separating. His older sister is going to college. So where is Ethan? With grandparents he hardly knows in inner-city Washington, D.C. Their African American neighbors tell him to stay away from the Latinos. The Latinos don't like his black friends. Ethan is white and Jewish. Good luck. So he eats a wrinkled brown bag lunch on the school stairs and shares a mushy, dried-out dinner with his grandparents at 4:30 in the afternoon. He got himself into this multi-ethnic time warp, and he can get himself out— one decision at a time. He makes some friends. Not everybody worries about color. He joins the jazz band even if the only instrument left is the oboe. And he learns about his family, and himself—Ethan, in action and *Ethan, Suspended*.

Curriculum Connections

1. (Research, social studies) Using library resources, research the civil rights movement. Share the information with the group.
2. (Research, social action) Explore a Web site listed on page 266. Report on the site to the group.
3. (Discuss, language arts) Read Ethan's lists on pages 253 and 254 for staying and leaving Washington. Did he make the right decision? Consider the book title.

Related Works

1. Curtis, Christopher Paul. **Bucking the Sarge.** New York: Wendy Lamb Books, 2004. $15.95. ISBN 0 385 32307 7. [fiction] MJS, CG with high interest for boys. (*Booktalks and Beyond,* 2009, pages 9 to 12.) Fourteen-year-old Luther T. Farrell earns college money by working for his tyrannical and dishonest slumlord mother. He leaves with a man who encourages him to act independently.

2. Garfinkle, D. L. **Storky: How I Lost My Nickname and Won the Girl.** New York: G. P. Putnam's Sons, 2005. 184p. $16.99. ISBN 0 399 24284 8. [fiction] MJ, CG with high interest for boys. (*Booktalks and Beyond,* pages 63 to 65.) High School freshman Michael "Storky" Pomerantz learns the power of decision in his school and family.

3. Koja, Kathe. **Buddha Boy.** New York: Farrar, Straus and Giroux/ Frances Foster Books, 2003. 117p. $16.00. ISBN 0 374 30998 1. [fiction] MJS, CG with high interest for boys. (*Booktalks and Beyond,* 2007, pages 40 to 43.) Helping a new student nicknamed Buddha Boy, a fellow student discovers his own inner strength.

4. Lubar, David. **Sleeping Freshmen Never Lie.** New York: Penguin Group/Speak, 2005. 279p. $6.99pa. ISBN-13: 978 0 14 240780 6. [fiction] MJ, CG with high interest for boys. (*Genre Talks for Teens,* 2009, pages 49 to 51.) Freshman Scott Hudson discovers his writing, organizational, and interpersonal talents.

5. Spinelli, Jerry. **Stargirl.** New York: Alfred A. Knopf, 2000. 186p. $15.95. ISBN 0 679 88637 0. [fiction] MJ, CG with high interest for girls. (*Booktalks and More,* pages 8 to 10.) Leo Borlock recalls the mysterious Stargirl, the new student who captivated, alienated, and hypnotized him and the rest of the student body.

ᘓᘔ

Voorhees, Coert. The Brothers Torres.

New York: Disney Book Group/Hyperion, 2008. 316p. $16.99.
ISBN-13: 978 142310304 2. [fiction] S, CG with high interest for boys

Themes/Topics: brothers, gang culture, coming of age, friendship, New Mexico

Summary/Description

Sophomore Frankie Towers looks up to his brother Steve, a charming, athletic, and popular senior. Steve has a girlfriend and a soccer scholarship but seeks respect from the local *cholas*. Frankie fights John Dalton, the richest kid in their New Mexican high school. Steve and the *cholas* defend him. The escalating confrontation brings Frankie status and his dream girl date. At the homecoming dance, Steve and a drunk John Dalton fight. Frankie pulls Steve away. The *cholas* beat Steve to the point of hospitalization for backing down and force Frankie to watch. Frankie decides that good and evil are not easily sorted and defines himself as independent of his brother's ambitions. The language and situations could be controversial.

Values: Frankie redefines family, friendship, honor, and personal responsibility.

Read Aloud/Reader Response

1. Chapter 2, pages 29, beginning "There are many benefits . . ." and ending ". . . Sensation." Frankie considers racist nicknames.
2. Chapter 6, pages 90 to 91, beginning "'Freaks . . .'" and ending ". . . first period history." Frankie recalls how he became friends with Zach.
3. Chapter 6, pages 98 to 99, beginning "'Frankie . . .'" and ending with the chapter. Frankie challenges the idea that Julius Caesar was too ambitious.
4. Chapter 21, pages 296 to 297, beginning "My dad told me . . ." and ending ". . . make a decision." Frankie reflects on his father's advice.
5. Chapter 22, pages 309 to 310, beginning "Steve and I . . ." and ending ". . . before they happen." Frankie concludes that a superhero needs hindsight to make good decisions.

Booktalk

Sixteen-year-old Frankie is the less important Torres brother. Popular, handsome, and athletic, older brother Steve is the man. Frankie waits tables in his family's hole-in-the-wall restaurant. Steve stars on the soccer field. Both want more. Frankie wants to date beautiful Rebecca. Steve wants respect from the local *cholos*. Their ambitions collide when Frankie fights John Dalton, the richest kid in their New Mexican high school, for Rebecca. Frankie wins the girl but not the three-against-one fight. Steve wants revenge. It's going to be preppy big city Dalton and friends vs. the local boy Steve and his *cholos*. Where is Frankie? Waiting on his tables and the sidelines. He could tell his parents about the fight. He could tell Rebecca's father, the local police chief. If he does, he risks losing the girl, protection, and popularity. So Frankie and Steve are both going to learn something more—what it means to be *The Brothers Torres*.

Curriculum Connections

1. (Research, language arts) Using library resources, explain the difference between a superhero and a Shakespearean hero. Act as a resource person for the group.
2. (Discuss, language arts) In chapter 21, the *cholos* beat Steve for cutting short the beating of Dalton. On page 298, Frankie compares this scene to the betrayal of Caesar in Shakespeare's *Julius Caesar.* Do you agree with this comparison?
3. (Discuss, language arts) In chapter 22, Cheo takes responsibility for Steve's beating, but Frankie feels that everyone is responsible. Do you agree?

Related Works

1. Alexie, Sherman (text), and Ellen Forney (illus.). **The Absolutely True Diary of a Part-Time Indian.** New York: Little, Brown & Co., 2007. 228p. $16.99. ISBN-13: 978 0 316 01368 0. [fiction] JS, CG with high interest for boys. (*Genre Talks for Teens*, 2009, pages 269 to 272.) Physically challenged and intellectually gifted Arnold Spirit overcomes white prejudice and Indian resentment when he attends a white high school.
2. Dunton-Downer, Leslie, and Alan Riding. **Essential Shakespeare Handbook.** New York: DK Press, 2004. 480p. $25.00. ISBN 0 7894 9333 0. [nonfiction] JS, CG This user-friendly Shakespeare reference includes plot summaries and analysis of all thirty-nine plays. *Julius Caesar* appears on pages 314 to 323.
3. Martinez, Victor. **Parrot in the Oven.** New York: Harper Trophy/Joanna Colter Books, 1996. 216p. $5.95pa. ISBN 0 06 447186 1. [fiction] JS, CG with high interest for boys. (*Booktalks Plus*, 2001, pages 112 to 114.) Manny Hernandez journeys through work, school, family, gang, and friendship and decides his family is most important.
4. Soto, Gary. **The Afterlife.** New York: Harcourt, 2003. 161p. $16.00. ISBN 0 15 204774 3. [fiction] JS, CG with high interest for boys. (*Teen Genre Connections*, 2005, pages 294 to 296.) Stabbed in a restroom when he comments on a man's yellow shoes, eighteen-year-old Jesús moves from life to after-life and sees what he means to friends and family. This book is the prequel to *Buried Onions.*
5. Soto, Gary. **Buried Onions.** New York: Harcourt Brace, 1997. 149p. $17.00. ISBN 0 15 201333 4. [fiction] JS, CG with high interest for boys. (*Booktalks Plus*, 2001, pages 124 to 126.) Living in a community

mired in crime and gang life, nineteen-year-old Eddie struggles to be free from the deadly code of "honor."

Empathy

❦

Alvarez, Julia. **Return to Sender.**
New York: Alfred A. Knopf, 2009. 322p. $16.99.
ISBN-13: 978 0 375 85838 3. [fiction] MJS, CG

Themes/Topics: farm life, Vermont, friendship, migrant workers, illegal aliens

Summary/Description

Eleven-year-old Tyler's family hires illegal Mexican workers to maintain their farm after the grandfather dies and the father suffers a horrible accident. The workers include three daughters whose mother has returned to Mexico for her mother's funeral. The families bond, and Tyler and the oldest daughter become close friends. When *coyotes* demand a ransom for the mother who was kidnapped trying to return, Tyler helps the family gather money and execute the pick-up. Eventually, the Mexicans are arrested by immigration and returned to Mexico. The families maintain their friendship, the workers hope for a stronger Mexico in which they can earn a living, and Tyler's family sells the farm to Tyler's uncle.

Value: Tyler learns compassion, true patriotism, friendship, and self-sacrifice.

Read Aloud/Reader Response

1. Chapter 1, page 9, beginning "Tyler remembered . . ." and ending "'. . . by our children.'" Tyler remembers the Abenaki chief's remark about land.
2. Chapter 2, pages 56 to 57, beginning "'Are we doing . . .'" and ending with the chapter. Tyler realizes that hiring the Mexicans is illegal.
3. Chapter 3, pages 75 to 80, beginning with the chapter and ending with ". . . the sky." Tyler experiences grief and moral confusion.
4. Chapter 8, pages 283 to 293, beginning "On Friday . . ." and ending ". . . to explain." Mari meets the immigration agent.

5. Chapter 9, pages 299 to 318. These are Tyler's and Mari's closing letters.

Booktalk

Ask how many people are in favor of allowing illegal aliens to stay in the United States.

Some say that allowing them to stay is un-American. Others say that sending them back to Mexico is inhumane. Eleven-year-old Tyler has a simple answer. Follow the law. It is the American way. Then his grandfather dies. His father almost dies in an accident. They will lose their farm, *unless* they can get some cheap labor. They can get it, but it is illegal labor, a Mexican family. What should Tyler do? Ignore them? Report them? They seem to be good people. They too have lost family, worry about money, dream on the stars. And while he struggles with his patriotism, he finds friendship. Mari, just his age, talks to him and asks him for help. Quickly, Tyler is in the middle of a violent world where no laws or rules apply, where gangsters thrive on murder and slavery, and where governments treat people like unread letters and stamp them all *Return to Sender.*

Curriculum Connections

1. (Research, social studies) Prepare a debate on illegal immigration from Mexico.
2. (Discuss, language arts) After reading the story, how do you feel about returning illegal aliens to Mexico? Be sure to draw on specifics from the novel.
3. (Discuss, language arts) How do the stars and swallows affect the story? Use specifics from the novel.

Related Works

1. DeFelice, Cynthia. **Under the Same Sky.** New York: Farrar, Straus and Giroux, 2003. 215p. $16.00. $26.95. ISBN 0 374 38032 5. [fiction] MJS, CG Fourteen-year-old Joe Pedersen matures as he works with the migrant workers on his father's farm.
2. Johnston, Tony. **Any Small Goodness: A Novel of the Barrio.** New York: The Blue Sky Press, 2001. 128p. $5.95. ISBN 0 439 18936 5. [fiction] MJS, CG Eleven-year-old Arturo Rodriguez struggles to hang on to the best of his culture in his East Lost Angeles barrio.
3. Phillip, Neil (comp.), and Jacqueline Mair (illus.). **Horse Hooves and Chicken Feet: Mexican Folktales.** New York: Clarion

Books, 2003. 83p. $19.00. ISBN 0 618 19463 0. [fiction] MJS, CG
This folktale collection includes "tale types" that are told with a
distinctive Mexican flavor.

4. Ryan, Pam Muñoz. **Becoming Naomi León.** New York: Scholastic
    Press, 2004. 256p. $16.95. ISBN 0 439 26969 5. [fiction] MJS, CG
    (*Booktalks and Beyond*, 2007, pages 249 to 251.) Naomi Soledad León
    Outlaw and her physically challenged brother reconnect with their
    Mexican heritage when their abusive mother returns to take custody.

5. Ryan, Pam Muñoz. **Esperanza Rising.** New York: Scholastic Press,
    2000. 272p. $15.95. ISBN 0 43929 3. [fiction] MJS, CG with high
    interest for girls. (*Booktalks and More*, 2003, pages 42 to 44.) In this
    Depression journey, Mexican immigrant workers and one formerly
    wealthy girl join their fate and welfare.

☙❧

Myers, Walter Dean. **Riot.**

New York: Egmont, 2009. 164p. $16.99.
ISBN 978 1 60684 000 9. [screenplay] JS, CG

Themes/Topics: Draft Riot, New York City, 1863,
African Americans, Irish Americans, Civil War,
racially mixed people, identity

Summary/Description

Fifteen-year-old Claire and her friend Priscilla are caught up in the
New York race riots precipitated by Lincoln's draft policy, which
allowed any Northern man to buy out his draft obligation for $300.
Throughout the violence, Claire questions her identity: black/white/
Irish/African American or just American. After the rioting, she empa-
thizes with the Irish who lost loved ones but now realizes danger in skin
color. A timeline leading up to the rioting, an author's note, and a set of
pictures of the time period are included. One of the pictures is of two
girls that Myers sees as his two characters.

Values: Each group, like Claire, seeks equal treatment and security.
The rioting prevents both.

Read Aloud/Reader Response

The screenplay can be acted on a stage or taped.

1. Pages 25 to 31, beginning "Oh, he's all . . ." and ending "Maybe I'll
    be back . . ." Maeve reveals her prejudices against the "coloreds"
    and the "swells."

2. Pages 58 to 65, beginning "A thin white man . . ." and ending ". . . either, ma'am." Walt Whitman reflects on the events,
3. Pages 66 to 67, Claire's voice-over. Whitman makes Claire ponder her identity.
4. Pages 89 to 90, beginning "If it's my skin . . ." and ending "Where is it?" Claire wonders if she can ever be safe again.
5. Page 98, "Old Irish Woman." She sees an end to hope if the young men die.

Booktalk

In 1863, the Civil War is raging. The Union needs soldiers. They institute a draft. The Union also needs money. The wealthy can escape the draft by paying $300. Irish immigrant families in New York feel the blows from both the war and the $300 waiver. Freed slaves will take their jobs. The wealthy will avoid the draft, and the Irish will be fighting the Confederates. What do the Irish do? They strike back. They target the blacks and the wealthy. They aim to destroy the people they think will destroy them. Fifteen-year-old Claire isn't sure where she fits in this fight. Her mother is Irish. Her father is black. They are prosperous. She has many questions to ask about hate and the color of her skin, but not many answers come back in a *Riot*.

Curriculum Connections

1. (Research, history) Using library resources, learn more about the 1863 New York riots. Act as a resource person for the group.
2. (Research, language arts) Using library resources, learn more about Walt Whitman. Act as a resource person for the group.
3. (Discuss, language arts) How would you answer Claire's questions about her identity? Be sure to use specifics from the play and your experience in your answer.

Related Works

1. Aronson, Marc. **Race: A History Beyond Black and White.** New York: Atheneum Books for Young Readers/Ginee Seo Books, 2007. 322p. $18.99. ISBN-13: 978 0 689 86554 1. [nonfiction] S, CG. Aronson traces the history of man persecuting man from the survival instincts of primitive tribes to a multi-cultural modern-day world
2. McKissack, Patricia. **Color Me Dark: The Diary of Nellie Lee Love, the Great Migration North.** New York: Scholastic, 2000. 224p. (Dear America) $10.95. ISBN 0 590 1159 9. [fiction] MJ, G

(*Booktalks and More,* 2003, pages 10 to 12.) Eleven-year-old Nellie Lee Love's family moves to Chicago after World War I, and they are caught up in the rioting of "The Red Summer."

3. McKissack, Patricia C., and Fredrick L. McKissack. **Days of Jubilee: The End of Slavery in the United States.** New York: Scholastic Press, 2003. 144p. $18.95. ISBN 0 590 10764 X [nonfiction] MJS, CG Civil War diaries, letters, and slave narratives describe how slaves gained freedom through the Underground Railroad, rebellion, military service, the Emancipation Proclamation, and the Thirteenth Amendment.

4. McMullan, Margaret. **How I Found the Strong: A Novel of the Civil War**. Boston, MA: Houghton Mifflin Co., 2004. 136p. $15.00. ISBN 0 618 35008 X [fiction] MJS, CG (*Booktalks and Beyond,* 2007, pages 210 to 213.) When his father and older brother join the Confederacy, ten-year-old Shanks runs the farm with his mother, grandparents, and their slave.

5. Taylor, Mildred D. **The Land: Prequel to Roll of Thunder, Hear My Cry.** New York: Penguin Putnam/Phyllis Fogelman Books, 2001. 275p. $17.99. ISBN 0 8037 1950 7. [fiction] JS, CG with high interest for boys. (*Teen Genre Connections,* 2005, pages 267 to 269.) The friendship between a biracial boy and an African American boy ends in the tragic death of the African American in the post–Civil War world.

෬෬

Li, Moying. **Snow Falling in Spring: Coming of Age in China during the Cultural Revolution.**

New York: Farrar, Straus and Giroux/Melanie Kroupa Books, 2008. 176p. $16.00.
ISBN-13: 978 0 374 39922 1. [nonfiction] JS, CG

Themes/Topics: China's Cultural Revolution,
family, conduct of life

Summary/Description

Moying Li recalls her early life with a successful family that supports Chairman Mao and are labeled traitors during the Cultural Revolution. Twelve-year-old Moying Li attends a Beijing language school. She leaves when the headmaster hangs himself and the guard forces a child to denounce her father. Moying's home is ransacked, and her father taken away. She educates herself with a reading list smuggled from her father. Her school becomes a vocational high school for language teachers. Moying Li studies there and is selected to teach language at an international school for five years. After Chairman Mao's death in 1976, the national exam is offered for college enrollment. Twenty-three-year-old Moying Li is permitted to study in the United States. A forward explains events leading to Mao's regime. The epilogue recounts the author's return after twenty-six years. "A Chronology" lists significant events from 1912 to 1979. A glossary defines terms, historical events, and pivotal people.

Values: Moying Li's life illustrates diligence, faith, and love.

Read Aloud/Reader Response

1. "The Great Leap," pages 6 to 10, beginning "Early that summer . . ." and ending "'. . . Lao Lao first.'" This passage illustrates the dedication of the entire family to China's success.
2. "The Gathering Storm," pages 42 to 60. This chapter depicts gang violence.
3. "Hunan Mummy," pages 116 to 121. Moying Li's ancestor suggests rebirth.
4. "Temple of the Sun," page 138, beginning "During another visit . . ." and ending "'. . . short but effective.'" Mr. Hu gives Moying Li a formula for writing well.
5. "Turning Point," pages 154 to 161, beginning "My first day . . ." and ending ". . . to study in America." This section demonstrates that Moying Li values education.

Booktalk

Ask the group to share what they know about China.

In the early twentieth century, Chinese warlords create chaos. In 1931, the Japanese invade China. By 1937, China is at war with the Japanese. The Nationalists and Communists fight them for eight years and win. Those two groups wage four years of civil war. The Communists win. Chairman Mao, the Communist leader, announces that China controls its destiny, but the Korean War slows progress. Finally, in 1958, the government crafts an economic plan, the Great Leap Forward. It fails. When China's next chapter begins, Moying is twelve. Her family is successful. Moying is a top student at a prestigious Beijing language school. But, the Great Proletarian Cultural Revolution decides that haves must become have-nots. The government sees people as cogs in a powerful machine. Thinkers are suspect, even criminals. Moying and her family are thinkers. Will this movement mean the family's destruction, or will it, like the others, disappear like *Snow Falling in Spring*?

Curriculum Connections

1. (Research, social studies) Using library resources, learn more about the Cultural Revolution and the Japanese invasion. Act as a resource person for the group.
2. (Research, social studies) Using library resources, learn about China today. Act as a resource person for the group.
3. (React, language arts) Choose the passage from the memoir that touched or surprised you. Share it with the group and explain your choice.

Related Works

1. Park, Linda Sue. **When My Name Was Keoko: A Novel of Korea in World War II.** New York: Clarion Books, 2002. 199p. $16.00. ISBN 0 618 13335 6. [fiction] JS, CG (*Teen Genre Connections, 2005,* pages 235 to 237.) Told through the eyes of Sun hee and her older brother, the story recounts the World War II Japanese occupation of Korea.
2. Sís, Peter. **The Wall: Growing Up behind the Iron Curtain**. New York: Farrar, Straus and Giroux/Frances Foster Books, 2007. 56p. $18.00. ISBN-13: 978 0 374 34701 7. [graphic, nonfiction] MJS, CG (*Genre Talks for Teens,* 2009, pages 255 to 257.) In this illustrated memoir, Sís describes growing up in Soviet-controlled Czechoslovakia.
3. Whelan, Gloria. **Chu Ju's House.** New York: HarperCollins Publishers, 2004. 227p. $16.89. ISBN 0 06 050725 X. [fiction] MJS, CG (*Booktalks and Beyond,* 2009, pages 239 to 241.) At the end of the Cultural Revolution, fourteen-year-old Chu Ju leaves home so that her parents will keep her baby sister. She builds an independent life.
4. Yan, Ma. Pierre Haske (ed.). Lisa Appignanesi (trans.). **The Diary of Ma Yan: The Struggles and Hopes of a Chinese Schoolgirl.** New York: HarperCollins Publishers, 2004. 176p. $16.89. ISBN 0 06 076496 1. [nonfiction] MJS, CG with high interest for girls. Living in a barren region of China, Ma Yan records family's poverty, harsh living conditions, hunger, and physical challenges she must overcome to study.
5. Yen Mah, Adeline. **Chinese Cinderella and the Secret Dragon Society.** New York: HarperCollins Publishers, 2005. 242p. $16.99. ISBN 0 06 056735-X. [fiction] MJ, CG When her step-mother abuses her, twelve-year-old Chinese Cinderella (CC) seeks shelter at a martial arts school, joins a secret dragon society, and works with the Chinese Resistance against the Japanese.

☙❧

Marston, Elsa. **Santa Claus in Baghdad and Other Stories about Teens in the Arab World.**

Bloomington, IN: Indiana University Press, 2008. 198p. $15.95.
ISBN-13: 978 0 253 22004 2. [short stories] JS, CG

Themes/Topics: Middle Eastern social life and customs,
coming of age, conduct of life

Summary/Description

E ight short stories express the personal crises of Arab teens who live in societies with challenges different than our own, but universal coming-of-age choices and desires. "Santa Claus in Baghdad: A Story from Iraq (2000)" portrays a family trying to keep hope alive under dire financial pressure. "Faces: A Story from Syria" tells about a male-dominated divorce. "The Hand of Fatima: A Story from Lebanon" portrays a girl who loves her father but wants her own life rather than an arranged marriage. In "The Olive Grove: A Story from Palestine," a young man learns the true meaning of jihad. "In Line: A Story from Egypt" tells about a young woman choosing friends against her family's preferences. "Scenes in a Roman Theater: A Story from Tunisia" depicts a boy who begins as a lackey but then aspires to be an artist. "Honor: A Story from Jordon" involves the archaic codes of honor that allow a girl to be killed for flirting. "The Plan: A Story from a Palestinian Refugee Camp in Lebanon" demonstrates that a young man whose family is ravaged by war still believes in hope, beauty, and love. Explanatory notes for each story are included at the back of the book.

Values: The teenagers struggle with love, family, tolerance, tradition, and independence.

Read Aloud/Reader Response

Each story is an excellent read aloud. After eliciting the group's responses to the story, the leader might read aloud each author's note for a follow-up response.

Booktalk

Ask the group what they picture when they hear the word Arab. *Using a map, point out the countries included in the short stories—Iraq, Syria, Lebanon, Palestine, Egypt, Tunisia, and Jordan—and emphasize that the Arab world is larger than what appears on televisions and in headlines. You might want to display newspaper stories and headlines.*

Real people are behind pictures on televisions, in newspapers, and in our minds, and many of them are teenagers. They face wars, poverty, and political uncertainty. But they also ask many of the same questions that teenagers in the non-Arab world face. Who can I date? Who will I marry? Where will I go to school? If I move, will the new school be friendly? Too difficult? Can I make my own choices? Will I make the right choices? How should I choose friends? Can I earn enough money? How do I handle parents who make bad choices? And while dealing with all those questions, they also see a new world invading theirs—the West. Often, they view our world the same way we view theirs, through television, newspapers, and movies. These eight short stories talk about the struggles with tradition and change going on in the lives of eight teenagers. That Arab world is a great deal like ours, except when it isn't. And there is no better place to start understanding that confusing statement than with the first story in this book of short stories, "Santa Claus in Baghdad."

Curriculum Connections

1. (Research, social studies) Using your library resources, learn more about the dating customs, women's rights, and terrorism groups in the Middle East. Act as a resource person for the group.
2. (React, language arts) Which story is your favorite? Why?
3. (React, language arts) Which story did you find most disturbing or challenging? Why?

Related Works

1. Abdell-Fattah, Randa. **Does My Head Look Big in This?** New York: Scholastic/Orchard Books, 2007. 352p. $16.99. ISBN-13: 978 0 439 91947 0 [fiction] JS, G (*Genre Talks for Teens*, 2009, pages 259 to 262.) Eleventh-grader Amal Mohamed Nasrullah Abdel-Hakim wears the *hijab* and begins a journey of identity and faith.
2. Barakat, Ibtisam. **Tasting the Sky: A Palestinian Childhood.** New York: Farrar, Straus and Giroux/Melanie Kroupa Books, 2007. 176p. $16.00. ISBN-13: 978 0 374 35733 7. [nonfiction] JS, CG (*Genre Talks for Teens*, 2009, pages 283 to 287.) Parts I and III address the author's frustration and hope (1981). Part II, the main story, extends from the Six Days' War to the family's finding a permanent home (1967 to 1971).
3. Johansen, Jonathan (ed.). **Critical Perspectives on Islam and the Western World.** New York: The Rosen Publishing Group, 2006. 182p. (Critical Anthologies of Nonfiction Writing) $30.60. ISBN 1 4042 0538 1. [nonfiction] JS, CG This series of selected documents, essays, and articles explains the background of East/

West relations and the rise of Islamist or Islamic fundamentalist movements.

4. Lat. **Kampung Boy.** New York: Roaring Brook Press/First Second, 2006. 142p. $16.95. ISBN 1 59643 121 0. [graphic] MJS, CG (*Genre Talks for Teens*, 2009, pages 264 to 266.) Starting with his parents' marriage and ending with his journey to school, this first book in the *Kampung Boy* series outlines the life of a Muslim boy within a disappearing rural family life.

5. Satrapi, Marjane. **Persepolis.** New York: Random House/Pantheon, 2003. 153p. $11.95pa. ISBN 0 375 71457 X. [graphic memoir] JS/A, CG The great-granddaughter of one of Iran's emperors, Satrapi recounts eight years of her life that witnessed the overthrow of the shah, the Islamic Revolution, and the war with Iraq.

ৎৣ৾

Wyatt, Melissa. **Funny How Things Change.**

New York: Farrar, Straus and Giroux, 2009. 195p. $16.95.
ISBN-13: 978 0 374 30233 2. [fiction] JS, CG

Themes/Topics: interpersonal relations, West Virginia, Appalachian Mountains, identity

Summary/Description

Eighteen-year-old Remy Walker will follow his girlfriend when she leaves West Virginia for Dickinson College, Pennsylvania. Working as a mechanic, he will support them in an apartment. His father questions the decision. The girlfriend's family opposes it. When a young artist comes to town, Remy begins to question his plan too. He is physically attracted to her and fascinated about how positively she sees the area and the things that are important to him: a vintage car, his career as a mechanic, and the Walker family's mountain. When Remy's father decides to sell the mountain to support his son's dream, Remy realizes that he wants to stay in the mountains, go to the local technical school, and delay any permanent romantic relationships. He breaks off with his girlfriend and reconnects with his father and family heritage.

Values: Remy realizes the importance of his own identity formed by his heritage and aspirations.

Read Aloud/Reader Response

1. Chapter 3, pages 32 to 33, beginning "He hadn't been home . . ." and ending ". . . maybe it was." This passage illustrates the father's character and the trust they share.

2. Chapter 4, page 49, beginning "Lisa had disappeared" and ending ". . . in more ways than one." Dana tells Lisa that Remy will drag her down at school. Remy overhears.
3. Chapter 5, pages 63 to 66, beginning "What was she interested in?" and ending with the chapter. Remy realizes that he does not really know Lisa's plans, and that he sees good in his life and area.
4. Chapter 10, pages 110 to 112, beginning "Lisa shrugged" and ending with the chapter. Remy realizes that Lisa does not respect who he is.
5. Chapter 17, page 167, beginning "He sat down . . ." and ending ". . . to be enough." Remy reflects on his relationship to the mountain and his family.

Booktalk

Remy Walker is a senior, ready to graduate and leave his home, Walker Mountain, in the Appalachians. (*Try to show positive and negative pictures of Appalachia.*) Next year, he will be in Pennsylvania with his girlfriend Lisa. He won't be leaving much. His dad and he live in a trailer that doesn't even have an inside bathroom. Remy can fix any car made. That's what he will do in Pennsylvania. When Lisa finishes college, they will make more plans for their life together. Then he meets an artist, an outsider. She isn't much older than he is, but she has a government grant to paint the local water tower. Like the other visitors to their town, she gushes about how she loves the mountains. He knows she'll go back to her other life when that water tower is finished, but he can't stop looking at her or listening. Suddenly, his rock-solid future plans don't look so solid. *Funny How Things Change.*

Curriculum Connections

1. (Research, social studies) Using your library resources, learn more about Appalachia. Act as a resource person for your group.
2. (React, language arts) Do you agree with Remy's decision to stay?
3. (Discuss, language arts) What do you think the role of a high school teacher in the community should be?

Related Works

1. Anderson, Laurie Halse. **Prom.** New York: Viking, 2005. 215p. $16.99. ISBN 0 670 05974 9. [fiction] JS, G (*Booktalks and Beyond*, 2007, pages 56 to 58.) Eighteen-year-old Ashley Hannigan just tolerates school until she saves the prom and discovers her executive talents.

2. Deuker, Carl. **Runner.** New York: Houghton Mifflin Co., 2005. 216p. $16.00. ISBN 0 618 54298 1. [fiction] JS, CG with high interest for boys. (*Booktalks and Beyond,* 2007, pages 70 to 73.) Chance delivers packages to a marina locker for $200 per week, discovers he works for a terrorist ring, loses his father who defends him, and stays true to his family roots by joining the service.

3. Moriarty, Jaclyn. **The Year of Secret Assignments.** New York: Arthur A. Levine Books, 2004. 352p. $16.95. ISBN 0 439 49881 3. [fiction] JS, CG Three high school friends in an upscale private school acquire pen pals through their high school English class and discover their inaccurate stereotypes.

4. Nye, Naomi Shihab. **Going Going**. New York: Harper Collins/Greenwillow Books, 2005. 232p. $16.89. ISBN 0 06 029366 7. [fiction] JS, G (*Genre Talks for Teens,* 2009, pages 59 to 61.) Sixteen-year-old Florrie crusades to save small, unique buildings and discovers that she should have the same appreciation for people.

5. Paulsen, Gary. **Brian's Return.** New York: Delacorte Press, 1999. 117p. $13.50. ISBN 0 385 32500 2. [fiction] JS, CG with high interest for boys. (*Booktalks and More,* 2003, pages 40 to 42.) In this supposedly concluding volume of the Brian series, Brian discovers that he is no longer comfortable in civilization and returns to the wilderness to discover himself in relation to nature.

Faith

༄ༀ

Baskin, Nora Raleigh.
The Truth about My Bat Mitzvah.

New York: Simon & Shuster Books for Young Readers, 2008. 138p. $15.99.
ISBN-13: 978 1 4169 3558 2. [fiction] MJS, G

Themes/Topics: Jews, identity, prejudice, grandmothers, rituals and symbols

Summary/Description

After her grandmother dies and leaves her a gold Star of David, twelve-year-old Caroline Weeks explores her Jewish heritage. Caroline's best friend is planning a Bat Mitzvah celebration. When a new, popular girl invites her to an overnight and expresses prejudice against Jews, Caroline doesn't feel strong enough to wear the Star of David in front of her. Caroline's faith journey intertwines with learning her family history, which includes conflicts and prejudice within the Jewish community. She concludes that Bat Mitzvah is not a party but a signal of her adult identity. She wears the star, discovers that the boy she likes is Jewish, and perceives her friend's Bat Mitzvah celebration as a bonding and clarification for them both.

Values: Caroline learns self-respect and tolerance as she discovers her identity.

Read Aloud/Reader Response

1. Chapter 1, pages 1 to 4. Caroline recalls her grandmother's funeral.
2. Chapter 13, pages 52 to 53, beginning "About a year ago . . ." and ending with the chapter. Carolyn recalls her realization that wearing a cross is a declaration of identity.
3. Chapter 15, pages 58 to 61. In this chapter, the grandmother tells the story about her encounter, as a little girl, with a rich girl who stuck out her tongue at her.
4. Chapter 20, pages 79 to 81. In this chapter, Caroline recalls a field trip in which she encountered Orthodox Jews.
5. Chapter 33, pages 126 to 127, beginning "'You know . . .'" and ending with the chapter. Caroline realizes that one can hold people through memories.

Booktalk

I'm twelve. My name is Carolyn, and I am a Jew—and a Gentile. My mother is Jewish. My father is not. Nobody talks religion in our house. Nobody talks religion in my Jewish grandma and grandpa's apartment either. The closest that we get to talking even about nationality at my grandparents is making out the order for the Chinese take-out. So when my grandmother dies, and I feel so bad that I can hardly think, I am puzzled by many things. My grandpa gives me my grandma's Star of David necklace. (*Hold up a similar necklace or a picture of a Star of David.*) Why did she leave it to me? What is she saying to me? At her funeral, I meet a great aunt I never knew. Why is this person important? I learn that my grandparents weren't so happy about their daughter's marriage. Was it because the groom wasn't Jewish? Suddenly, I am defending my best friend Rachel from anti-Jewish remarks. Why would anyone try to hurt or exclude Rachel? I can't answer these questions when I don't have my dear grandma to help me. But as I look for answers, I learn *The Truth about My Bat Mitzvah*.

Curriculum Connections

1. (Research, multiple cultures) Using your library resources, learn more about the Bat Mitzvah. Act as a resource person for your group.
2. (Discuss, social studies or language arts) Do you think wearing jewelry and clothing as religious symbols is a good idea? Use specifics from the novel and your own life to support your opinion.
3. (Discuss, language arts) How does Carolyn grow through the novel?

Related Works

1. Abdel-Fattah, Randa. **Does My Head Look Big in This?** New York: Scholastic/Orchard Books, 2007. 352p. $16.99. ISBN-13: 978 0 439 91947 0. [fiction] JS, G (*Genre Talks for Teens*, 2009, pages 259 to 262.) Eleventh-grader Amal Mohamed Nasrullah Abdel-Hakim, an Australian/Muslim/Palestinian, begins a faith journey by wearing the *hijab*, the Muslim head scarf, full time.
2. Bloom, Judy. **Are You There, God? It's Me, Margaret.** New York: Simon and Shuster Children's Books, 2001. 160p. $17.95. ISBN-13: 978 0 6898 4158 3. [fiction] In this reprint of Bloom's 1970 publication, twelve-year-old Margaret struggles with puberty and religion.
3. Fraustino, Lisa Rowe (ed.). **Soul Searching: Thirteen Stories about Faith and Belief.** New York: Simon & Schuster Books for Young Readers, 2002. 267p $17.95. ISBN 0 689 83484 5. [fiction] JS, CG The stories talk about how faith supports people in all cultures.
4. Hautman, Pete. **Godless.** New York: Simon & Schuster Books for Young Readers, 2004. 198p. $15.95. ISBN 0 689 86278 4. [fiction] JS, CG (*Genre Talks for Teens*, 2009, pages 27 to 29.) Jason Bock, disillusioned by his parents' religion, starts a new one centered on the town water tower and triggers events that spiral out of control.
5. Singer, Marilyn (ed.). **I Believe in Water: Twelve Brushes with Religion.** New York: HarperCollins, 2000. 280p. $24.89. ISBN 0 06 028398 X. [fiction] JS, CG Twelve short stories examine how real life and spiritual beliefs can complement and collide.

ᘓᘔ

Edwardson, Debby Dahl. **Blessing's Bead.**
New York: Farrar, Straus and Giroux/Melanie Kroupa Books, 2009. 178p. $16.99.
ISBN-13: 978 0 374 30805 6. [fiction] JS, CG with high interest for girls

Themes/topics: Iñupiaq culture; village life; tundra; influenza; alcoholism; Ice Curtain; Iron Curtain; Alaska, 1917–1989

Summary/Description

In Book I, 1917, Nutaaq's family travels to the trade fair where her sister marries a Siberian Eskimo, gives Nutaaq two magical blue beads, and promises to return with beads for the entire family, but a flu epidemic ravages Nutaaq's village. Nutaaq marries and moves to the Far North. Book II, Blessing's Story, 1989 is about Nutaaq's great-granddaughter. After a domestic battle between Blessing's alcoholic mother and partner, the police send Blessing and her brother to their grandmother. Blessing eases into the Eskimo culture through dancing, village customs, and family life and becomes attached to the blue bead in her grandmother's sewing box. A "Friendship Flight" from the newly opened Siberian territory brings a man and boy, descendents of Nutaaq's sister. They have a blue bead for each member of the original family. Blessing's rehabilitated mother returns to her family, and Blessing realizes the support of her culture's stories and symbols. An "Author's Note" explains the story's background. An "Iñupiaq Glossary" provides definitions and pronunciations.

Values: Blessing discovers her identity and self-respect through openness and tolerance.

Read Aloud/Reader Response

1. "The Ones We Lost," pages 52 to 57. In this chapter, the "boot soles" match up the epidemic survivors in forced marriages. Tupaaq claims Nutaaq.
2. "Eskimo Dancing," pages 95 to 99. Blessing has culture conflict in Eskimo dance.
3. "Telling Stories," pages 106 to 108. In this chapter, the lemming story distinguishes change from growth. It links to the first ("Old Stories," pages 10 to 12) and the last ("Tarva," pages 168, beginning "I'm remembering . . ." and ending with the novel) chapters.
4. "Blessing's Bead," pages 122 to 123. In this chapter, Blessing blends into the community.
5. "Good Things and Bad Things," pages 144 to 145. Blessing sorts negatives and positives.

Booktalk

This novel is two stories set in remote Alaska. The first occurs in 1917. Nutaaq sees her life change by the "boot soles," the white men, who bring new ideas and diseases to the Eskimos. The second occurs in 1989. Nutaaq's great-granddaughter Blessing and great-grandson Isaac live in Anchorage, Alaska, with their mother. A disease, alcoholism, changes that world too. When a drunken battle drives Blessing and her brother out of their Anchorage home, they find the remote village their great-grandmother fled to years ago. A new beginning, again. Blessing becomes part of a story spanning the past, present, and future, and it comes in a simple blue bead, maybe like this one (*Possibly show a blue bead or point to the bead on the book cover*), *Blessing's Bead.*

Curriculum Connections

1. (Research, language arts) Using library resources, learn more about storytelling in oral cultures. Act as a resource person for your group.
2. (Discuss, language arts) Discuss how the bead supports the story.
3. (Compare, social studies) Describe the concept of family in *Blessing's Bead.* Compare that with your own concept of family. What does the comparison say about values?

Related Works

1. Bastedo, Jamie. **On Thin Ice.** Calgary, AB, Canada: Fitzhenry & Whiteside Co./Red Deer Press, 2006. 348p. $10.95pa. ISBN 0 88995 337 6. [fiction] JS, CG with high interest for girls. (*Genre Talks for Teens,* 2009, pages 262 to 264.) Sixteen-year-old Ashley, a mix of Irish, French Canadian, and Inuk, shares her uncle's mystical gifts.
2. Norfolk, Sherry, Jane Stenson, and Diane Williams (ed.). **Literacy Development in the Storytelling Classroom.** Santa Barbara, CA: ABC-CLIO/ Libraries Unlimited, 2009. 342p. $40.00. ISBN 978 1 59158 694 4. [professional reference] S/A, CG This reference includes suggestions for younger storytellers. The article "Grandma—My First Teacher: Lessons Learned Outside of School" by Dovie Thomason, pages 86 to 88, explains how Kiowa Apache stories guide behavior and attitudes.
3. Orenstein, Denise Gosliner. **Unseen Companion.** New York: Harper Collins Publishers/Katherine Tegen Books, 2003. 357p. $16.89. ISBN 0 06 052057 4. [fiction] JS, CG In 1959 Bethel, Alaska, four teenagers tell about a beaten half-breed teenage rebel, Dove, who disappears after being arrested.
4. Sís, Peter. **The Wall: Growing Up behind the Iron Curtain.** New York: Farrar, Straus and Giroux/Frances Foster Books, 2007. 56p. $18.00. ISBN-13: 978 0 374 34701 7. [graphic, nonfiction] MJS, CG (*Genre Talks for Teens,* 2009, pages 255 to 257.) Sís's illustrated memoir of growing up behind the Iron Curtain relates to Blessing's experience behind the Ice Curtain.

5.   Sullivan, Paul. **Maata's Journal.** New York: Atheneum Books for
     Young Readers, 2003. 240p. $16.95. ISBN 0 689 83463 2 [fiction]
     JS, G Seventeen-year-old Maata, an Inuit, records her survival in an
     Arctic expedition from April to July of 1924.

❧❧

Frost, Helen. Diamond Willow.
New York: Farrar, Straus and Giroux/Frances Foster Books, 2008. 109p. $16.00.
ISBN-13: 978 0 374 31776 8. [novel in verse] M, G

Themes/Topics: spirits, dogs, family life, Alaska, popularity,
Athabascan Indians, friendship

Summary/Description

In a series of diamond-shaped verses with small bolded messages
within them, twelve-year-old Willow, a girl with one friend, tells
about her coming of age tied to her birth. Willow drives the dog team
to her grandparents' house for the first time. On her return, she fails to
slow on a blind curve, and a tree limb blinds the lead dog, Roxy. Her
parents plan to put the dog to sleep. With her friend's help, she takes
Roxy to her grandparents. The group encounters a storm. Cora, the
new lead dog, takes the wrong trail. They camp overnight, and in the
morning, Willow's friend is rescued by her boyfriend. Willow pushes
on, arrives at her grandparents' house, and ultimately persuades her
parents to keep Roxy as a house dog. The animals, the young people's
ancestors, keep the party safe. Roxy is the reincarnation of Willow's
twin. As Roxy's eyes heal, she runs lead with Cora and becomes closer
to Willow. Willow learns that her social problems begin with her own
attitudes.

Values: Cora learns that popularity depends on cooperation and a
positive attitude.

Read Aloud/Reader Response

The entire book is appropriate for read aloud/reader response. Below
are a few suggestions.

1.   Page 4. In this poem, Willow explains her name.
2.   Pages 76 to 78. In this passage, Roxy tells the story of her short life
     as Diamond.
3.   Page 87. Willow reflects on how to make friends.

4. Page 88. Willow's name, the baby's ashes, the place of overnight refuge, and the origin of Willow's name all come together.
5. Page 91. Willow finds the diamond inside herself and joins Kaylie and Richard at lunch.

Booktalk

Twelve-year-old Willow lives in Old Fork, Alaska. She is part Athabascan Indian. Only 600 people live in her town, and Willow gets along better with her sled dogs than most of the citizens of Old Fork. She would rather live in the wilderness with her grandparents. She persuades her parents that she can drive the sled to her grandparents' house. Maybe she will persuade them to let her stay. But her grandparents think that it is a better idea for Willow to live in Old Fork, and on the return trip, she goes too fast, too long—and boom! Roxy, the lead dog and Willow's favorite, is hit. Willow has to get her home and make her better. Is that possible? This accident puts her on another journey. One that makes her travel inside herself, makes her re-think the word *friend*, and leads her to family secrets. It is also one that teaches her the full meaning of her name, *Diamond Willow*.

Curriculum Connections

1. (Research, social studies) Using your library resources, learn more about the characteristics of sled dogs. Act as a resource person for the group.
2. (Research, social studies) Using your library resources, learn more about religious beliefs of the Indians of North America. Act as a resource person for the group.
3. (Discuss, language arts) Willow reveals herself as she speaks. She is using a personal narrative. What do you find out about her? Would she be your friend?

Related Works

1. Bastedo, Jamie. **On Thin Ice.** Calgary, AB, Canada: Fitzhenry & Whiteside Co./Red Deer Press, 2006. 348p. $10.95pa. ISBN 0 88995 337 6. [fiction] JS, CG with high interest for girls. (*Genre Talks for Teens*, 2009, pages 262 to 264.) Sixteen-year-old Ashley, a mix of Irish, French Canadian, and Inuit bloodlines, lives in a northern small town with her extended family and is gifted with powers similar to her uncle's.
2. Bruchac, Joseph. **Wabi: A Hero's Tale.** New York: Dial Books, 2006. 198p. $16.99. ISBN 0 8037 3098 5. [fiction] MJS, CG (*Genre*

Talks for Teens, 2009, pages 189 to 191.) Wabi, born a great horned owl, tells the story of his life, from his hatching to his performing heroic human deeds in human form.

3. Hobbs, Valerie. **Sheep.** New York: Farrar, Straus and Giroux/ Frances Foster Books, 2006. 115p. $16.00. ISBN 0 374 36777 9. [fiction] MJ, CG with high interest for boys. Jack, a runt sheepdog, finds kind and sadistic owners, and finally, the boy he calls his own.

4. Hobbs, Will. **Wild Man Island.** New York: HarperCollins Publishers, 2002. 184p. $15.95. ISBN 0 688 17473 6. [fiction] MJ, CG with high interest for boys. (*Teen Genre Connections,* 2005, pages 92 to 94.) Fourteen-year-old Andy Galloway, the youngest member of an Adventure Alaska program, leaves the group to find where his father died and encounters a stray Newfoundland dog who saves his life.

5. Martin, Ann M. **A Dog's Life: The Autobiography of a Stray.** New York: Scholastic Press, 2005. 182p. $16.99. ISBN 0 439 71559 8. [fiction] MJ, CG (*Booktalks and Beyond,* 2007, pages 81 to 83.) A female stray dog leads a life filled with abuse and hostility until she is taken in by an eighty-two-year-old farm lady.

ᘓᘔ

Spires, Elizabeth. **I Heard God Talking to Me: William Edmondson and His Stone Carvings.**

New York: Farrar, Straus and Giroux, 2009. 56p. $17.95.
ISBN-13: 978 0 374 33528 1. [biography in verse] JS, CG

Themes/Topics: African American life, poetry, religion, stonecutting

Summary/Description

In twenty-three poems, Elizabeth Spires personifies the creations and expresses the vision of William Edmondson. After God spoke to him, Edmondson, the son of two former slaves, began carving in the early 1930s when he was in his late fifties. For Edmondson, carving set spirits free within pieces of limestone. He sold the carvings for a few dollars from his shed in Nashville, Tennessee. In 1937, he became the first black artist to have a solo show at the Museum of Modern Art in New York. Edmondson's words form four of Spires's poems. A photograph of Edmondson or his work accompanies each poem. Ten of the photos are by Edward Weston and Louis Dahl-Wolfe.

"About William Edmondson" describes the man, his thinking, and his recognition. Spires includes a bibliography and "Photo Credits and Acknowledgments."

Values: Edmondson demonstrates the importance of following one's talent and vision.

Read Aloud/Reader Response

Each poem is suitable for a Read Aloud/Reader Response.

Booktalk

Read aloud "The Gift" on page 4 or "A Conversation" on page 6. Show the picture of Edmondson on the opposite page. As you talk, turn the pages of the book and show the pictures.

Yes, God told William Edmondson to carve. The message came in the early 1930s. The United States was in the middle of the Great Depression. Edmondson was the son of two former slaves. He was poor and in his late fifties. The world around him told him that the idea was silly. Edmondson picked up his tools and began to release the spirits of stones, first in tombstones, then in figures. His first carvings were inexpensive tombstones for poor black families in his segregated Nashville, Tennessee. Then wealthy white people began to notice his work. A professor introduced him to art collectors who introduced him to a famous photographer. Soon the world saw his carvings. William Edmondson became the first African American to have a solo show at the Museum of Modern Art in New York. How could this happen to a poor black man in the middle of the Depression? Edmondson has the answer in *I Heard God Talking to Me*.

Curriculum Connections

1. (Research, art) Using library resources, learn more about Edmondson's work and why he is considered a great artist. Share the information that you find with the group.
2. (Research, language arts) Using library resources, find other poems written in reaction to visual art. Share those works with the group.
3. (Create, language arts) Choose an art work. Write your own poem in reaction to it.

Related Works

1. Bacho, Peter. **Boxing in Black and White.** New York: Henry Holt and Co., 1999. 122p. $18.95. ISBN 0 8050 5779 X. [nonfiction] MJS, CG Bacho discusses how boxing, a means for the poor

to earn money, became a metaphor for black/white relations in the United States. Chapter 3 explains how the Jack Johnson vs. Jim Jeffries fight of 1910 proved that a black man, under fair conditions, could defeat a white man. The fighter is the subject of one of Edmondson's carvings. A photograph of the carving and a poem in reaction to it appear on pages 14 and 15.

2. Cooper, Michael L. **Slave Spirituals and the Jubilee Singers.** New York: Clarion, 2001. 86p. $16.00. ISBN 0 395 97829 7. [nonfiction] MJS, CG This history of the Jubilee Singers from Fisk University reveals the post–Civil War efforts in African American education. The singers are referred to in the poem "Eleanor Roosevelt," page 19, in *I Hear God Talking to Me.*

3. Daly, Jude (reteller and illus.) **Sivu's Six Wishes: A Taoist Tale.** Grand Rapids, MI: Eerdmans Books for Young Readers, 2010. 32p. $16.99. ISBN 978 0 8028 5369 1. [fiction] C, CG Sivu, a stonecutter, wishes for more powerful roles and discovers the stonecutter's power. The thought-provoking tale examines identity and value.

4. Freedman, Russell. **Eleanor Roosevelt: A Life of Discovery.** New York: Clarion Books, 1993. $17.95. ISBN-13: 978 0 89919 862 0. [nonfiction] MJS, CG This biography expands on the causes suggested in Spires's poem "Eleanor Roosevelt," page 19.

5. Nelson, Marilyn. **Carver: A Life in Poems.** Asheville, NC: Front Street, 2001. 103p. $16.95. ISBN 1 8869 10 53 7. [biography in verse] MJS, CG (*Teen Genre Connections,* 2005, pages 42 to 44.) This series of poems emphasizes Carver's dedication to nature and education, outstanding mental ability, artistic talent, religious faith, work ethic, love of nature, and humbling generosity.

ങ്ട

Stork, Francisco X. Marcelo in the Real World.

New York: Scholastic/Arthur A. Levine Books, 2009. 320p. $17.99.
ISBN-13: 978 0 545 05474 4. [fiction] S, CG

Themes/Topics: autism, family, love, faith, conduct of life, choices, the study of God

Summary/Description

Eighteen-year-old Marcelo has an autistic-like disorder and has grown up in a sheltered environment. His father wants him to work in his law office for the summer, attend a regular high school, and enter college. Marcelo works for nineteen-year-old Jasmine. They bond.

Wendell, the partner's son, pressures Marcelo to work for him and persuade Jasmine to sleep with him. In Wendell's office, Marcelo becomes obsessed with the picture of a girl harmed by a faulty windshield manufactured by the firm's biggest client. Jasmine finds proof that the company knew the risk. Marcelo gives the proof to the girl's lawyer and refuses to help Wendell coerce Jasmine. He believes that God will eventually use his actions for good. Marcelo is fired and plans to attend regular high school so that he can become a nurse and work with those in the real world whom he sees as more handicapped than those in special institutions. Some content may be considered controversial.

Value: Marcelo values truth even if it might hurt his father and family.

Read Aloud/Reader Response

1. Chapter 4, pages 30 to 35, beginning "'When I was your age . . .'" and ending with the chapter. Marcelo's mother shares the story of a life-changing summer experience.
2. Chapter 12, pages 115 to 120, beginning "'Marcelo has a question . . .'" and ending with the chapter. Rabbi Heschel explains how sex can be used for both good and evil.
3. Chapter 14, pages 140 to 143, beginning "You seem angry . . ." and ending ". . . those two." Jasmine tells about the horse that killed her brother.
4. Chapter 26, pages 270 to 279, beginning "I remember . . ." to the end of the chapter. Rabbi Heschel and Marcelo discuss the relationship between God's will and faith.
5. Chapter 30, page 302, beginning *"Why the change?"* and ending ". . . overwhelmed by it?" Marcelo explains why he wants to go to school in the real world.

Booktalk

Eighteen-year-old Marcelo's world is safe. He has music in his head. He cares for animals at his special school, and he is figuring out God. He can always retreat to a tree house built for him by his parents. His father decides that Marcelo should go to a regular school for his senior year and then college. He will work in the father's law firm for the summer. If he does all the jobs requested, then Marcelo will have his school choice for his senior year. If he does not, his father will choose. Marcelo agrees. His father is fair and loving. Marcelo starts in the mail room, a little job. His boss, Jasmine, doesn't want him there. Wendell, the partner's son, calls

Marcelo a "retard." But Marcelo will try. Then he fishes a picture of a mangled face from a wastebasket. It teaches him about greed, deception, jealousy, and hate. Marcelo wonders how God can allow such things and wonders if God exists. Marcelo is out of the tree house now. His music is gone, and he is learning about someone new, *Marcelo in the Real World.*

Curriculum Connections

1. (Research, science) Using library resources, learn more about an autistic person's ability to work in the real world. Share your information with the group.
2. (Discuss, language arts) Are there any clearly good or bad people in the story?
3. (React, language arts) What does this book say to you personally? Compose a brief presentation that you might want to share with the group.

Related Works

1. Albom, Mitch. **The Five People You Meet in Heaven.** New York: Hyperion, 2003. 196p. $19.95. ISBN 0 7868 6871 6. [fiction] JS/A (*Booktalks and Beyond,* 2007, pages 35 to 37.) Eighty-three-year-old Eddie dies saving a little girl's life during an amusement park accident and learns every act is important.
2. Brooks, Martha. **Mistik Lake.** New York: Farrar, Straus and Giroux/Melanie Kroupa Books, 2007. 207p. $16.00. ISBN-13: 978 0 374 34985 1. [fiction] S,G (*Genre Talks for Teens,* 2009, pages 4 to 6.) At her family's summer retreat, seventeen-year-old Odella unravels the secrets that grips her family and discovers her own love in the process.
3. Edwards, Michele Engel. **Autism: Diseases and Disorders.** San Diego, CA: Lucent Books, 2001. 112p. $28.70. ISBN 1 56006 829 9. [nonfiction] MJS, CG Edwards defines autism, specifies cause and treatment, presents social options, describes possibilities for autistic adults, and distinguishes between autistic savants and persons suffering from Asperger's syndrome. Organization addresses and Web sites, source notes, further reading, and a bibliography provide additional sources.
4. Haddon, Mark. **The Curious Incident of the Dog in the Night-Time.** New York: Vintage Contemporaries, 2003. 226p. $12.00. ISBN 1 4000 3271 7. [fiction] S/A, CG (*Booktalks and Beyond,* 2007, pages 119 to 121.) A brilliant autistic teenager investigates the murder of his neighbor's dead dog and discovers family secrets.

5.   Hautman, Pete. **Godless.** New York: Simon & Shuster Books for Young Readers, 2004. 198p. $15.95. ISBN 0 689 86278 4. [fiction] JS, CG (*Genre Talks for Teens,* 2009, pages 27 to 29.) Jason Bock starts a new religion centered on the town water tower, and after dangerous complications, learns to distinguish between faith and religion.

Index

About the Author

LUCY SCHALL is a retired high school and middle school English teacher, a book reviewer for *VOYA,* and the author of five other acclaimed booktalking guides, including *Genre Talks for Teens* (Libraries Unlimited, 2009) and *Teen Genre Connections* (Libraries Unlimited, 2005), a selection for the VOYA Five Foot Bookshelf award. Ms. Schall holds a Bachelor of Arts with a major in English and a Master of Arts in Education from Allegheny College.